Study Guide

for use with

Managerial Accounting
Creating Value in a Dynamic Business Environment

Fifth Edition

Ronald W. Hilton
Cornell University

Prepared by
Douglas deVidal
University of Texas at Austin

McGraw-Hill
Irwin

Boston   Burr Ridge, IL   Dubuque, IA   Madison, WI   New York   San Francisco   St. Louis
Bangkok   Bogotá   Caracas   Kuala Lumpur   Lisbon   London   Madrid   Mexico City
Milan   Montreal   New Delhi   Santiago   Seoul   Singapore   Sydney   Taipei   Toronto

McGraw-Hill Higher Education

A Division of The McGraw-Hill Companies

Study Guide for use with
MANAGERIAL ACCOUNTING: CREATING VALUE IN A DYNAMIC BUSINESS ENVIRONMENT
Ronald W. Hilton

Published by McGraw-Hill/Irwin, an imprint of the McGraw-Hill Companies, Inc., 1221 Avenue of the Americas, New York, NY 10020.

1 2 3 4 5 6 7 8 9 0 QPD/QPD 0 9 8 7 6 5 4 3 2 1

ISBN 0-07-239482-X

www.mhhe.com

PREFACE

This Study Guide was developed to help you study more effectively. It incorporates many of the accounting survival skills essential to your success. It is designed to accompany the fifth edition of *Managerial Accounting* by Ronald W. Hilton, but is not a substitute for your textbook. Its purpose is to supplement the textbook by helping you learn. Each chapter of the Study Guide contains the following sections: *Chapter Focus Suggestions; Read and Recall Questions; Self-Test Questions and Exercises; Solutions to Self-Test Questions and Exercises;* and *Ideas for Your Study Team.*

AN ACCOUNTING SURVIVAL PLAN (Preview, Read, Recall, Test & Review)

Before you read a chapter, preview it. Start by reading the *Chapter Focus Suggestions* included in the Study Guide, and the learning objectives that appear at the beginning of the chapter in your textbook. Next, thumb through the chapter, noting the names of each of the section headings. Finally, read the chapter summary, and the list of key terms at the end of the chapter.

Now that you know what to expect, start reading. As you finish reading each section of the chapter, answer the related *Read and Recall Questions* included in the Study Guide. Check your answers by referring to the related section in your textbook. If you were not able to answer all of the questions, read the related section of the chapter in your textbook again. If you can answer the *Read and Recall Questions,* you understand and can recall what you just read. To move that information into long-term memory, you'll need to practice and apply what you have just learned.

You can do this, in part, by completing the *Self-Test Questions and Exercises* included in the Study Guide. Test your vocabulary skills by matching the key terms with the textbook definitions. Complete the true-false, fill-in-the-blank and multiple choice questions, and check your answers in the *Solutions to Self-Test Questions and Exercises* section. Work through the exercises. Finally, complete all of the end-of-chapter questions, exercises and problems assigned by your instructor.

Remember that you're not alone. Develop your own support system by forming a study team with three or four of your classmates. Each chapter of the Study Guide contains *Ideas for Your Study Team.* You'll retain the material by discussing it with the members of your study team, and develop valuable interpersonal skills.

Use the Study Guide on a daily basis as you prepare for exams. The *Read and Recall Questions* can be used to review the essential concepts covered in each chapter. The *Self-Test Questions and Exercises* are likely to be similar to the materials you will encounter on exams. And don't forget to use positive self-talk as you visualize your success in this accounting class

TABLE OF CONTENTS

CHAPTER 1

THE CHANGING ROLE OF MANAGERIAL ACCOUNTING IN A DYNAMIC BUSINESS ENVIRONMENT

CHAPTER FOCUS SUGGESTIONS

This chapter provides an overview of managerial accounting. The fundamental management processes and types of information needed by decision-makers to achieve the goals of the organization are described. The role of managerial accounting in the management information system is explained, and it is compared and contrasted with financial accounting. The continuous evolution of the role of managerial accounting in organizations and various contemporary themes are addressed. Finally, career opportunities for managerial accountants are explored.

If you have not yet worked as a member of the management team of a large organization, you will probably not be familiar with many of the terms used in this chapter. A listing of key terms appears at the end of the chapter. You will need to be able to define each of these key terms. However, you should also make sure that you are familiar with other terms that are used in this chapter. These terms will be used throughout the course.

READ AND RECALL QUESTIONS

MANAGERIAL ACCOUNTING: A BUSINESS PARTNERSHIP WITH MANAGEMENT

LEARNING OBJECTIVE #1
After studying this section of the chapter, you should be able to:
• Define managerial accounting and describe its role in the management process.

What is managerial accounting? What is its role in the management process?

How has managerial accounting changed in the last decade?

MANAGING RESOURCES, ACTIVITIES AND PEOPLE

> **LEARNING OBJECTIVE #2**
> *After studying this section of the chapter, you should be able to:*
> - Explain four fundamental management processes that help organizations attain their goals.

Who sets the goals for an organization?

What steps does an organization take in pursuing its goals?

What four basic activities comprise the day-to-day work of the management team of an organization?

HOW MANAGERIAL ACCOUNTING ADDS VALUE TO THE ORGANIZATION

> **LEARNING OBJECTIVE #3**
> *After studying this section of the chapter, you should be able to:*
> - List and describe five objectives of managerial accounting activity.

Objectives of Managerial Accounting Activity

What are the five major objectives of managerial accounting activity?

How does managerial accounting information serve as an attention-directing function?

What is "employee empowerment?"

What is measured by a managerial accounting system? How are these measures used in an organization?

What four questions can be asked in order to assess an organization's competitive position?

LEARNING OBJECTIVE #4
After studying this section of the chapter, you should be able to:
• Explain the major differences between managerial and financial accounting.

Managerial Versus Financial Accounting

What is financial accounting? What is a common output of a financial-accounting system?

What is an accounting system? What is the function of a cost-accounting system?

How does managerial accounting differ from financial accounting (i.e., in terms of users, regulation, source of data and nature of reports and procedures)?

WHERE ARE MANAGERIAL ACCOUNTANTS LOCATED IN AN ORGANIZATION?

LEARNING OBJECTIVES #5 & #6
After studying this section of the chapter, you should be able to:
- Explain where managerial accountants are located in an organization, in terms of formal organization, deployment in cross-functional teams, and physical location.
- Describe the roles of an organization's chief financial officer (CFO) or controller, treasurer, and internal auditor.

Line and Staff Positions

What is the role of a manager in a line position? What is the role of a manager in a staff position?

What are the responsibilities of the chief financial officer (CFO) of an organization? What other names is this position sometimes called?

What are the responsibilities of the treasurer of an organization?

What are the responsibilities of the internal auditor of an organization?

Cross-Functional Deployment, Physical Location

What is cross-functional deployment? Where do management accountants actually do their work?

MAJOR THEMES IN MANAGERIAL ACCOUNTING

LEARNING OBJECTIVE #7
After studying this section of the chapter, you should be able to:
• Briefly describe some of the major contemporary themes in managerial accounting.

Information and Incentives, Behavioral Issues

What two functions are served by managerial accounting information? How do these two functions differ? Why does a managerial accountant need to have an understanding of human behavior?

Costs and Benefits

What is the "cost-benefit trade-off?"

Evolution and Adaptation in Managerial Accounting

What is e-business?

What are two major differences between service and manufacturing firms?

What is a "multinational company?" What type of challenge is faced by both a manager of a multinational company and an American planning a trip in a foreign county?

What is a "product's value" to the customer?

What purpose do cross-functional managerial teams serve? What holds a cross-functional team together?

What is "time to market?" Why is time to market a critical objective for many companies?

How did Chrysler Corporation successfully apply the concepts of time-based competition to reorganize its design and development process?

What is an intranet? What is the internet?

How does a traditional manufacturing setting differ from a just-in-time (or JIT) production system?

What is the "pull" approach to controlling manufacturing? How does a "pull" system of production management result in a smooth flow of production and significantly reduced inventory levels?

What is "total quality management" (or TQM)?

What is meant by "continuous improvement?"

Cost Management Systems

What are the four objectives of a cost management system?

What is "activity-based costing?" How are the costs of the organization's significant activities accumulated and then assigned to goods or services when activity-based costing is used?

STRATEGIC COST MANAGEMENT AND THE VALUE CHAIN

What is the "value chain?" What entities would be included in a hospital's value chain?

What are two ways a company can achieve a sustainable competitive advantage?

What are "cost drivers?"

What is "strategic cost management?"

What is the "theory of constraints?"

MANAGERIAL ACCOUNTING AS A CAREER

LEARNING OBJECTIVE #8
After studying this section of the chapter, you should be able to:
• Discuss the professional organizations, certification process, and ethical standards in the field of managerial accounting.

What types of knowledge and skills are needed by managerial accountants in order to perform their duties effectively?

Professional Organizations

What professional organizations do managerial accountants join?

Professional Certification

How can a managerial accountant become a Certified Management Accountant (CMA)?

Professional Ethics

What are the four major types of ethical standards for managerial accountants?

SELF-TEST QUESTIONS AND EXERCISES

MATCHING

Match each of the key terms listed below with the appropriate textbook definition:

___ 1. Activity accounting	___ 17. E-commerce
___ 2. Activity-based costing (ABC)	___ 18. Empowerment
___ 3. Activity-based management (ABM)	___ 19. Financial accounting
	___ 20. Internal auditor
___ 4. Attention-directing function	___ 21. Just-in-time (JIT) production system
___ 5. Balanced scorecard	
___ 6. Certified Management Accountant (CMA)	___ 22. Line positions
	___ 23. Managerial accounting
___ 7. Chief financial officer (CFO)	___ 24. Non-value-added costs
___ 8. Continuous improvement	___ 25. Planning
___ 9. Controller (or comptroller)	___ 26. Staff positions
___ 10. Controlling	___ 27. Strategic cost management
___ 11. Cost-accounting system	___ 28. Supply-chain management
___ 12. Cost driver	___ 29. Theory of constraints
___ 13. Cost management system	___ 30. Total quality management (TQM)
___ 14. Cross-functional management teams	
	___ 31. Treasurer
___ 15. Decision making	___ 32. Value chain
___ 16. Directing operational activities	

A. The constant effort to eliminate waste, reduce response time, simplify the design of both products and processes, and improve quality and customer service.

B. Using an activity-based costing system to improve the operations of an organization.

C. The top managerial and financial accountant in an organization. Supervises the accounting department and assists management at all levels in interpreting and using managerial-accounting information.

D. Running an organization on a day-to-day basis.

E. Developing a detailed financial and operational description of anticipated operations.

F. An accountant who reviews the accounting procedures, records, and reports in both the controller's and treasurer's areas of responsibility.

G. An accountant who has earned professional certification in managerial accounting.

H. The broad set of management and control processes designed to focus an entire organization and all of its employees on providing products or services that do the best possible job of satisfying the customer.

I. Positions held by managers who are directly involved in providing the goods or services that constitute an organization's primary goals.

J. The concept of encouraging and authorizing workers to take their own initiative to improve operations, reduce costs, and improve product quality and customer service.

K. The collection of financial or operational performance information about significant activities in an enterprise.

L. A management approach that focuses on identifying and relaxing the constraints that limit an organization's ability to reach a higher level of goal attainment.

M. An organization's set of linked, value creating activities, ranging from securing basic raw materials and energy to the ultimate delivery of products and services.

N. A characteristic of an event or activity that results in the incurrence of costs by that event or activity.

O. A management planning and control system that measures the cost of significant activities, identifies non-value-added costs, and identifies activities that will improve organizational performance.

P. An accountant in a staff position who is responsible for managing an organization's relationships with investors and creditors and maintaining custody of the organization's cash, investments, and other assets.

Q. Part of the basic accounting system that accumulates cost data for use in both managerial and financial accounting.

R. Choosing between alternatives.

S. A two-stage procedure used to assign overhead costs to products or services produced. In the first stage, significant activities are identified, and overhead costs are assigned to activity cost pools in accordance with the way resources are consumed by the activities. In the second stage, the overhead costs are allocated from each activity cost pool to each product line in proportion to the amount of the cost driver consumed by the product line.

T. The costs of activities that can be eliminated without deterioration of product quality, performance, or perceived value.

U. Ensuring that an organization operates in the intended manner and achieves its goals.

V. Positions held by managers who are only indirectly involved in producing an organization's product or service.

W. The use of accounting information for reporting to parties outside the organization.

X. The process of identifying, measuring, analyzing, interpreting and communicating information in pursuit of an organization's goals.

Y. The function of managerial-accounting information in pointing out to managers issues that need their attention.

Z. A comprehensive inventory and manufacturing control system in which no materials are purchased and no products are manufactured until they are needed.

AA. Overall recognition of the cost relationships among the activities in the value chain, and the process of managing those costs relationships to a firm's advantage.

BB. A model of business performance evaluation that balances measures of financial performance, internal operation, innovation and learning, and customer satisfaction.

CC. Another name for the chief financial officer.

DD. Teams that use individuals with varied expertise and experience to address management issues.

EE. The coordination of order generation, order taking, order fulfillment, and distribution of products and services.

FF. The buying and selling over digital media.

TRUE-FALSE QUESTIONS

For each of the following statements, enter a T or F in the blank to indicate whether the statement is true or false.

___**1.** Managers rely on managerial-accounting information to prepare financial statements.

___**2.** A chief purpose of managerial accounting is to motivate managers toward achieving the goals of the organization.

___**3.** Production-cost data are used exclusively for managerial-accounting purposes.

___**4.** In order to understand the role of a managerial accountant in an organization, it is necessary to know the structure of that organization.

___**5.** Making a managerial decision means choosing among the alternative goals of the organization.

___**6.** Planning involves developing a detailed financial and operational description of past operations.

____7. A main purpose of managerial accounting is to motivate managers to direct their efforts toward achieving the goals of an organization.

____8. A means of motivating people toward an organization's goals is to measure their performance in achieving those goals.

____9. In some organizations, internal auditors make a broad performance evaluation of middle management.

____10. The effectiveness of a managerial accountant in providing information does not depend on his or her understanding of human behavior.

____11. Information is a commodity.

____12. The main difference between service and manufacturing organizations is that in service organizations most services are consumed as they are generated.

____13. An implication of the just-in-time inventory philosophy is the need to de-emphasize product quality.

____14. The Institute of Management Accountants sponsors the Certified Management Accountant (CMA) program.

____15. Recognizing important cost relationships among activities in a value chain and managing those relationships to the firm's advantage is known as optimal cost management.

FILL-IN-THE-BLANK QUESTIONS

For each of the following statements, fill in the blank to properly complete the statement.

1. In pursuing the goals of an organization, managers need_____.

2. The system which accumulates cost data for use in both managerial accounting and financial accounting is called a(n)_____system.

3. Ensuring that the organization operates in the intended manner and achieves its goals means that management is engaged in_____.

4. The focus of_____accounting is on the needs of managers within the organization.

5. _____managers are directly involved in the specific operations of an organization.

6. In many organizations the _____is the chief managerial and financial accountant.

7. In_____accounting the emphasis is on reporting to parties outside the organization.

8. Managers in_____positions supervise activities that support the goals of the organization.

9. The_____of an organization is responsible for safeguarding its assets.

10. The_____of the organization is the set of linked, value-creating activities ranging from getting raw materials to the delivery of products.

MULTIPLE-CHOICE QUESTIONS

Circle the best answer or response.

1. Which of the following would *not* typically be a goal of an organization?
   (a) Profitability
   (b) Product quality
   (c) Cost maximization
   (d) Market diversification

2. In pursuing an organization's goals, which of the following is *not* a basic activity of managers?
  (a) Decision making
  (b) Financial reporting to stockholders
  (c) Directing operations
  (d) Controlling

3. Which of the following is true of financial accounting?
  (a) Users of its information are primarily outside the organization.
  (b) It is not regulated by outside agencies.
  (c) Only a small portion of its data is drawn from the organization's basic accounting system.
  (d) Its reports are seldom based on historical transaction data.

4. The controller of an organization
  (a) supervises the accounting department.
  (b) prepares all reports for external parties.
  (c) is responsible for preparing reports for internal users.
  (d) does all of the above.

5. The objectives of a cost management system do *not* include
  (a) measuring the cost of resources used in performing significant activities.
  (b) eliminating the non-value-added costs.
  (c) eliminating the need for financial reporting.
  (d) determining the effectiveness and efficiency of all major organizational activities.

6. Which of the following is an area of concern in the ethical standards set forth by the Institute of Management Accountants?
  (a) Confidentiality
  (b) Integrity
  (c) Objectivity
  (d) All of the above

EXERCISES

Record your answers to each part of the exercises in the space provided. Show your work.

Exercise 1.1

Included in the inventory of Carter's Home Products, Inc. (CHP) are various health care items that became obsolete early in the year and now have a market value well below cost (the amounts originally paid for these inventory items). CHP's controller has been aware of the obsolescence problem since the beginning of the year. While closing the company's books, the controller decided not to make an adjustment in the accounting records to reduce the obsolete inventory items to their net realizable values. The adjustment, if made, would have had a material effect on, or would have significantly reduced the amount of, the amount of net income reported by the company for the year.

The controller reports directly to the chief executive officer, and is eligible for a bonus that is directly tied to the amount of the company's net income. The controller did not discuss the decision not to make an adjustment with the chief executive officer, and was relieved when the chief executive officer did not raise the obsolescence problem.

Write a brief essay that addresses the ethical considerations of the decision made by the controller. Address the controller's motivation, how the company's financial accounting information is affected, how its managerial accounting information is affected, and the impact on decision-makers.

SOLUTIONS TO SELF-TEST QUESTIONS AND EXERCISES

MATCHING

1. K	7. C	13. O	19. W	25. E	31. P
2. S	8. A	14. DD	20. F	26. V	32. M
3. B	9. CC	15. R	21. Z	27. AA	
4. Y	10. U	16. D	22. I	28. EE	
5. BB	11. Q	17. FF	23. X	29. L	
6. G	12. N	18. J	24. T	30. H	

TRUE-FALSE QUESTIONS

1. F Managers rely on financial-accounting information to prepare financial statements.
2. T
3. F These data are also used for financial-accounting purposes.
4. T
5. F Managerial decisions are made by choosing among the alternative courses of action available to the manager.
6. F Planning pertains to future operations, not past operations.
7. T
8. T
9. T
10. F Understanding human behavior is an important factor in contributing to the effectiveness of a managerial accountant in providing information.
11. T
12. T
13. F The just-in-time philosophy implies that product quality must be emphasized.
14. T
15. F This is known as strategic cost management, not optimal cost management.

FILL-IN-THE-BLANK QUESTIONS

1. information
2. cost-accounting
3. control
4. managerial
5. Line
6. controller
7. financial
8. staff
9. treasurer
10. value chain

MULTIPLE-CHOICE QUESTIONS

1. **(c)** An organization would most likely be interested in cost minimization.
2. **(b)** Financial reporting to stockholders is primarily an activity of financial accountants.
3. **(a)** The FASB and the SEC regulate financial accounting. The major portion of its data comes from the basic accounting system, and its reports are based chiefly on historical transaction data.
4. **(d)** The controller's work involves each of the items indicated in choices (a), (b), and (c).
5. **(c)** A cost management system seeks to improve the quality of financial reporting.
6. **(d)** Each of the items in (a), (b), and (c) is of concern in the ethical standards of the IMA.

EXERCISES

Exercise 1.1

The company has a significant number of inventory items that are obsolete. However, an adjustment to reduce the obsolete inventory items to their net realizable values has not been made to the company's records. As a result, the total assets and net income are both overstated. The controller is eligible for a bonus that is directly tied to the amount of the company's net income. As such, it is possible that the controller's decision not to make the adjustment was based on the negative impact that this adjustment would have had on the amount of the bonus awarded to the controller.

The adjustment to reduce the obsolete inventory items to their net realizable value is required by generally accepted accounting principles (GAAP). Current and prospective investors, lenders, and other users of the company's financial-accounting information may make inappropriate decisions based on the company's financial statements, which are not in accordance with GAAP. In addition, throughout the year, incorrect managerial accounting information was being provided to the company's managers.

This incorrect information may have affected decision making (e.g., choices between continuing or discontinuing selected inventory items), planning (e.g., the pricing of these inventory items), directing of operational activities (e.g., the continued production of these items) and controlling (e.g., ensuring that the company meets its budgetary goals for the year). The controller had an ethical obligation to record the necessary adjustment and communicate the related information to management in a timely manner.

IDEAS FOR YOUR STUDY TEAM

1. Rewrite each of the definitions of the key terms that appear at the end of the chapter using your own words. Imagine that you are trying to explain each key term to a friend who has not taken any accounting classes. Then, get together with the other members of your study team and compare your definitions.

Activity accounting

Activity-based costing

Activity-based management

Attention-directing function

Balanced scorecard

Certified Management Accountant (CMA)

Chief financial officer (CFO)

Continuous improvement

Controller (or comptroller)

Controlling

Cost-accounting system

Cost driver

Cost management system

Cross-functional management teams

Decision-making

Directing operational activities

E-commerce

Empowerment

Financial accounting

Internal auditor

Just-in-time (JIT) production system

Line positions

Managerial accounting

Non-value-added costs

Planning

Staff positions

Strategic cost management

Supply chain management

Theory of constraints

Total quality management (TQM)

Treasurer

Value chain

2.   Try to predict the types of questions, exercises and problems that you will encounter on the quizzes and exams that cover this chapter. Review the *Read and Recall Questions* and the *Self-Test Questions and Exercises* that are set forth in this Study Guide. Work through the end-of-chapter review problem(s), if applicable, and the end-of-chapter questions, exercises and problems that were assigned by your instructor. As you perform these tasks, identify the terms, concepts, formulas, etc. that you are responsible for knowing. After you develop the list of questions, exercises and problems that you expect to encounter on quizzes and exams, review the learning objectives that appear at the beginning of the chapter in your textbook to ensure that you have not overlooked anything significant. After you have completed your review of your list, get together with the other members of your study team and compare your predictions.

CHAPTER 2
BASIC COST MANAGEMENT CONCEPTS AND ACCOUNTING FOR MASS CUSTOMIZATION OPERATIONS

CHAPTER FOCUS SUGGESTIONS

In order to ensure that you are successful in this course, you must gain an understanding of the various types of costs that are incurred by organizations and how these costs are managed. This chapter describes the cost terms, concepts, and classifications used by managerial accountants.

Again, you may not be familiar with many of the terms used in this chapter. A listing of key terms appears at the end of the chapter. Become familiar with each of these key terms. You should especially focus your attention on the following: product and period costs; manufacturing costs (i.e., direct material, direct labor and manufacturing overhead costs); cost drivers; fixed and variable costs; direct and indirect cost; and controllable and uncontrollable costs. You will need to know how to categorize costs by function (e.g., manufacturing, selling and administrative) and apply various economic concepts to describe costs (e.g., opportunity cost, sunk cost, differential or incremental cost, marginal cost, and average cost per unit). You will also need to know how to prepare a schedule of cost of goods manufactured, a schedule of cost of goods sold, and an income statement.

READ AND RECALL QUESTIONS

WHAT DO WE MEAN BY A COST?

LEARNING OBJECTIVE #1
After studying this section of the chapter, you should be able to: • Explain what is meant by the word "cost."

What is the most basic definition of a "cost?"

LEARNING OBJECTIVE #2
After studying this section of the chapter, you should be able to: • Distinguish among product costs, period costs, and expenses.

Product Costs, Period Costs, and Expenses

In general, how can the term "expense" be defined?

What is a "product cost?"

What term is used to describe product cost in the period in which the product is sold?

What costs comprise the product cost of a retailer?

What costs comprise the product cost of a manufacturer?

What is an "inventoriable cost?"

What is a "period cost?" How are period costs reflected in the financial statements?

What are "research and development costs?" Should research and development costs be treated as product costs or period costs?

What are "selling costs?" Should selling costs be treated as product costs or period costs?

What are "administrative costs?" Should administrative costs be treated as product costs or period costs?

COSTS ON FINANCIAL STATEMENTS

LEARNING OBJECTIVE #3
After studying this section of the chapter, you should be able to:
• Describe the role of costs on published financial statements.

Income Statement

How are period costs reflected in the financial statements?

How are product costs reflected in the financial statements? When do product costs become cost of goods sold?

What are "operating expenses?" Should operating expenses be treated as product costs or period costs?

Balance Sheet

What is "raw-material inventory?" What is "work-in-process inventory?" What is finished-goods inventory?"

MANUFACTURING OPERATIONS AND MANUFACTURING COSTS

LEARNING OBJECTIVE #4
After studying this section of the chapter, you should be able to:
- List five types of manufacturing operations and describe mass customization.

What are the five generic types of manufacturing processes? Describe the process for each type.

Mass-Customization Manufacturing

What is mass-customization? What is a production cell module (mod)?

Manufacturing Costs

What is "direct material?" Why is this cost considered a direct cost?

What is "direct labor?" Why is this cost considered a direct cost?

What is "manufacturing overhead?" What are the three types of manufacturing overhead? Why is each considered an indirect cost?

What are "service department costs?"

What is an "overtime premium?" What is "idle time?" Why are overtime premiums and the cost of idle time classified as manufacturing overhead?

What two types of costs are called "conversion costs?"

What two types of costs are called "prime costs?"

MANUFACTURING COST FLOWS

LEARNING OBJECTIVE #6
After studying this section of the chapter, you should be able to: • Prepare a schedule of cost of goods manufactured, a schedule of cost of goods sold, and an income statement for a manufacturer.

What two schedules are prepared to summarize the flow of manufacturing costs during an accounting period?

What are the three types of manufacturing costs reflected on a schedule of cost of goods manufactured?

What formula can be used to compute the cost of goods manufactured?

What formula can be used to compute the cost of goods sold?

Production Costs in Service Industry Firms and Nonprofit Organizations

What distinguishes service industry firms and many nonprofit organizations from manufacturing firms?

What costs comprise the direct materials of a service firm, such as an airline?

What costs comprise the direct labor costs of a service firm, such as an airline?

What costs comprise the overhead costs of a service firm, such as an airline?

BASIC COST MANAGEMENT CONCEPTS: DIFFERENT COSTS FOR DIFFERENT PURPOSES

Why does the managerial accountant need to understand cost concepts and classifications?

The Cost Driver Team

What is meant by the term "activity?"

What is a "cost driver?" What factors should the managerial accountant consider when identifying a cost driver? Give some examples of cost drivers in manufacturing firms.

As the number of cost drivers that are used in explaining an organization's cost behavior increases, what happens to the accuracy of the resulting information? Why? What happens to the cost of information?

After studying this section of the chapter, you should be able to:
• Describe the behavior of variable and fixed costs, both in total and on a per-unit basis.

Variable and Fixed Costs

What is a "variable cost?" What is the relationship between a variable cost and the level of activity?

In terms of total cost, what happens to a variable cost when the level of activity increases? What happens to the total amount of a variable cost when the level of activity decreases?

On a per unit basis, does a variable cost remain the same or change as the level of activity changes?

Assume that the cost of paper napkins and other paper products increases directly and proportionately with the level of the patronage of a Pizza Hut franchise. How would this cost appear on a graph? Label each axis, and graph this cost. (Compare your graph to the illustration in Exhibit 2-8.)

What is a "fixed cost?" What is the relationship between a fixed cost and the level of activity?

In terms of total cost, what happens to a fixed cost when the level of activity increases? What happens to the total amount of a fixed cost when the level of activity decreases?

On a per unit basis, does a fixed cost remain the same or change as the level of activity changes?

Assume that the cost of property taxes at a Ramada Inn does not change when the hotel's occupancy rate changes. How would this cost appear on a graph? Label each axis, and graph this cost. (Compare your graph to the illustration in Exhibit 2-9.)

After studying this section of the chapter, you should be able to:
- Distinguish among direct, indirect, controllable, and uncontrollable costs.

The Cost Management and Control Team

What is "responsibility accounting?"

What is the definition of a "direct cost?" What is the definition of an "indirect cost?"

The textbook indicates that a cost may be considered a direct or indirect cost of a "department" depending on the nature of the department being considered. What cost might be categorized as an indirect cost of a given department in a manufacturing plant but as a direct cost of the manufacturing plant itself? Why?

What is an important objective of a cost management system? What is "activity accounting?"

What are "non-value-added costs?"

What is a "controllable cost?" What is an "uncontrollable cost?"

What is an example of a cost that is controllable in the long run but uncontrollable in the short run?

LEARNING OBJECTIVES #11 & #12
After studying this section of the chapter, you should be able to:
- Define and give examples of an opportunity cost, an out-of-pocket cost, a sunk cost, a differential cost, a marginal cost, and an average cost.
- Explain the behavioral tendencies many people show when they encounter opportunity costs and sunk costs.

The Outsourcing Action Team

What is an "opportunity cost?"

What are "out-of-pocket costs?"

What is a "sunk cost?"

What is a "differential cost?"

What is an "incremental cost?"

What is a "marginal cost?"

How is the average cost per unit computed?

SELF-TEST QUESTIONS AND EXERCISES

MATCHING

Match each of the key terms listed below with the appropriate textbook definition:

____ 1. Activity
____ 2. Average cost per unit
_A._ 3. Controllable costs
____ 4. Conversion costs
____ 5. Cost
____ 6. Cost drivers
____ 7. Cost of goods sold
____ 8. Differential cost
_F._ 9. Direct cost
____ 10. Direct-labor cost
_B._ 11. Direct material
____ 12. Direct sales
____ 13. Expense
____ 14. Finished goods
____ 15. Fixed costs
____ 16. Idle time
_D._ 17. Incremental costs
____ 18. Indirect cost
____ 19. Indirect labor
____ 20. Indirect material

_C._ 21. Inventoriable cost
____ 22. Manufacturing costs
____ 23. Manufacturing overhead
____ 24. Marginal cost
____ 25. Mass customization
____ 26. Operating expenses
____ 27. Opportunity cost
____ 28. Out-of-pocket cost
____ 29. Overtime premium
____ 30. Period costs
____ 31. Prime costs
____ 32. Product cost
____ 33. Raw material
____ 34. Schedule of cost of goods Manufactured
____ 35. Schedule of cost of goods sold
____ 36. Service (support) departments
____ 37. Sunk costs
____ 38. Variable cost
____ 39. Work in process

A. A cost that is subject to the control or substantial influence of a particular individual.

B. Materials that are physically incorporated in the finished product.

C. Costs incurred to purchase or manufacture goods. (See also product costs.)

D. The amount by which the cost of one action exceeds that of another. (See also differential cost.)

E. Costs that are expensed during the time period in which they are incurred.

F. A cost that can be traced to a particular department or other subunit of an organization.

G. Materials that either are required for the production process to occur but do not become an integral part of the finished product, or are consumed in production but are insignificant in cost.

H. The extra cost incurred in producing one additional unit of output.

I. A detailed listing of the manufacturing costs incurred during an accounting period and showing the change in Work-in-Process.

J. The potential benefit given up when the choice of one action precludes selection of a different action.

K. A cost that does not change in total as activity changes.

L. Direct-labor cost plus manufacturing-overhead cost.

M. The expense measured by the cost of the finished goods sold during a period of time.

N. The extra compensation paid to an employee who works beyond the normal period of time.

O. A detailed schedule showing the cost of goods sold and the change in finished-goods inventory during an accounting period.

P. Partially completed products that are not yet ready for sale.

Q. The consumption of assets for the purpose of generating revenue.

R. The differences in a cost item under two decision alternatives.

S. A measure of an organization's output of goods or services.

T. Costs incurred in a manufacturing process, which consist of direct material, direct labor, and manufacturing overhead.

U. Unproductive time spend by employees due to factors beyond their control, such as power outages and machine breakdowns.

V. The costs incurred to produce and sell services, such as transportation, repair, financial, or medical services.

W. Costs that were incurred in the past and cannot be altered by any current or future decision.

X. All manufacturing costs other than direct-material and direct-labor costs.

Y. Material entered into a manufacturing process.

Z. Costs incurred that require the expenditure of cash or other assets.

AA. The total cost of producing a particular quantity of product divided by the number of units produced.

BB. A cost that changes in total in direct proportion to a change in an organization's activity.

CC. A cost that cannot be traced to a particular department.

DD. At the most basic level, the sacrifice made, usually measured by the resources given up, to achieve a particular purpose.

EE. All costs of compensating employees who do not work directly on the firm's product but who are necessary for production to occur.

FF. The cost of salaries, wages, and fringe benefits for personnel who work directly on the manufactured products.

GG. A subunit in an organization that is not involved directly in producing the organization's output of goods or services.

HH. The costs of direct material and direct labor.

II. Costs that are associated with goods for sale until the time period during which the products are sold, at which time the costs become expenses. See also inventoriable costs.

JJ. A characteristic of an event or activity that results in the incurrence of costs by that event or activity.

KK. Completed products awaiting sale.

LL. Production process in which many standardized components are combined to produce custom-made products to customer order.

MM. Sales approach in which the consumer orders directly from the manufacturer (often via the internet).

TRUE-FALSE QUESTIONS

For each of the following statements, enter a T or F in the blank to indicate whether the statement is true or false.

___1. Cost data classified in one way for a given purpose may be inappropriate for other purposes.

___2. If the unit variable cost is $45 to make one unit of product, then the total variable cost to make 100 units is $4,500.

___3. Costs that are not directly traceable to a particular department are known as uncontrollable costs.

___4. An important objective of a cost management system is to trace as many costs as possible directly to activities that caused those costs.

___5. Raw materials that are consumed in making a product and are physically added to the finished product are known as direct materials.

___ 6. The total fixed costs during the period to make 5,000 units is $35,000. Based on this information, the unit fixed cost (or fixed cost per unit) is $7.

___ 7. Activities that are caused by the incurrence of cost are called cost drivers.

___ 8. Costs that are controllable in the long run are also controllable in the short run.

___ 9. If a product cost is neither direct labor nor direct materials, then it must be manufacturing overhead.

___ 10. Direct-material cost plus conversion cost is known as prime cost.

___ 11. Period costs are recognized as expenses during the time period in which they are incurred.

___ 12. Overtime premiums are part of direct-labor costs.

___ 13. Operating expenses are period costs.

___ 14. Work-in-process inventory includes the cost of products that have been completed and are ready for sale.

___ 15. Total cost divided by the quantity of units related to that total cost is the marginal cost per unit.

___ 16. As the number of cost drivers increases, the accuracy of the cost information goes down.

FILL-IN-THE-BLANK QUESTIONS

For each of the following statements, fill in the blank to properly complete the statement.

1. The measure of an organization's output of products or services is known as _____.

2. _____cost per unit does not change as the level of the cost driver varies.

3. Tracing costs to particular work centers is known as _____accounting.

4. The cost of salaries, wages, and fringe benefits of personnel who do not work directly on the product but who are needed for the production process is called _____ cost.

5. Direct labor plus manufacturing overhead make up _____costs.

6. The relative proportion of an organization's fixed and variable costs is called the _____ of the organization.

7. Total _____cost changes in direct proportion to the level of the cost driver.

8. A cost that can be traced to a particular work center is known as a(n) _____cost.

9. When an asset is used up or sold for the purposes of generating revenue, the cost incurred is called a(n)_____.

10. A(n) _____cost is the same as a product cost.

11. All materials acquired to be used in production constitute _____ inventory.

12. _____costs are those costs that require the payment of cash or other assets as the result of their incurrence.

13. _____costs are those costs that have been incurred in the past.

14. _____inventory is made up of all goods completed and ready for sale.

15. A(n) _____cost is the economic benefit foregone when one action is chosen over an alternative course of action.

16. The cost incurred to make one additional unit is known as the_____ cost.

MULTIPLE-CHOICE QUESTIONS

Circle the best answer or response.

1. Which of the following is correct? As the level of a cost driver varies,

   (a) unit variable costs change.
   (b) total variable costs change.
   (c) fixed cost in total changes.
   (d) unit fixed cost does not change.

2. Which of the following are manufacturing costs:

   I. direct materials
   II. indirect labor
   III. depreciation on plant and equipment

   (a) Only I
   (b) Only I and II
   (c) Only II and III
   (d) I, II, and III

3. Marketing costs do *not* include
   (a) sales commissions.
   (b) shipping costs.
   (c) the president's salary.
   (d) advertising costs.

4. Which of the following statements is (are) true?

   I. Beginning inventory of finished goods, plus cost of goods manufactured, less the cost of goods sold equals the ending inventory of finished goods.
   II. Beginning inventory of finished goods, plus the cost of goods manufactured, less ending inventory of finished goods equals the cost of goods sold.

   (a) Only I
   (b) Only II
   (c) Both I and II
   (d) Neither I nor II

5. The cost of goods manufactured does *not* include
   (a) the cost of distributing the goods from the warehouse during the period.
   (b) direct-labor costs incurred during the period.
   (c) manufacturing-overhead costs incurred during the period.
   (d) the cost of direct materials used in production during the period.

6. The total cost to produce 500 units of finished product is $75,000. This total cost is made up of $60,000 variable cost and $15,000 fixed cost. Which of the following is true?
   (a) The average cost per unit is $120.
   (b) The unit fixed cost is $30.
   (c) The variable cost per unit is the same as the average cost per unit.
   (d) The variable cost per unit is $150.

EXERCISES

Record your answers to each part of the exercises in the space provided. Show your work.

Exercise 2.1

Smokey Mountain Furniture Company makes wooden lawn furniture in its Lawndale Division. Several of the costs incurred by this division are set forth in the table below: Complete the table by classifying each of the costs listed according to the following categories: *(Note:* Each cost may be assigned to more than one category.)

Description of Cost	Product	Period	Operating Expense	Manuf. Cost	Direct Material	Direct Labor	Manuf. Overhead
1. Salaries of workers who cut the wood to form chair arms and legs							
2. Electricity used in the Assembly Department							
3. Salary of the sales manager							
4. Oil used to lubricate the cutting machines							
5. Wood used to make the furniture							
6. Property taxes on the plant							
7. Depreciation on the equipment in the division sales manager's office							
8. Fringe benefits for the workers who assemble the furniture							
9. Small amounts of paint used in the Finishing Department							
10. Sandpaper used in the Finishing Department							
11. Overtime premiums paid to Assembly Department workers							

Description of Cost	Product	Period	Operating Expense	Manuf. Cost	Direct Material	Direct Labor	Manuf. Overhead
12. Fire insurance on the finished goods warehouse							
13. Salaries of janitors in the plant							
14. Fringe benefits of the general office workers							
15. Repairs made to the cutting machines							
16. Shipping costs for sending furniture to retail outlets							
17. Billing costs for furniture sold							
18. Cartons used to ship the finished furniture							
19. Travel expenses of salespeople							
20. Cost to ship lumber to the Lawndale plant							

Exercise 2.2

The Taber Company makes and sells clay pottery. The following cost data were recorded for 19x2:

Direct materials used in production	$482,000
Salaries of salespersons	67,000
Property taxes on factory building	8,000
General office salaries	105,000
Factory supervision	50,000
Depreciation on general office equipment	6,000
Wages paid for direct labor	291,000
Factory utilities	34,000
Advertising expense	93,000
Miscellaneous administrative expenses	17,000
Depreciation on factory plant and equipment	85,000
Fringe benefits for direct laborers	73,000

There were no beginning or ending inventories, except for an ending finished-goods inventory of $83,000. Compute the following costs for 19x2:

(a) Total conversion costs

(b) Total prime costs

(c) Total cost of goods manufactured

(d) Total cost of goods sold

(e) Total administrative costs

(f) Total selling costs

(g) Total period costs

Exercise 2.3

The cost of the electricity at the Helman Company each month is $400 plus $.02 for each kilowatt-hour used. During the month of March the company used 8,000 kilowatt-hours. Compute the following:

(a) Total variable cost of electricity for March.

(b) Unit fixed cost of electricity for March.

(c) Average cost of electricity per kilowatt-hour for March.

Exercise 2.4

Compute the missing amounts using the information set forth in the following table:

Beginning inventory, raw materials	$ 15,000
Ending inventory, raw materials	10,000
Purchases of raw materials	Unknown (1)
Raw materials used	Unknown (2)
Direct labor.	175,000
Manufacturing overhead	112,000
Total manufacturing costs	377,000
Beginning inventory, work in process	Unknown (3)
Ending inventory, work in process	16,000
Cost of goods manufactured	389,000
Beginning inventory, finished goods	Unknown (4)
Cost of goods available for sale	462,000
Ending inventory, finished goods	61,000
Cost of goods sold	Unknown (5)
Sales	741,000
Gross margin	Unknown (6)
Selling and administrative expenses	Unknown (7)
Income before taxes	143,000
Income tax expense	Unknown (8)
Net income	98,000

(Hint: Consider solving for the unknowns by setting up a schedule of cost of goods manufactured, a schedule of cost of goods sold, and an income statement. Alternatively, you could use an equation approach.)

SOLUTIONS TO SELF-TEST QUESTIONS AND EXERCISES

MATCHING

1. S	9. F	17. D	25. LL	33. Y
2. AA	10. FF	18. C C	26. V	34. I
3. A	11. B	19. EE	27. J	35. O
4. L	12. MM	20. G	28. Z	36. GG
5. DD	13. Q	21. C	29. N	37. W
6. JJ	14. KK	22. T	30. E	38. BB
7. M	15. K	23. X	31. HH	39. P
8. R	16. U	24. H	32. II	

TRUE-FALSE QUESTIONS

1. **T**
2. **T**
3. **F** These costs are called indirect costs.
4. **T**
5. **T**
6. **T**
7. **F** Activities that cause cost are called cost drivers.
8. **F** Costs that are controllable in the long run may be uncontrollable in the short run.
9. **T**
10. **F** Prime cost is direct-material cost plus direct-labor cost.
11. **T**
12. **F** Overhead premiums are part of manufacturing overhead.
13. **T**
14. **F** Work-in-process inventory includes only the cost of partially completed products.
15. **F** Total cost divided by the corresponding quantity of units is called average cost. Marginal cost is the cost to make one extra unit.
16. **F** The accuracy of the cost information goes up.

FILL-IN-THE-BLANK QUESTIONS

1. activity
2. Variable
3. responsibility
4. indirect-labor
5. conversion
6. cost structure
7. variable
8. direct
9. expense
10. inventoriable
11. raw-materials
12. Out-of-pocket
13. Sunk
14. Finished-goods
15. opportunity
16. marginal

MULTIPLE-CHOICE QUESTIONS

1. **(b)** When the cost driver level varies, unit variable costs and total fixed costs remain constant, whereas unit fixed cost changes.
2. **(d)** All three of these costs are manufacturing costs.
3. **(c)** The president's salary is an administrative expense.
4. **(c)** Both statements are true.
5. **(a)** The costs of distributing goods from the warehouse are marketing costs.
6. **(b)** Unit fixed cost = $15,000/500=$30. (Note that average cost per unit = $75,000/500 = $150; variable cost per unit = $60,000/500 = $120.)

EXERCISES

Exercise 2.1

Description of Cost	Product	Period	Operating Expense	Manuf. Cost	Direct Material	Direct Labor	Manuf. Overhead
1. Salaries of workers who cut the wood to form chair arms and legs	X			X		X	
2. Electricity used in the Assembly Department	X			X			X
3. Salary of the sales manager		X	X				
4. Oil used to lubricate the cutting machines	X			X			X
5. Wood used to make the furniture	X			X	X		
6. Property taxes on the plant	X			X			X
7. Depreciation on the equipment in the division sales manager's office		X	X				

Description of Cost	Product	Period	Operating Expense	Manuf. Cost	Direct Material	Direct Labor	Manuf. Overhead
8. Fringe benefits for the workers who assemble the furniture	X			X		X	
9. Small amounts of paint used in the Finishing Department	X			X			X
10. Sandpaper used in the Finishing Department	X			X			X
11. Overtime premiums paid to Assembly Department workers	X			X			X
12. Fire insurance on the finished goods warehouse		X	X				
13. Salaries of janitors in the plant	X			X			X
14. Fringe benefits of the general office workers		X	X				
15. Repairs made to the cutting machines	X			X			X
16. Shipping costs for sending furniture to retail outlets		X	X				
17. Billing costs for furniture sold		X	X				
18. Cartons used to ship the finished furniture		X	X				
19. Travel expenses of salespeople		X	X				
20. Cost to ship lumber to the Lawndale plant	X			X	X		

Exercise 2.2

(a) Total conversion costs = direct labor and manufacturing overhead

($291,000 + $73,000) + ($8,000 + $50,000 + $34,000 + $85,000) = $541,000

(b) Total prime costs = direct materials used and direct labor

$482,000 + ($291,000 + $73,000) = $846,000

(c) Total cost of goods manufactured = direct materials used + direct labor + manufacturing   overhead + beginning work-in-process inventory – ending work-in-process inventory

$482,000 + ($291,000 + $73,000) + ($8,000 + $50,000 + $34,000 + $85,000) + $0 - $0 = $1,023,000

(d) Total cost of goods sold = cost of goods manufactured + beginning finished-goods inventory – ending finished-goods inventory

$0 + $1,023,000 - $83,000 = $940,000

(e) Total administrative costs

$105,000 + $6,000 + $17,000 = $128,000

(f) Total selling costs

$67,000 + $93,000 = $160,000

(g) Total period costs = total administrative costs + total selling costs

$128,000 + $160,000 = $288,000

Exercise 2.3

(a) Total variable cost of electricity for March.

8,000 kilowatt-hours x $.02 per kilowatt-hour = $160

(b) Unit fixed cost of electricity for March.

$400/8,000 kilowatt-hours = $.05 per kilowatt-hour

(c) Average cost of electricity per kilowatt-hour for March.

($160 + $400)/8,000 kilowatt-hours = $.07 per kilowatt-hour

Exercise 2.4

Schedule of Cost of Goods Manufactured

Beginning inventory, raw materials	$ 15,000	
Add: Raw-materials purchases (1)	85,000	
Raw materials available for use	100,000	
Less: Ending inventory, raw materials	10,000	
Raw materials used (2)		$ 90,000
Direct labor		175,000
Manufacturing overhead		112,000
Total manufacturing costs		$377,000
Add Beginning inventory, work in process (3)		28,000
Subtotal		405,000
Less: Ending inventory, work in process		16,000
Cost of goods manufactured		$389,000

Schedule of Cost of Goods Sold

Cost of goods manufactured	$389,000
Add: Beginning inventory, finished goods (4)	73,000
Cost of goods available for sale	462,000
Less: Ending inventory, finished goods	61,000
Cost of goods sold (5)	$401,000

Income Statement

Sales	$741,000
Less: Cost of goods sold	401,000
Gross margin (6)	340,000
Selling and administrative expenses (7)	197,000
Income before taxes	143,000
Income tax expenses (8)	$45,000
Net income	$ 98,000

Note: Alternatively, the missing amounts can be calculated using equations as follows in the order indicated:

(8) 143,000 - 98,000 = 45,000

(7) 340,000 - 143,000= 197,000

(6) 741,000 - 401,000 = 340,000

(5) 462,000 - 61,000 = 401,000

(4) 462,000 - 389,000 = 73,000

(3) 389,000 + 16,000 - 377,000 = 28,000

(2) 377,000 - 112,000 - 175,000 = 90,000

(1) 90,000 + 10,000 - 15,000 = 85,000

IDEAS FOR YOUR STUDY TEAM

1.   Rewrite each of the definitions of the key terms that appear at the end of the chapter using your own words. Imagine that you are trying to explain each key term to a friend who has not taken any accounting classes. Then, get together with the other members of your study team and compare your definitions.

Activity

Average cost per unit

Controllable cost

Conversion costs

Cost

Cost drivers

Cost of goods sold

Differential cost

Direct cost

Direct-labor cost

Direct material

Direct sales

Expense

Finished goods

Fixed costs

Idle time

Incremental costs

Indirect cost

Indirect labor

Indirect material

Inventoriable cost

Manufacturing costs

Manufacturing overhead

Marginal cost

Mass customization

Operating expenses

Opportunity cost

Out-of-pocket costs

Overtime premium

Period costs

Prime costs

Product cost

Raw material

Schedule of cost of goods manufactured

Schedule of cost of goods sold

Service departments

Sunk costs

Variable cost

Work in process

2.   Try to predict the types of questions, exercises and problems that you will encounter on the quizzes and exams that cover this chapter. Review the *Read and Recall Questions* and the *Self-Test Questions and Exercises* that are set forth in this Study Guide. Work through the end-of-chapter review problem(s), if applicable, and the end-of-chapter questions, exercises and problems that were assigned by your instructor. As you perform these tasks, identify the terms, concepts, formulas, etc. that you are responsible for knowing. After you develop the list of questions, exercises and problems that you expect to encounter on quizzes and exams, review the learning objectives that appear at the beginning of the chapter in your textbook to ensure that you have not overlooked anything significant. After you have completed your review of your list, get together with the other members of your study team and compare your predictions.

CHAPTER 3
PRODUCT COSTING AND COST ACCUMULATION
IN A BATCH PRODUCTION ENVIRONMENT

CHAPTER FOCUS SUGGESTIONS

This chapter begins an in-depth discussion of product-costing systems and includes coverage of job-order costing systems. The next chapter covers process-costing and hybrid product-costing systems.

Initially, this chapter addresses the various uses of product-costing systems. After a brief introduction to the flow of costs through the general ledger accounts of manufacturing firms, job-order costing systems are compared and contrasted with process-costing systems. The various source documents used in a job-order costing system to capture information related to direct-material and direct-labor costs are described, as is the use of a predetermined overhead rate to apply manufacturing-overhead costs to productions jobs. Job-order costing in nonmanufacturing organizations is also explored.

You will need to know how to use journal entries to record direct-material, direct-labor and manufacturing-overhead costs. You must also be able to prepare a schedule of cost of goods manufactured, a schedule of cost of goods sold, and an income statement. Your success in this course will depend, in part, on your appreciation for and understanding of the application (or assignment) of manufacturing-overhead costs to products. You will need to understand how to: choose a cost driver, calculate a predetermined overhead rate, and use the predetermined overhead rate to assign manufacturing-overhead costs to products. You will need to be able to distinguish plantwide overhead rates from departmental overhead rates, and be familiar with a two-stage cost allocation process. Finally, you will need to understand the meaning and disposition of the ending balance in the manufacturing-overhead account.

READ AND RECALL QUESTIONS

PRODUCT AND SERVICE COSTING

> **LEARNING OBJECTIVE #1**
> *After studying this section of the chapter, you should be able to:*
> - Discuss the role of product and service costing in manufacturing and nonmanufacturing firms.

What is the purpose of a product-costing system?

How are product costs used in financial accounting? How are product costs used in managerial accounting and cost management? Why are product costs sometimes separately provided (i.e., not only via the company's financial statements) to other external decision-makers?

Product Costing in Nonmanufacturing Firms

Why do service organizations need information about the costs of producing services?

FLOW OF COSTS IN MANUFACTURING FIRMS

LEARNING OBJECTIVE #2
After studying this section of the chapter, you should be able to:
- Diagram and explain the flow of costs through the manufacturing accounts used in product costing.

What are the three types of manufacturing costs?

What is Work-in-Process Inventory? Which costs are added to the work in process account? When products are completed, what happens to the related product costs? Then, when products are sold, what happens to the related product costs? What journal entry is used to transfer the costs?

TYPES OF PRODUCT-COSTING SYSTEMS

LEARNING OBJECTIVE #3
After studying this section of the chapter, you should be able to:
• Distinguish between job-order costing and process costing.

Job-Order Costing Systems

What types of companies use job-order costing? What is a "job" or "job order?"

How are costs accumulated in a job-order costing system? How is the average cost per unit computed when job-order costing is used?

Process Order Costing Systems

What types of companies use process costing? How are costs accumulated in a process costing system? How is the average cost per unit computed when process costing is used?

ACCUMULATING COSTS IN A JOB-ORDER COSTING SYSTEM

What is the subsidiary ledger account called that is assigned to each job in a job-order costing system?

Job-Cost Record

What are the five sections of a job-cost record?

Direct-Materials Cost

What is a material requisition form? What is a bill of materials? What is each one used for?

Direct-Labor Costs

What is a time ticket? What is it used for?

Should shop cleanup duties be classified as direct labor or manufacturing overhead? Why?

After studying this section of the chapter, you should be able to:

• Compute a predetermined overhead rate, and explain its use in job-order costing for job-shop and batch-production environments.

Manufacturing-Overhead Costs

What is "overhead application" (or overhead absorption)? Why is it necessary to assign manufacturing-overhead costs to production jobs?

Overhead Application

Why not wait until the end of an accounting period so that actual costs of manufacturing overhead can be determined before applying overhead costs to the firm's products?

What is a "volume-based cost driver" (or activity base)?

What estimates must be made in order to compute the predetermined overhead rate? How is a predetermined overhead rate computed?

How is overhead applied to production jobs? What formula is used to determine the amount of overhead that should be applied?

ILLUSTRATION OF JOB-ORDER COSTING

LEARNING OBJECTIVE #5
After studying this section of the chapter, you should be able to:
- Prepare journal entries to record the costs of direct labor, direct material, and manufacturing overhead in a job-order costing system.

Purchase of Material

What entry to used to record the purchase of materials?

Use of Direct Material

What entry is used to record the release of raw materials to production for use in specific jobs?

Use of Indirect Material

Why didn't Adirondack Outfitters attempt to trace the cost of glue to specific jobs? Was the glue considered a direct material or an indirect material?

What entry is used to record the requisition of indirect materials?

Use of Direct Labor

What entry is used to record the direct labor costs of each job at the end of the pay period?

Use of Indirect Labor

What entry is used to record the use of indirect labor at the end of the pay period?

Incurrence of Manufacturing-Overhead Costs

What entry is used to record the incurrence of manufacturing-overhead costs (such as rent on factory building, depreciation on factory equipment, and utilities, property taxes and insurance related to the factory)?

Application of Manufacturing Overhead

What entry is used to add (or apply) manufacturing overhead to work-in-process inventory?

Summary of Overhead Accounting

When is overhead budgeted? When is overhead applied? When is actual overhead measured?

What is accumulated on the left side of the Manufacturing-Overhead account? What is accumulated on the right side of the account?

Selling and Administrative Costs

Are selling and administrative costs product costs or period costs? Are such costs capitalized as incurred or expensed?

Completion of a Production Job

What entry is used to record the transfer of job costs from work-in-process inventory to finished-goods inventory?

Sale of Goods

What entry is used to record the cost of the units sold during the period?

Underapplied and Overapplied Overhead

What is underapplied overhead? What is overapplied overhead? Why doesn't the amount of actual overhead typically equal the amount of overhead that has been applied to production? What causes this situation?

If the manufacturing-overhead account has a debit balance at the end of the accounting period, was overhead underapplied or overapplied? What if the account has a credit balance?

What entry is *commonly* used to close the balance of the manufacturing-overhead account? Why do most firms use this approach? When do most firms record this entry?

Technically speaking, what three accounts have been affected (or misstated) when overhead was underapplied or overapplied during an accounting period? What is "proration?" How is the amount of underapplied or overapplied overhead prorated to the three accounts that were affected?

What entry is used to close a debit balance of the manufacturing-overhead account when proration is used? In this situation, was overhead underapplied or overapplied during the accounting period? What entry is used to close a credit balance of the manufacturing-overhead account when proration is used? In this situation, was overhead underapplied or overapplied during the accounting period?

LEARNING OBJECTIVE #6
After studying this section of the chapter, you should be able to:
• Prepare a schedule of cost of goods manufactured, a schedule of cost of goods sold, and an income statement for a manufacturer.

Schedule of Cost of Goods Manufactured

What three types of manufacturing costs appear on the schedule of cost of goods manufactured?

Which two types of inventory appear on the schedule of cost of goods manufactured?

Where can you find the amount that was transferred from Work-in-Process Inventory to Finished-Goods Inventory on the schedule of cost of goods manufactured? (*Hint*: Trace the amount used in journal entry (9) to Exhibit 3-9.)

Schedule of Cost of Goods Sold

Which type of inventory appears on the schedule of cost of goods sold?

What is the relationship between the schedule of cost of goods manufactured and the schedule of cost of goods sold? (*Hint*: Locate the amount on the schedule of cost of goods manufactured in Exhibit 3-9 that also appears in the schedule of cost of goods sold in Exhibit 3-10.)

Can you trace the total of the two amounts used in journal entries (11) and (12) to the total cost of goods sold figure that appears on Exhibit 3-10?

FURTHER ASPECTS OF OVERHEAD APPLICATION

LEARNING OBJECTIVE #7

After studying this section of the chapter, you should be able to:
- Discuss the cost-benefit issue of accuracy versus timeliness of information in accounting for overhead.

Accuracy versus Timeliness of Information: A Cost-Benefit Issue

What are the "costs" of applying actual overhead to production? What are the "benefits" of applying actual overhead to production?

Why do managerial accountants generally recommend the use of a predetermined overhead rate instead of an actual overhead rate? Why would inconsistency in product costs result if an actual overhead rate was used and recomputed monthly?

What is a "normalized overhead rate?" Why do managerial accountants use normalized overhead rates?

What is "normal costing?" How is the amount of overhead applied to production determined when normal costing is used?

What is an "actual-costing system?" How is the amount of overhead applied to production determined when actual costing is used?

Choosing the Cost Driver for Overhead Application

Assume that a single, volume-based cost driver (or activity base) is used in calculating the predetermined overhead rate. In addition, assume that all of the firm's products required direct labor, but only some products require machine time. Is direct labor or machine time the preferable activity base? What would happen if the other activity base were used instead?

Why should there be a correlation between the incurrence of overhead costs and the use of the cost driver?

What are the two most common volume-based cost drivers?

What happens to the makeup of production (or manufacturing) costs as the production process becomes increasingly automated? Which manufacturing cost increases? Which manufacturing cost decreases? Why has direct labor become less appropriate as a cost driver?

What other volume-based cost drivers are being used by firms that no longer use direct labor as the volume-based cost driver?

What is "throughput (or cycle) time?"

Department Overhead Rates

What is a "plantwide overhead rate?" What is a "departmental overhead rate?"

TWO-STAGE COST ALLOCATION

LEARNING OBJECTIVE #8
After studying this section of the chapter, you should be able to:
• Describe the two-stage allocation process used to compute departmental overhead rates.

What two types of departments are the manufacturing-overhead costs assigned to in the first stage of a two-stage cost allocation? What is this step called?

What is a "service department?" What is "service department cost allocation?" How are service department costs allocated to the various production departments in the first stage of a two-stage cost allocation?

What happens in the second stage of a two-stage cost allocation? What is this process called?

LEARNING OBJECTIVE #9
After studying this section of the chapter, you should be able to:
• Diagram the two-stage allocation process used in activity-based costing.

Activity-Based Costing: An Introduction

Why do departmental overhead rates provide more accurate product costs than a single plantwide overhead rate?

What is an "activity-based costing (or ABC) system?" What change is made in the second stage of a two-stage cost allocation when activity-based costing is used?

What types of significant activities comprise the production process of many manufacturers?

Why does activity-based costing result in increased product-costing accuracy?

What are the costs of an activity-based costing system? What are the benefits of this system?

PROJECT COSTING:
JOB-ORDER COSTING IN NONMANUFACTURING ORGANIZATIONS

LEARNING OBJECTIVE #10

After studying this section of the chapter, you should be able to:

- Describe the process of project costing used in service industry firms and nonprofit organizations.

Why should job-order costing be used in nonmanufacturing organizations? How would costs be accumulated when a service firm uses a job-order costing system? That is, what term would be used instead of "job?"

CHANGING TECHNOLOGY IN MANUFACTURING OPERATIONS

Electronic Data Interchange

What is "electronic data interchange" or (EDI)? What are the benefits of the use of EDI?

Use of Bar Codes

How can bar codes be used to record data in the manufacturing process?

APPENDIX TO CHAPTER 3: DIFFERENT OVERHEAD RATES UNDER PLANT-WIDE, DEPARTMENTAL, AND ACTIVITY-BASED COSTING SYSTEMS

LEARNING OBJECTIVE #9
Determine whether or not you are responsible for this appendix. If so, after studying this section of the chapter, you should be able to:
- Diagram the two-stage allocation process used in activity-based costing.

Generally, why is a single, plantwide overhead rate based on only one volume-related cost driver the least accurate? When should multiple departmental overhead rates be used instead?

What is a "plantwide overhead rate?" How is a plantwide overhead rate determined? What is a "departmental overhead rate?" How is a departmental overhead rate determined? How does the use of departmental overhead rates differ from a plantwide overhead rate?

How does the assignment of overhead costs under activity-based costing differ from the use of departmental overhead rates?

Which method of assigning overhead costs (that is, the use of a single plantwide overhead rate, departmental overhead rates, or overhead rates developed under activity-based costing) yields the most accurate product cost? Why?

SELF-TEST QUESTIONS AND EXERCISES

MATCHING

Match each of the key terms listed below with the appropriate textbook definition:

____ 1. Activity base
____ 2. Activity-based costing (ABC) system
____ 3. Actual costing
____ 4. Actual manufacturing overhead
____ 5. Actual overhead rate
____ 6. Applied manufacturing overhead
____ 7. Bill of materials
____ 8. Cost distribution (sometimes called cost allocation)
____ 9. Cost of goods manufactured
____ 10. Cycle time
____ 11. Departmental overhead centers
____ 12. Departmental overhead rate
____ 13. Job-cost record
____ 14. Job-order costing
____ 15. Material requisition form
____ 16. Normal costing
____ 17. Normalized overhead rate
____ 18. Overapplied overhead

____ 19. Overhead application (or absorption)
____ 20. Plantwide overhead rate
____ 21. Predetermined overhead rate
____ 22. Process-costing system
____ 23. Product-costing system
____ 24. Proration
____ 25. Schedule of cost of goods manufactured
____ 26. Schedule of cost of goods sold
____ 27. Service departments
____ 28. Service department cost allocation
____ 29. Source document
____ 30. Throughput time
____ 31. Time ticket
____ 32. Two-stage cost allocation
____ 33. Underapplied overhead
____ 34. Volume-based cost driver

A. The total cost of direct labor, direct material, and overhead transferred from Work-In-Process Inventory to Finished-Goods Inventory during an accounting period.

B. A list of all the materials needed to manufacture a product or product component.

C. A measure of an organization's activity that is used as a basis for specifying cost behavior. The activity base also is used to compute a predetermined overhead rate. The current trend is to refer to the activity base as a volume-based cost driver.

D. The third step in assigning manufacturing-overhead costs. All costs associated with each production department are assigned to the product units on which a department has worked.

E. A document on which the costs of direct material, direct labor, and manufacturing overhead are recorded for a particular production job or batch. The job-cost sheet is a subsidiary ledger account for the Work-In-Process Inventory account in the general ledger.

F. A product-costing system in which actual direct-material, actual direct labor, and applied manufacturing-overhead costs are added to Work-In-Process Inventory.

G. An overhead rate calculated for a single production department.

H. A product-costing system in which actual direct-material, direct-labor, and actual manufacturing-overhead costs are added to Work-In-Process Inventory.

I. The amount by which the period's applied manufacturing overhead exceeds actual manufacturing overhead.

J. The rate at which overhead costs are actually incurred during an accounting period, calculated as follows: actual manufacturing-overhead divided by actual cost driver (or activity base).

K. The first step in assigning manufacturing-overhead costs. Overhead costs are assigned to all departmental overhead centers.

L. An overhead rate calculated by averaging manufacturing-overhead costs for the entire production facility.

M.   The amount by which the period's actual manufacturing overhead exceeds applied manufacturing overhead.

N.   The second step in assigning manufacturing overhead costs. All costs associated with a service department are assigned to the departments that use the services it produces.

O.   A product-costing system in which production costs are averaged over a large number of product units. Used by firms that produce large numbers of nearly identical products.

P.   The average amount of time required to convert raw materials into finished goods ready to be shipped to customers.

Q.   A product-costing system in which costs are assigned to batches or job orders of production. Used by firms that produce relatively small numbers of dissimilar products.

R.   A document that is used as the basis for an accounting entry. Examples include material requisition forms and direct-labor time tickets.

S.   A detailed schedule showing the cost of goods sold and the change in finished-goods inventory during an accounting period.

T.   The amount of manufacturing-overhead costs added to Work-In-Process Inventory during an accounting period.

U.   The process of allocating underapplied or overapplied overhead to Work-In-Process Inventory, Finished-Goods Inventory, and Cost of Goods Sold.

V.   A two-stage procedure used to assign overhead costs to products or services produced. In the first stage, significant activities are identified, and overhead costs are assigned to activity cost pools in accordance with the way resources are consumed by the activities. In the second stage, the overhead costs are allocated from each activity cost pool to each product line in proportion to the amount of the cost driver consumed by the product line.

W.   A document upon which the production department supervisor requests the release of raw materials for production.

X.   Same as throughput time.

Y.   The process of accumulating the costs of a production process and assigning them to the products that comprise the organization's output.

Z.   Any department to which overhead costs are assigned via overhead cost distribution.

AA. The rate used to apply manufacturing overhead to Work-In-Process Inventory, calculated as follows: estimated manufacturing overhead cost divided by estimated amount of cost driver (or activity base).

BB. The actual costs incurred during an accounting period for manufacturing overhead. Includes actual indirect material, indirect labor, and other manufacturing costs.

CC. A document that records the amount of time an employee spends on each production job.

DD. A cost driver that is closely associated with production volume, such as direct-labor hours or machine hours.

EE. A two-step procedure for assigning overhead costs to products or services produced. In the first stage, all production costs are assigned to the production departments. In the second stage, the costs that have been assigned to each production department are applied to the products or services produced in those departments.

FF. A detailed listing or the manufacturing costs incurred during an accounting period and showing the change in Work-In-Process.

GG. An overhead rate calculated over a relatively long time period.

HH. A subunit in an organization that is not involved directly in producing the organization's output of goods or services.

TRUE-FALSE QUESTIONS

For each of the following statements, enter a T or F in the blank to indicate whether the statement is true of false.

___1. Work-in-Process Inventory is partially completed inventory.

___2. In job-order costing the costs assigned to each job are averaged over the units of production in a job to get an average cost per unit.

___3. Manufacturing overhead is a homogeneous pool of indirect production costs.

___4. In financial accounting, product costs are needed for planning and cost control and to provide managers with data for decision making.

___5. A document, such as a material requisition form, which is used as the basis for an accounting entry, is called a source document.

___6. In job-order costing the predetermined overhead rate is used to apply manufacturing overhead costs to service departments.

___7. In managerial accounting, product costs are needed to value inventory on the balance sheet and to compute cost-of-goods-sold expense on the income statement.

___8. Procedures similar to those used in job-order costing are also used in many service organizations.

___9. A time ticket is a form that records the length of time needed to manufacture a product.

___10. If actual overhead is more than applied overhead, the difference is called underapplied overhead.

___11. A schedule of cost of goods sold shows the cost of goods sold during an accounting period and details the changes in Work-in-Process Inventory during the period.

___12. If an actual overhead rate is used in job-order costing, it can be computed only at the end of the accounting period.

___13. When direct materials and direct labor are added to Work-in-Process Inventory at their actual amounts and overhead is applied to Work-in-Process Inventory based on a predetermined overhead rate, this product-costing system is called actual costing.

___14. There should be a correlation between the incurrence of overhead costs and use of the chosen cost driver for overhead application.

___15. When multiple cost drivers and overhead rates instead of a single plantwide rate are used in overhead application, the resulting product-cost information is more accurate and more useful for decision making.

___16. Job-order costing is not used in nonmanufacturing organizations.

___17. Greater accuracy in product costs can be achieved with activity-based costing than with just the use of departmental overhead rates.

FILL-IN-THE-BLANK QUESTIONS

For each of the following statements, fill in the blank to properly complete the statement.

1. _____costing is used in organizations where goods are produced in distinct batches and there are significant differences among the batches.

2. In a job-order costing system, the cost of direct materials, direct labor, and manufacturing overhead are the _____to this product-costing system.

3. The first step in assigning manufacturing overhead costs to jobs is called _____.

4. The second step in assigning manufacturing overhead costs to jobs is through a process called _____.

5. The third step in assigning manufacturing overhead costs to jobs consists of applying the overhead costs accumulated in a production department to the _____ _____ that department has worked on.

6. The subsidiary-ledger account assigned to each job in job-order costing is a document called a(n) _____.

7. A(n) _____ lists all the materials needed to make a product that is produced routinely.

8. The left-hand side of the Manufacturing-Overhead Account is used to accumulate _____ manufacturing overhead costs as they are incurred throughout the accounting period.

9. If actual overhead is less than applied overhead, the difference is called _____ overhead.

10. When underapplied or overapplied overhead is allocated among Work-in-Process Inventory, Finished-Goods Inventory, and Cost of Goods Sold, the process is called _____.

11. A schedule of _____ shows the manufacturing costs incurred during an accounting period and the change in Work-in-Process Inventory.

12. If an overhead rate is computed over a long period of time to smooth out fluctuations in this rate, we call this a(n) _____ overhead rate.

13. _____ is the average amount of time needed to convert raw materials into finished goods ready to be shipped to customers.

14. _____ is the process of assigning manufacturing overhead costs to production jobs.

MULTIPLE-CHOICE QUESTIONS

Circle the best answer or response.

1. When direct materials are used in production,
    (a) Work-in-Process Inventory is credited.
    (b) Work-in-Process Inventory is debited.
    (c) Direct-Materials Inventory is debited.
    (d) Finished-Goods Inventory is debited.

2. In the application of manufacturing overhead, the predetermined overhead rate is computed as the estimated manufacturing overhead cost
    (a) divided by the estimated amount of the cost driver.
    (b) multiplied by the estimated amount of the cost driver.
    (c) divided by the actual amount of the cost driver.
    (d) multiplied by the actual amount of the cost driver.

3. Suppose the predetermined overhead rate is $5 per machine hour. If Job K31 required 10 machine hours, then the overhead applied to Job K31 is
    (a) $2
    (b) $5
    (c) $15
    (d) $50

4.	The journal entry to record the use of indirect labor in production includes a
	(a)	debit to Manufacturing Overhead
	(b)	credit to Manufacturing Overhead.
	(c)	debit to Work-in-Process Inventory.
	(d)	credit to Work-in-Process Inventory.

5.	The journal entry to record the transfer of job costs from Work-in-Process Inventory to Finished-Goods Inventory includes a
	(a)	debit to Cost of Goods Sold
	(b)	credit to Finished-Goods Inventory.
	(c)	debit to Work-in-Process Inventory.
	(d)	credit to Work-in-Process Inventory.

6.	The journal entries to record the sale of products made for a particular job order include a
	(a)	credit to Finished-Goods Inventory.
	(b)	credit to Accounts Receivable.
	(c)	credit to Cost of Goods Sold.
	(d)	debit to Sales Revenue

EXERCISES

Record your answers to each part of the exercises in the space provided. Show your work.

Exercise 3.1

The Standard Furniture Company makes and sells customized computer furniture and uses job-order costing. Prepare journal entries for each the following events that occurred during the month of September: T-Account

(a) Lumber costing $135,000 was purchased on account.

(b) Various indirect-material supplies costing $4,800 were used in production.

(c) Utility bills for plant operations totaling $9,000 were received, but not paid.

(d) Lumber and other direct materials amounting to $95,000 were used in production.

(e) Depreciation on the plant and production equipment amounted to $12,000 for the month.

(f) Direct labor of $30,000 for 2,500 direct-labor hours was used in production and paid for in cash.

(g) Indirect labor of $4,000 was used in production and paid for in cash.

(h) Manufacturing overhead was applied to jobs on the basis of $12.80 per direct-labor hour.

(i) Furniture completed and transferred to finished-goods amounted to $123,000.

(j) The cost of furniture sold amounted to $105,900.

Exercise 3.2

The Matthews Company makes and sells lamps and lighting fixtures. The following data are for their operations in 20x5.

Budgeted machine hours	12,000
Budgeted direct-labor hours	18,000
Budgeted manufacturing overhead	$375,000
Budgeted direct-labor rate	$12
Actual direct-labor hours	17,000
Actual machine hours	10,000
Actual direct-labor rate	$13.50
Actual manufacturing overhead	$394,000

(a) Compute the predetermined overhead rate for 20x5 using each of the following cost drivers:

(1) Direct-labor hours

(2) Direct-labor cost

(3) Machine hours

(b) For each cost driver given in part (a), compute the underapplied or overapplied overhead for 20x5:

(1) Direct-labor hours

(2) Direct-labor cost

(3) Machine hours

Exercise 3.3

The accounting records of Bramer Company showed the following recorded amounts as of December 31, 20x3:

Plant utilities	$ 78,000
Raw-materials inventory,12/31/x2	51,600
Work-in-process inventory, 12/31/x3	72,000
Plant supervision	75,000
Direct-labor cost incurred	336,000
Finished-goods inventory,12/31/x3	130,800
Purchase of raw materials	168,000
Finished-goods inventory,12/31/x2	144,000
Work-in-process inventory,12/31/x2	78,000
Other manufacturing overhead	12,000
Selling and administrative expenses	187,100
Indirect-labor cost incurred	60,000
Raw-materials inventory, 12/31/x3	31,200
Indirect materials used	42,000
Depreciation on plant and equipment	54,000
Sales Revenue	1,342,000

Prepare the following for the year ended December 31, 20x3:

(a) Schedule of cost of goods manufactured

(b) Schedule of cost of goods sold

(c) Income statement

SOLUTIONS TO SELF-TEST QUESTIONS AND EXERCISES

MATCHING

1. C	8. K	15. W	22. O	29. R
2. V	9. A	16. F	23. Y	30. P
3. H	10. X	17. GG	24. U	31. C C
4. BB	11. Z	18. I	25. FF	32. EE
5. J	12. G	19. D	26. S	33. M
6. T	13. E	20. L	27. HH	34. DD
7. B	14. Q	21. AA	28. N	

TRUE-FALSE QUESTIONS

1. T
2. T
3. F   Manufacturing overhead is a heterogeneous pool of indirect costs.
4. F   In managerial accounting, product costs are needed for planning, cost control, and decision making.
5. T
6. F   The predetermined overhead rate is used to apply overhead costs to products.
7. F   In financial accounting, product costs are needed to value inventory and to compute the cost-of-goods-sold expense.

8. **T**
9. **F** A time ticket is a record of the time a worker spends on a job.
10. **T**
11. **F** A schedule of cost of goods sold details the changes in Finished-Goods Inventory, as well as the cost of goods sold during the period.
12. **T**
13. **F** This costing system is called normal costing.
14. **T**
15. **T**
16. **F** It is used by various nonmanufacturing organizations.
17. **T**

FILL-IN-THE-BLANK QUESTIONS

1. Job-order
2. inputs
3. cost distribution (cost allocation)
4. service department cost allocation
5. jobs
6. job-cost sheet
7. bill of materials
8. actual
9. overapplied
10. proration
11. cost of goods manufactured
12. normalized
13. Throughput time
14. Overhead application

MULTIPLE-CHOICE QUESTIONS

1. **(b)** To record direct materials used in production, Work-in-Process Inventory is debited and Raw-Materials Inventory is credited.
2. **(a)** For the rate to be predetermined rate, we must divide by the estimated or planned amount of the cost driver.
3. **(d)** $50 = $5 x 10.
4. **(a)** This entry consists of a debit to Manufacturing Overhead and a credit to Wages Payable.
5. **(d)** This entry consists of a debit to Finished-Goods Inventory and a credit to Work-in-Process Inventory.
6. **(a)** The two entries to record the credit sale of products made are: (1) a debit to Cost of Goods Sold and a credit to Finished Goods Inventory and (2) a debit to Accounts Receivable and a credit to Sales Revenue.

EXERCISES

Exercise 3.1

(a)	Raw Materials	$135,000	
	Accounts Payable		$135,000
(b)	Manufacturing Overhead	4,800	
	Manufacturing Supplies Inventory		4,800
(c)	Manufacturing Overhead	9,000	
	Accounts Payable		9,000
(d)	Work-in-Process Inventory	95,000	
	Raw-Materials Inventory		95,000
(e)	Manufacturing Overhead	12,000	
	Accumulated Depreciation: Plant & Equipment		12,000
(f)	Work-in-Process Inventory	30,000	
	Cash		30,000
(g)	Manufacturing Overhead	4,000	
	Cash		4,000
(h)	Work-in-Process Inventory	32,000	
	Manufacturing Overhead		32,000
(i)	Finished-Goods Inventory	123,000	
	Work-in-Process Inventory		123,000
(j)	Cost of Goods Sold	105,900	
	Finished-Goods Inventory		105,900

Exercise 3.2

(a)(1)

$375,000/18,000 DLH = $20.83 per direct-labor hour

(a)(2)

$375,000/$216,000= $1.74 per direct labor dollar
(or overhead will applied at a rate of 174% of direct-labor cost)

(a)(3)

$375,000/12,000 MH = $31.25 per machine hour

(b)(1)

Applied overhead: =
17,000 actual direct-labor hours x $20.83 per direct-labor hour = $354,110
$394,000 actual overhead - $354,110 applied = $39,890 of underapplied overhead

(b)(2)

Applied overhead: =
(17,000 actual direct labor hours x $13.50 per direct labor hour) x 1.74 = $399,330
$399,330 applied overhead - $394,000 actual = $5,330 of overapplied overhead

(b)(3)

Applied overhead: =
10,000 machine hours x $31.25 per machine hour = $312,500
$394,000 actual overhead - $312,500 applied = $81,500 of underapplied overhead

Exercise 3.3

(a)

THE BRAMER COMPANY

Schedule of Cost of Goods Manufactured

For the Year Ended December 31, 20x3

Direct material:		
Raw-materials inventory, 1/1/x3	$ 51,600	
Add: Purchases of raw materials	168,000	
Raw materials available for use	219,600	
Less: Raw-materials inventory, 12/31/x3	31,200	
Raw material used		$188,400
Direct labor		336,000
Manufacturing overhead:		
Plant utilities	$78,000	
Plant supervision	75,000	
Indirect labor	60,000	
Indirect materials	42,000	
Depreciation on plant and equipment	54,000	
Other manufacturing overhead	12,000	321,000
Total manufacturing costs		845,400
Add: Work-in-process inventory, 1/1/x3		78,000
Subtotal		923,400
Less: Work-in-process inventory, 12/31/x3		72,000
Cost of goods manufactured		$851,400

(b)

THE BRAMER COMPANY
Schedule of Cost of Goods Sold
For the Year Ended December 31, 20x3

Finished goods inventory, 1/1/x3	$144,000
Add: Cost of goods manufactured	851,400
Cost of goods available for sale	995,400
Less: Finished-goods inventory, 12/31/x3	130,800
Cost of goods sold	$864,600

(c)

THE BRAMER COMPANY
Income Statement
For the Year Ended December 31, 20x3

Sales revenue	$1,342,000
Less: Cost of goods sold	864,600
Gross margin	477,400
Selling and administrative expenses	187,100
Net income before taxes	$ 290,300

IDEAS FOR YOUR STUDY TEAM

1. Rewrite each of the definitions of the key terms that appear at the end of the chapter using your own words. Imagine that you are trying to explain each key term to a friend who has not taken any accounting classes. Then, get together with the other members of your study team and compare your definitions.

Activity base

Activity-based costing (ABC) system

Actual costing

Actual manufacturing overhead

Actual overhead rate

Applied manufacturing overhead

Bill of materials

Cost distribution (sometimes called cost allocation)

Cost of goods manufactured

Cycle time

Departmental overhead centers

Departmental overhead rate

Job-cost record

Job-order costing

Material requisition form

Normal costing

Normalized overhead rate

Overapplied overhead

Overhead application (or absorption)

Plant-wide overhead rate

Predetermined overhead rate

Process-costing system

Product-costing system

Proration

Schedule of cost of goods manufactured

Schedule of cost of goods sold

Service departments

Service department cost allocation

Source document

Throughput time

Time ticket

Two-stage cost allocation

Underapplied overhead

Volume-based cost driver

2. Try to predict the types of questions, exercises and problems that you will encounter on the quizzes and exams that cover this chapter. Review the *Read and Recall Questions* and the *Self-Test Questions and Exercises* that are set forth in this Study Guide. Work through the end-of-chapter review problem(s), if applicable, and the end-of-chapter questions, exercises and problems that were assigned by your instructor. As you perform these tasks, identify the terms, concepts, formulas, etc. that you are responsible for knowing. After you develop the list of questions, exercises and problems that you expect to encounter on quizzes and exams, review the learning objectives that appear at the beginning of the chapter in your textbook to ensure that you have not overlooked anything significant. After you have completed your review of your list, get together with the other members of your study team and compare your predictions.

CHAPTER FOCUS SUGGESTIONS

This chapter continues the discussion of product-costing systems and includes coverage of process-costing systems. This chapter begins by reinforcing the similarities and differences between job-order and process-costing systems. After a discussion of the flow of costs through the system, the departmental production report is introduced. The departmental production report accounts for all units flowing into and out of the department; sets forth the calculations of material equivalent units, conversion equivalent units, and cost per equivalent unit for materials and conversion; and accounts for all costs flowing into and out of the department.

A clear understanding of the concept of an equivalent unit will help to ensure that you understand the other process-costing concepts presented in this chapter. You may or may not be responsible for knowing how to prepare a departmental production report from scratch, but you will definitely need to be familiar with the various calculations that are set forth on that report. You will need to know how to calculate the equivalent units for both materials and conversion, and the cost per equivalent unit for materials and conversion. You will also need to know how to determine the production costs for units transferred out to the next department during the period, and the costs that remain in Work-in-Process Inventory at the end of the period. You will need to be familiar with the journal entries used in a process-costing system, and the relationship between those journal entries and the departmental production report.

READ AND RECALL QUESTIONS

COMPARISON OF JOB-ORDER COSTING AND PROCESS COSTING

> **LEARNING OBJECTIVE #1**
> *After studying this section of the chapter, you should be able to:*
> • List and explain the similarities and important differences between job-order and process costing.

What are the two functions that are performed by a product-costing system?

What is a "repetitive production" environment?

What types of companies would use process costing?

In terms of the flow of costs through the manufacturing accounts, how is process costing similar to job-order costing? How is it different from job-order costing in this regard?

LEARNING OBJECTIVE #2
After studying this section of the chapter, you should be able to:
- Prepare journal entries to record the flow of costs in a process-costing system with sequential production departments.

Flow of Costs

What entry is used to record the use of direct materials and direct labor and the application of overhead in a production department?

How is the predetermined overhead rate determined in a process-costing system?

What are "transferred-in costs?" What entry is used to record the transfer of goods from one department to the next?

What entry is used to record the transfer of goods from the final production department to the finished-goods warehouse?

What entry is used to record the cost of the units sold during the period?

Differences between Job-Order and Process Costing

How are costs accumulated in a job-order costing system?

How are costs accumulated in a process-costing system?

EQUIVALENT UNITS: A KEY CONCEPT

LEARNING OBJECTIVE #3
After studying this section of the chapter, you should be able to:
- Prepare a table of equivalent units under weighted-average process costing.

What are conversion costs?

Equivalent Units

How are equivalent units computed?

What is an equivalent unit?"

How is the cost per equivalent unit for conversion computed?

How is the cost per equivalent unit for direct material computed?

ILLUSTRATION OF PROCESS COSTING

What is a "departmental production report?"

What job-order cost report is replaced by a departmental production report when process costing is used?

What are the four steps in the preparation of a departmental production report?

Which method (weighted-average or first-in, first-out) do most companies with process-costing systems use? Which method is described in detail in this chapter of the textbook?

Weighted-Average Method of Process Costing

Step 1: Analysis of Physical Flow of Units

What formula is used to prepare a table summarizing the physical flow of production units during the period?

Step 2: Calculation of Equivalent Units

What formula is used to calculate the total number of equivalent units?

LEARNING OBJECTIVE #4
After studying this section of the chapter, you should be able to:
• Compute the cost per equivalent unit under the weighted-average method of process costing.

Step 3: Computation of Unit Costs

How is the cost per unit for direct material computed?

What are conversion costs? How is the cost per unit for conversion costs computed?

LEARNING OBJECTIVE #5

After studying this section of the chapter, you should be able to:
- Analyze the total production costs for a department under the weighted-average method of process costing.

Step 4: Analysis of Total Costs

What formula is used to make sure that the total costs have been accounted for? (*Hint*: Examine the Analysis of Total Costs Report in Exhibit 4-8, and answer the following questions. First, what two subtotals in that exhibit add up to the "total costs accounted for" amount shown at the bottom of that report? Second, what are the two components of the "total costs accounted for" amount?)

LEARNING OBJECTIVE #6

After studying this section of the chapter, you should be able to:
- Prepare a departmental production report under weighted-average process costing.

What entry is used to record the transfer of goods from one department to the next department when the first department completes its production process? Where does the dollar amount that is used in this journal entry appear in the Analysis of Total Costs Report in Exhibit 4-8?

OTHER ISSUES IN PROCESS COSTING

Actual versus Normal Costing

What is the difference between a normal costing system and an actual-costing system in terms of the determination of the amounts of direct material, direct labor, and manufacturing overhead that are added to each Work-in-Process Inventory account?

Can normal costing be used in a process-costing system? Can actual costing be used in a process-costing system?

When normal costing is used, there may be overapplied or underapplied overhead at the end of the period. What are the two methods for closing the balance of the manufacturing overhead account?

Other Costs for Overhead Application

Commonly, direct labor and manufacturing overhead are combined and identified as conversion costs. When would overhead costs be accounted for separately from direct-labor costs in the process-costing calculations? Why?

HYBRID PRODUCT-COSTING SYSTEMS

LEARNING OBJECTIVE #7
After studying this section of the chapter, you should be able to: • Describe how an operation costing system accumulates and assigns the costs of direct-material and conversion activity in a batch manufacturing process.

Operation Costing for Batch Manufacturing Processes

What is a "batch manufacturing" process?

When is a hybrid product-costing system required? What is a "hybrid product-costing" system?

What is "operation costing?"

How are conversion costs accumulated in an operation costing system?

How are direct-material costs accumulated in this type of costing system? What method is then used to assign material costs to products in an operation costing system?

When operation costing is used, how is the predetermined application rate for conversion costs computed?

When operation costing is used, what entry is used to record the requisition of raw material by a production department under an operation costing system?

When operation costing is used, what entry is used to record the application of conversion costs to the production department's Work-in-Process Inventory account?

When operation costing is used, what entry is used to record the transfer of partially completed goods from one production department to the next?

When operation costing is used, what entry is used to record the transfer of completed goods from the last production department in the process to the finished goods department?

ADAPTING PRODUCT-COSTING SYSTEMS TO TECHNOLOGICAL CHANGE

Why does the amount of work-in-process inventory decline substantially when just-in-time (JIT) production and inventory management systems are installed?

Why did Hewlett-Packard combine its direct labor with manufacturing overhead in a single cost category? What benefit was realized by this change in procedure?

APPENDIX TO CHAPTER 4: PROCESS COSTING IN SEQUENTIAL PRODUCTION DEPARTMENTS

> **LEARNING OBJECTIVE #8**
> *Determine whether or not you are responsible for this appendix. If so, after studying this section of the chapter, you should be able to:*
> • Prepare process-costing calculations for a sequential manufacturing process.

In manufacturing operations with sequential production departments, a production department may have three cost elements: direct-material, conversion and transferred-in costs. What are "transferred-in costs?" What do these costs represent, in terms of the previous production department in the sequence?

SELF-TEST QUESTIONS AND EXERCISES

MATCHING

Match each of the key terms listed below with the appropriate textbook definition:

___	1. Batch manufacturing	___	6. Process-costing system
___	2. Departmental production report	___	7. Repetitive production
___	3. Equivalent units	___	8. Transferred-in costs*
___	4. Hybrid product-costing system	___	9. Weighted-average method
___	5. Operation costing		

*This key term is included in the appendix to the chapter.

A. The key document in a process-costing system. This report summarizes the physical flow of units, equivalent units of production, cost per equivalent unit, and analysis of total departmental costs.

B. A hybrid of job-order and process costing. Direct material is accumulated by batch of products using job-order-costing methods. Conversion costs are accumulated by department and assigned to product units by process-costing methods.

C. A measure of the amount of productive effort applied to a physical unit of production. For example, a physical unit that is 50 percent completed represents one-half of an equivalent unit.

D. High-volume production of several product lines that differ in some important ways but are nearly identical in others.

E. A production environment in which large numbers of identical or very similar products are manufactured in a continuous flow.

F. A system that incorporates features from two or more alternative product-costing systems, such as job-order and process costing.

G. A product-costing system in which production costs are averaged over a large number of product units. Used by firms that produce large numbers of nearly identical products.

H. Costs assigned to partially completed products that are transferred into one production department from a prior department.

I. A method of process costing in which the cost assigned to beginning work-in-process inventory is added to the current-period production costs. The cost per equivalent unit calculated under this process-costing method is a weighted average of the costs in the beginning work in process and the costs of the current period.

TRUE-FALSE QUESTIONS

For each of the following statements, enter a T or F in the blank to indicate whether the statement is true or false.

___1. The ultimate purpose of process costing is to assign production costs to units of output.

___2. In process costing, as products are produced, the manufacturing costs are accumulated in the Finished-Goods Inventory account.

___3. The most significant feature of process costing is that direct-material costs and conversion costs are assigned to equivalent units instead of physical units.

___4. The departmental production report for a department summarizes the flow of production quantities through the department.

___5. Nine hundred physical units that are 20 percent completed correspond to 720 equivalent units.

___6. In calculating equivalent units of activity under the weighted-average method, no distinction is made as to whether the activity occurred in the current period or in the previous period.

___7. The total cost per equivalent unit is the sum of the cost per equivalent unit of direct materials and the cost per equivalent unit of conversion.

___8. Process costing is used where relatively small numbers of products are made in distinct batches that are significantly different from one another.

___9. The flow of costs through the manufacturing accounts is the same in process costing as it is in job-costing.

___10. In preparing a departmental production report, either the FIFO method or the LIFO method may be used.

___11. The weighted average of process costing is more widely used in practice than is FIFO.

___12. Normal costing can be used with process costing, but actual costing cannot.

___13. If some driver other than direct labor is used for applying manufacturing overhead in a process-costing system, then overhead costs are accounted for separately from direct-labor costs in the process-costing computations.

___14. In operation costing, conversion costs are accumulated by batch or job order.

FILL-IN-THE-BLANK QUESTIONS

For each of the following statements, fill in the blank to properly complete the statement.

1. In sequential production departments, the manufacturing costs of the first department that are passed to the second department are called _____ ___ costs.

2. In process costing, costs are accumulated by _____; in job-order costing, costs are accumulated by _____.

3. The term _____ is used in process costing to refer to the amount of manufacturing activity that has been applied to a batch of physical units.

4. The departmental production report for a department shows the amount of production cost transferred out of the department's _____ account during the period.

5. Under the weighted-average method, the cost of goods completed and transferred out of a department is the number of units transferred out times the _____ ___.

6. The main document in a process-costing system is the _____ report.

7. If a predetermined overhead rate is used in a process-costing system, then this process-costing system is also a(n) _____ costing system.

8. _____ and _____ costing are the polar extremes of product costing.

9. _____ operations have features of both job-order costing and process-costing environments.

10. _____ costing is used when conversion activities are common across product lines, but the direct materials used in these products differ significantly.

11. In a sequential production process involving two departments, the second department in the sequence has three cost elements; they are _____ ___, _____ and conversion costs.

MULTIPLE-CHOICE QUESTIONS

Circle the best answer or response.

1. In a two-department sequential production process, A is the first department and B is the second. When partially completed goods are moved from A to B, the journal entry to record the transfer of production costs from A to B includes a
   (a) debit to Work-in-Process Inventory, Dept. A
   (b) debit to Work-in-Process Inventory, Dept. B
   (c) credit to Work-in-Process Inventory, Dept. B.
   (d) debit to Finished-Goods Inventory.

2. Assume 600 physical units are 80 percent complete with respect to direct materials and 30 percent complete with respect to conversion. Consider the following two statements, and determine which statement(s) is (are) true.

   I. There are 180 conversion equivalent units.
   II. There are 120 material equivalent units.

   (a) Only I
   (b) Only II
   (c) Both I and II
   (d) Neither I nor II

3. Preparing a production department report does *not* involve which of the following steps?
   (a) Analysis of physical flow units
   (b) Calculation of equivalent units
   (c) Computation of costs per equivalent unit
   (d) Preparation of the journal entry to account for the flow of cost

4. If beginning inventory of work in process has 3,000 physical units, 7,000 physical units were started during the period, and 8,000 physical units were completed and transferred out during the period, then the physical units in ending Work-in-Process Inventory amount to
   (a) 12,000.
   (b) 2,000.
   (c) 4,000.
   (d) 5,000

5. Consider the following statements and determine which statement(s) is (are) true.

   I. In operation costing, direct-material costs are accumulated by department.
   II. In operation costing, conversion costs are accumulated by job order or batch.

   (a) Only I
   (b) Only II
   (c) Both I and II
   (d) Neither I nor II

Exercises

Record your answers to each part of the exercises in the space provided. Show your work.

Exercise 4.1

The Clifford Company uses process costing and had the following data for the month of May:

Work-in-process inventory, May 1	3,000 units
Direct materials	100% complete
Conversion	40% complete
Finished and transferred out in May	78,000 units
Work-in-process inventory, May 31	5,000 units
Direct materials	100% complete
Conversion	70% complete

Using the weighted-average method, compute the equivalent units of direct material and conversion for May.

Exercise 4.2

The Rockwell Company makes latex paint and uses process costing. The following data are for the Mixing Department for the month of April:

Work-in-process, April 1	5,000 gal.
Direct materials	$22,000
Conversion	14,000
Costs incurred during April	
Direct materials	148,000
Conversion	350,000

The equivalent units (gallons) of activity for April were:

	Weighted Average	
	Materials	Conversion
Beginning work in process	5,000	5,000
Started and completed	35,000	35,000
Ending work in process	2,000	1,000
Total equivalent units	42,000	41,000

Units completed and transferred out in April: 40,000 gallons.

Use the weighted-average method to compute the:

(a) Cost of goods completed and transferred out during April

(b) Cost of work-in-process inventory on April 30

Exercise 4.3

The Kettler Company makes women's purses and uses operation costing. These purses are made of either leather or plastic. Both types of purses receive the same operations in the Cutting Department and the Assembly Department. However, only the leather purses receive a special type of stain-proofing in the Treatment Department. During June there were two batches started and finished, and there were no beginning or ending work-in-process inventories. Batch L consisted of 4,000 leather purses and batch P consisted of 6,000 plastic purses. Costs incurred were as follows:

Direct-material costs:

Batch L	$40,000
Batch P	24,000

Conversion costs:

Cutting Department	$30,000
Assembly Department	45,000
Treatment Department	8,000

Compute each of the following:

(a) The conversion cost per unit in the Cutting Department

(b) The conversion cost per unit in the Assembly Department

(c) The conversion cost per unit in the Treatment Department

(d) The product cost of a leather purse

(e) The product cost of a plastic purse

Exercise 4.4

The Assembly Department of the Fitz Company had the following results for July, in which some missing data are indicated:

Work in process, July 1 (in units)	18,000
Units started during July	?
Total units to account for	55,000
Units completed and transferred out in July	?
Work in process, July 31 (in units)	?
Total equivalent units for direct materials	55,000
Total equivalent units for conversion	?
Work in process, July 1, for direct materials	$ 90,000
Work in process, July 1, for conversion	?
Costs incurred during July for direct materials	?
Costs incurred during July for conversion	90,600
Work in process, July 1, cost in total	109,800
Total cost incurred during July	308,600
Total costs to account for	418,400
Cost per equivalent unit for direct materials	5.60
Cost per equivalent unit for conversion	?
Total cost per equivalent unit	8.00
Cost of goods completed and transferred out in July	?
Costs remaining in work process, July 31, for direct materials	?
Costs remaining in work in process, July 31, for conversion	7,200
Total cost of July 31 work in process	74,400

Additional information:

Direct material is added at the start of the production process, and conversion activity occurs uniformly throughout the process. Fitz uses weighted-average process costing.

The July I work in process was 50% complete as to conversion, and the July 31 work in process was 25% complete as to conversion.

There was no spoilage of any kind.

Calculate the missing data amounts and prepare a July production report for the Assembly Department.

SOLUTIONS TO SELF-TEST QUESTIONS AND EXERCISES

MATCHING

1. D   6. G
2. A   7. E
3. C   8. H
4. F   9. I
5. B

TRUE-FALSE QUESTIONS

1. T
2. F   They are accumulated in Work-in-Process Inventory.
3. T
4. T
5. F   They correspond to 180 equivalent units.
6. T
7. T
8. F   This description is for job-order costing, not process costing.
9. T
10. F   Either weighted average or FIFO can be used.
11. T
12. F   Both normal costing and actual costing can be used with process costing.
13. T
14. F   Conversion costs are accumulated by department.

FILL-IN-THE-BLANK QUESTIONS

1. transferred-in
2. department, job order (batch)
3. equivalent units
4. Work-in-Process Inventory
5. the total cost per equivalent unit
6. department production
7. normal
8. Job-order, process
9. Batch-manufacturing
10. Operation
11. transferred-in, direct-material

MULTIPLE-CHOICE QUESTIONS

1. **(b)** The journal entry involves a debit to Work-in-Process Inventory, Dept. B. and a credit to Work-in-Process Inventory, Dept. A.
2. **(a)** There are 480 material equivalent units and 180 conversion equivalent units.
3. **(d)**
4. **(b)** 7,000 - (8,000 - 3,000) = 2,000 units. Of the 8,000 units transferred out, 5,000 were started this period. This means that 7,000 - 5,000 = 2,000 are in ending Work-in- Process Inventory.
5. **(d)** In operation costing, direct-material costs are accumulated by batch and conversion costs are accumulated by department.

EXERCISES

Exercise 4.1

	Physical Units	Percent Complete in Conversion	Equivalent Units Direct Materials	Conversion
Work in process, May 1	3,000			
Units started in May	80,000			
Total units to account for	83,000			
Units completed and transferred out in May	78,000	100%	78,000	78,000
Work in process, May 31	5,000	70%	5,000	3,500
Total units accounted for	83,000			
Total equivalent units			83,000	81,500

Exercise 4.2

(a)

	Direct Material	Conversion	Total
Work in process, April 1	$ 22,000	$ 14,000	$ 36,000
Costs incurred in April	148,000	350,000	498,000
Total costs to account for*	$170,000	$364,000	$534,000
Total weighted-average equivalent units	42,000	41,000	
Cost per equivalent unit	$4.05	$8.88	$12.93

Cost of goods completed and transferred out
in April (40,000 x $12.93) $517,200

(b)

Costs remaining in work in process, April 30:	
Direct materials: (2,000 x $4.05)	8,100
Conversion: (1,000 x $8.88)	8,880
Total cost in work in process, April 30	16,980
Total costs accounted for*	$534,180

*Difference due to rounding.

Exercise 4.3

(a)

$30,000/(4,000 + 6,000) = $3.00

(b)

$45,000/(4,000 + 6,000) = $4.50

(c)

$8,000/4,000 = $2.00

(d)

Direct-material cost per unit = $40,000/4,000 = $10.00

Conversion cost per unit = $3.00 + $4.50 + $2.00 = $9.50

Total production cost per unit = $10.00 + $9.50 = $19.50

(e)

Direct-material cost per unit: $24,000/6,000 = $4.00

Conversion cost per unit: $3.00 + $4.50 = $7.50

Total production cost per unit = $4.00 + $7.50 = $11.50

Exercise 4.4

THE FITZ COMPANY
Production Report-Assembly Department
Weighted-Average Method
for the Month of July

	Physical Units	Percent Complete in Conversion	Equivalent Units Direct Materials	Conversion
Work in process, July 1	18,000	50%		
Units started in July	37,000 (1)			
Total units to account for	55,000			
Units completed and transferred out in July	43,000 (2)	100%	43,000	43,000
Work in process, July 31	12,000 (3)	25%	12,000	3,000
Total units accounted for	55,000			
Total equivalent units			55,000	46,000 (4)

	Direct Material	Conversion	Total
Work in process, July 1	$ 90,000	$ 19,800	$109,800
		(5)	
Costs incurred in July	218,000	90,600	308,600
	(6)		
Total costs to account for	$308,000	$110,400	$418,400
Total weighted-average equivalent units	55,00	46,000	
Cost per equivalent unit	$5.60	$2.40	$8.00
		(7)	
Cost of goods completed and transferred out in July			$344,000
			(8)
Costs remaining in work in process, July 31, Direct materials:			67,200
			(9)
Conversion:			7,200
Total cost in work in process, July 31			74,400
Total costs accounted for			$418,400

The numbers in parentheses in the above production report refer to the missing data and can be calculated as follows in the given sequence:

(9)   74,400 - 7,200 = 67,200

(8)   418,400 - 74,400 = 344,000

(7)   8.00 - 5.60 = 2.40

(6)   308,600 - 90,600 = 218,000

(5)   109,800 - 90,000 = 19,800

(4)   (19,800 + 90,600)/2.40 = 46,000

(3)   67,200/5.60 = 12,000

(2)   55,000 - 12,000 = 43,000

(1)   55,000 - 18,000 = 37,000

IDEAS FOR YOUR STUDY TEAM

1. Rewrite each of the definitions of the key terms that appear at the end of the chapter using your own words. Imagine that you are trying to explain each key term to a friend who has not taken any accounting classes. Then, get together with the other members of your study team and compare your definitions.

Batch manufacturing

Departmental production report

Equivalent units

Hybrid product-costing system

Operation costing

Process-costing system

Repetitive production

Transferred-in costs

Weighted-average method

2. Try to predict the types of questions, exercises and problems that you will encounter on the quizzes and exams that cover this chapter. Review the *Read and Recall Questions* and the *Self-Test Questions and Exercises* that are set forth in this Study Guide. Work through the end-of-chapter review problem(s), if applicable, and the end-of-chapter questions, exercises and problems that were assigned by your instructor. As you perform these tasks, identify the terms, concepts, formulas, etc. that you are responsible for knowing. After you develop the list of questions, exercises and problems that you expect to encounter on quizzes and exams, review the learning objectives that appear at the beginning of the chapter in your textbook to ensure that you have not overlooked anything significant. After you have completed your review of your list, get together with the other members of your study team and compare your predictions.

CHAPTER 5
ACTIVITY-BASED COSTING AND COST MANAGEMENT SYSTEMS

CHAPTER FOCUS SUGGESTIONS

This chapter provides an overview of the key characteristics of a traditional production process and plant layout. After reinforcing the computation of product costs under a traditional costing system, the shortcomings of this volume-based product-costing system are addressed.

A description of an activity-based costing system precedes an in-depth discussion of the two-stage procedure for cost assignment, the identification of cost pools, and the importance of the choice of cost drivers. The key features of a cost management system, including the elimination of non-value-added costs, are addressed, and the concept of activity-based management is introduced.

READ AND RECALL QUESTIONS

AEROTECH'S PHOENIX PLANT: TRADITIONAL PRODUCTION PROCESS

LEARNING OBJECTIVE #1
After studying this section of the chapter, you should be able to:
• Explain the key characteristics of a traditional manufacturing process and plant layout.

Plant Layout

What is a "process" or "functional" plant layout?

Traditional, Volume-Based Product-Costing System

How is overhead applied in a traditional, volume-based product-costing system?

Why are traditional product-costing systems often said to be "volume-based" (or throughput-based) costing systems?

LEARNING OBJECTIVE #2
After studying this section of the chapter, you should be able to:
• Compute product costs under a traditional, volume-based product-costing system and an activity-based costing system.

Activity-Based Costing System

An activity-based costing (ABC) system uses a two-stage procedure to assign overhead costs to products. What is performed in the first stage of the procedure?

What is an "activity cost pool?"

LEARNING OBJECTIVE #3
After studying this section of the chapter, you should be able to:
• Explain how an activity-based costing system operates, including the use of a two-stage procedure for cost assignment, the identification of activity cost pools, and the selection of cost drivers.

What are the four broad categories of activity cost pools that might be established in stage one?

What is performed in the second stage of the two-stage procedure to assign overhead costs to products?

Which activity cost pool category (i.e., unit level, batch level, product-sustaining level or facility level) would include a machinery cost pool? Why would machine hours be selected for the cost driver for this cost pool? How would the pool rate be computed for this cost pool?

Which activity cost pool category (i.e., unit level, batch level, product-sustaining level or facility level) would include a setup cost pool? Why would the number of production runs be selected for the cost driver for this cost pool? How would the pool rate be computed for this cost pool?

Which activity cost pool category (i.e., unit level, batch level, product-sustaining level or facility level) would include an engineering cost pool? What is an "engineering transaction?" Why would number of engineering transactions be selected for the cost driver for this cost pool? How would the pool rate be computed for this cost pool?

What is "transaction-based costing?"

Which activity cost pool category (i.e., unit level, batch level, product-sustaining level or facility level) would include a facility cost pool? Why might direct-labor hours be selected for the cost driver for this cost pool? How would the pool rate be computed for this cost pool?

Would it be appropriate to use transaction-based costing to select the cost driver for the following types of cost pools: receiving and inspection, material handling, quality assurance, and packaging and shipping? Why or why not?

LEARNING OBJECTIVE #4
After studying this section of the chapter, you should be able to:
• Explain why traditional, volume-based costing systems tend to distort product costs.

Why Traditional, Volume-Based Systems Distort Product Costs

Why did Aerotech's traditional, volume-based costing system overcost its high-volume product lines and undercost its complex, low-volume product line? Explain.

Why wasn't direct labor a suitable cost driver for Aerotech's overhead costs?

What type(s) of overhead costs is (are) incurred every time a unit is produced?

What type(s) of overhead costs is (are) *not* incurred every time a unit is produced?

What is a "consumption ratio?" Why does product diversity cause widely varying consumption ratios?

What two characteristics undermine the ability of a volume-based product-costing system to assign overhead costs accurately? Must both of these characteristics be present to undermine a volume-based product-costing system's ability to assign overhead costs accurately?

What type of costing system did Rockwell International use? How did Rockwell's costing system result in the overpricing of its high-volume truck axles? What cost driver was used?

What type of costing system did Compaq use? How did Compaq's costing system result in overcosting its high-volume products and undercosting its low-volume products? What cost driver was used?

ACTIVITY-BASED COSTING: SOME KEY ISSUES

LEARNING OBJECTIVE #5
After studying this section of the chapter, you should be able to:
- Discuss several key issues in activity-based costing, including criteria for choosing cost drivers, transaction costing, storyboarding, and indicators that a new costing system is needed.

Historically, what was the dominant element (direct materials, direct labor or overhead) in the cost structure of a typical manufacturer? What has been happening recently to that component of total production costs?

Why is the data required for activity-based costing more readily available than in the past?

Cost Drivers

What is a cost driver? What three factors are important in selecting appropriate cost drivers?

Why does the accuracy of the resulting cost assignment depend on the degree of correlation between consumption of the activity and consumption of the cost driver? How would the cost driver be identified?

What is the cost-benefit trade-off that must be considered in the design of an activity-based costing system? Why does the accuracy of the cost assignments increase when the number of activity cost pools in an activity-based costing system increases?

How can information systems positively influence the behavior of decision-makers? How can an information system result in dysfunctional behavioral effects?

Homogeneous Activity Cost Pools

What is a "homogeneous cost pool?"

Why should consumption ratios be the same for the individual components of a cost pool such as a combined receiving and inspection cost pool? What happens when significant deviations from homogeneity exist in combined cost pools?

Transaction Costing

How is transaction costing used to assign the costs of activities to product lines in an ABC system?

How did Aerotech obtain the transaction information that was used in its ABC system?

Storyboarding

What is "storyboarding?" Who participates in a storyboarding session?

Multidisciplinary ABC Project Teams

Who should be included on a typical ABC project team?

Activity Dictionary and Bill of Activity.

What is an activity dictionary? What is a bill of activity?

Direct versus Indirect Costs

Direct materials and direct labor are considered direct costs in traditional, volume-based costing systems? How are all other production costs treated? What basis is used to apply such production costs to products?

What is the goal of an ABC system in terms of the classification of direct and indirect costs?

When is a New Product-Costing System Needed?

What is the cost-benefit trade-off that is considered when an optimal information system is designed?

COST MANAGEMENT SYSTEMS

LEARNING OBJECTIVE #6
After studying this section of the chapter, you should be able to:
- Describe the key features of a cost management system, including the elimination of non-value-added costs.

What is "strategic cost analysis?" What is the "value chain?"

What is a "cost management system" (CMS)? What are the four objectives of a CMS?

Non-Value Added Costs

What is "process time?" What is "inspection time?" What is "move time?" What is "waiting time?" What is "storage time?"

Identifying Non-Value-Added Costs in the Phoenix Plant

Why does storage time have at least some potential for causing non-value-added costs? Why is waiting time indicative of potentially large non-value-added costs? Why does move time have at least some potential for causing non-value-added costs?

What is the goal of many manufacturers in terms of the costs of maintaining product quality? Why?

Could the actual production process that transforms raw materials into finished products (or process time) include some non-value-added costs? Explain.

ACTIVITY-BASED MANAGEMENT

What is "activity-based management" (ABM)? What is a key feature of activity-based costing systems?

What are the two motivating factors behind the collection of financial or operational performance information about significant activities in the enterprise?

ACTIVITY-BASED COSTING AND MANAGEMENT IN THE SERVICE INDUSTRY

What benefit was realized when Braintree Hospital implemented an activity-based costing system? What benefit was realized when American Express implemented an activity-based costing system? What benefit was realized when AT&T implemented an activity-based costing system?

SELF-TEST QUESTIONS AND EXERCISES

MATCHING

Match each of the key terms listed below with the appropriate textbook definition:

____ 1. Activity-based costing (ABC) system
____ 2. Activity-based management (ABM)
____ 3. Activity cost pool
____ 4. Activity dictionary
____ 5. Batch-level activity
____ 6. Bill of activities
____ 7. Consumption ratio
____ 8. Cost driver
____ 9. Cost management system (CMS)
____ 10. Facility (or general-operations) level activity
____ 11. Homogeneous cost pool
____ 12. Inspection time
____ 13. Move time
____ 14. Non-value added costs
____ 15. Pool rate
____ 16. Process (or functional) plant layout
____ 17. Process time
____ 18. Product-sustaining level activity
____ 19. Storage time
____ -20. Storyboarding
____ 21. Strategic cost analysis
____ 22. Transaction-based costing
____ 23. Unit-level activity
____ 24. Volume-based (or throughput-based) costing system
____ 25. Waiting time

A. The proportion of an activity consumed by a particular product.
B. The time spent on quality inspections of raw materials, partially completed products, or finished goods.
C. The cost per unit of the cost driver for a particular activity cost pool.
D. Using an activity-based costing system to improve the operations of an organization.
E. An activity that is required in order for an entire production process to occur.
F. An activity that must be accomplished for each batch of products rather than for each unit.
G. A product-costing system in which multiple cost drivers are identified, and costs of activities are assigned to products on the basis of the number of transactions they generate for the various cost drivers.
H. The time during which partially completed products wait for the next phase of production.
I. An activity that is needed to support an entire product tine, but is not always performed every time a new unit or batch of products is produced.
J. A two-stage procedure used to assign overhead costs to products or services produced. In the first stage, significant activities are identified, and overhead costs are assigned to activity cost pools in accordance with the way resources are consumed by the activities. In the second stage, the overhead costs are allocated from each activity cost pool to each product line in proportion to the amount of the cost driver consumed by the product line.
K. A grouping of overhead costs in which each cost component is consumed in roughly the same proportion by each product line.
L. The time during which raw materials or finished products are stored in stock.
M. The time spent moving raw materials, sub-assemblies, or finished products from one production operation to another.
N. A grouping of overhead costs assigned to various similar activities identified in an activity-based costing system.
O. An activity that must be done for each unit of production.
P. A broad-based managerial-accounting analysis that supports strategic management systems.

Q. A characteristic of an event or activity that results in the incurrence of costs by that event or activity.

R. The costs of activities that can be eliminated without deterioration of product quality, performance, or perceived value.

S. The amount of time during which a product is actually being worked on.

T. A product-costing system in which costs are assigned to products on the basis of a single activity base related to volume (e.g., direct-labor hours or machine hours).

U. A management planning and control system that measures the cost of significant activities, identifies non-value-added costs, and identifies activities that will improve organizational performance.

V. A method of organizing the elements of a production process, in which similar processes and functions are grouped together.

W. A procedure used to develop a detailed process flowchart, which visually represents activities and the relationships among the activities.

X. A complete listing of the activities identified and used in an organization's ABC analysis.

Y. A complete listing of the activities required for the product or service to be produced.

TRUE-FALSE QUESTIONS

For each of the following statements, enter a T or F in the blank to indicate whether the statement is true or false.

___**1.** Traditional product-costing systems are volume-based costing systems.

___**2.** The use of multiple overhead rates in the application of manufacturing overhead usually results in more accurate product-cost data than does a single overhead rate.

___**3.** In activity-based costing, a single cost driver is used for all manufacturing overhead costs.

___**4.** It would be unreasonable to assume that packing and shipping costs are driven by the number of production runs to be packed.

___**5.** The pressure of foreign competition is forcing U.S. manufacturers to strive for better understanding of their cost structures.

___**6.** Transactions provide a readily measurable gauge of the activity in a department.

___**7.** In ABC costing an effort is made to account for as few costs as possible as direct costs of production.

___**8.** A strategic analysis identifies the activities by which an organization creates a valuable product or service.

___**9.** The amount of time that raw materials or work in process spend waiting for the next operation is called move time.

___**10.** A possible cost driver of engineering costs is the number of engineering change orders.

___**11.** A possible cost driver of receiving and inspection costs is the number of shipments received and inspected.

___**12.** Nowadays, direct labor is becoming a much larger portion of total production costs than in the past.

___**13.** The cost structures of many manufacturers have changed significantly over the past decade.

___**14.** In an activity-based costing system, only those cost drivers that are related to the bulk of costs need to be identified and tracked.

___**15.** In an activity-based costing system, the costs of activities are assigned to product lines on the basis of the amount of cost driver consumed by each product.

___**16.** In stage two of an ABC system, overhead costs are assigned to activity cost pools.

FILL-IN-THE-BLANK QUESTIONS

For each of the following statements, fill in the blank to properly complete the statement.

1.   A(n) _____ is an event or activity that results in the incurrence of costs.

2.   _____ is a broad-based, managerial-accounting analysis that supports strategic management decisions.

3.   The time during which a product is undergoing conversion activity is called _____ _____.

4.   The time during which materials, partially completed products, or finished goods are held in stock before further processing or shipments to customers is called _____ _____.

5.   The amount of time spent moving raw materials, work in process, or finished goods between operations is called _____.

6.   The _____ is the proportion of an activity consumed by a product.

7.   In a plant layout when similar processes are grouped together, this type of layout is called a _____.

8.   In an ABC system the cost pool category that includes activities needed to support an entire product line is called the _____.

9.   When costs are assigned from an activity cost pool based on the relative proportion of the activity consumed by products as measured by transactions, this system is known as_____.

10.   Two reasons why volume-based costing systems can fail to assign overhead costs accurately in a manufacturing firm are a large proportion of nonunit-level activities and_____.

11.   _____ is a procedure in ABC analysis for collecting activity data and developing process flow charts for the activities.

12.   The set of linked activities by which an organization creates a valuable product or service is called the _____.

13.   The overall objectives of ABC and ABM in service firms are _____ as in manufacturing firms.

MULTIPLE-CHOICE QUESTIONS

Circle the best answer or response.

1.   Which of the following are cost drivers, as measured in terms of transactions?
      (a) Number of material moves
      (b) Number of units reworked
      (c) Number of vendors
      (d) All of the above

2.   Which of the following is *not* an objective of a cost management system?
      (a) Measuring the cost of resources used in performing the organization's significant activities
      (b) Identifying and creating non-value-added costs
      (c) Determining the effectiveness and efficiency of all major activities performed by the organization
      (d) Identifying and evaluating new activities that can improve the future performance of the organization

3. The category of activity cost pools where activities must be performed for a group of products rather than individual units of product is called
   (a) unit level
   (b) batch level
   (c) product-sustaining level
   (d) facility level

4. A company uses ABC and makes products P and Q. The total cost of the quality assurance activity cost pool is $120,000 of which $36,000 is consumed by product P. The consumption ratio of this activity for product Q is
   (a) 30 percent
   (b) 33 percent
   (c) 70 percent
   (d) 67 percent

5. The total cost of the machining activity cost pool is $600,000. The cost driver of machining is machine hours, and a total of 40,000 machine hours are consumed. If one unit of product X requires 1.5 machine hours, then the cost per unit of product X for machining is
   (a) $15.00
   (b) $18.75
   (c) $20.00
   (d) $22.50

EXERCISES

Record your answers to each part of the exercises in the space provided. Show your work.

Exercise 5.1

Mosher Abrasives, Inc., has two production departments, I and II, with the following overhead budget data for the forthcoming year:

	Total	Production Dept. I	Production Dept. II
Depreciation of equipment	$110,000	$20,000	$90,000
Occupancy costs	$30,000	$10,000	$20,000
Energy costs	$14,000	$6,000	$8,000
Machine hours	12,500	4,500	8,000
Direct-labor hours	15,000	10,500	4,500

The company makes two products, A and B, for sale. The production times per unit needed for these products (measured in direct-labor hours) are as follows:

	Labor Time		Machine Time	
	Dept. I	Dept. II	Dept. I.	Dept. II.
Product A	1.5	0.5	0.4	0.6
Product B	0.6	0.4	0.5	1.0

(a) Calculate a single predetermined overhead rate based on direct-labor hours.

(b) Determine how much overhead will be assigned to product A per unit and to product B per unit if the overhead rate in part (a) is used.

(c) Determine two overhead rates, one for Department I based on direct-labor hours and another for Department II based on machine hours.

(d) How much overhead will be assigned to product A per unit and to product B per unit if the overhead rates found in part (c) are used?

(e) Explain why the unit costs of overhead for each product in parts (b) and (d) are different.

Exercise 5.2

The Duncan Company makes and sells three products, A, B, and C. The company uses activity-based costing. The following budget data for overhead for next year are available:

	Total	Product A	Product B	Product C
Units to be made and sold		12,000	8,000	3,000
Manufacturing overhead costs:				
Engineering	$500,000	30%	50%	20%
Receiving and inspection	180,000	40%	30%	30%
Material handling	430,000	50%	30%	20%
Machining	960,000	60%	20%	20%
Packing	120,000	50%	20%	30%

The above percentages represent the proportion of transaction items for each overhead item that pertains to each product. The cost drivers for the overhead items are as follows:

Engineering—number of change orders

Receiving and inspection—number of inspections

Material handling—raw-material costs

Machining—machine hours

Packing—number of shipments made

Calculate the total overhead costs assigned to each product on a per-unit basis:

Exercise 5.3

The Hanson Manufacturing Company has recently installed new computerized devices to help monitor the quality of the output of their production processes. These devices, which are operated by three technically trained computer specialists, have replaced fifteen quality control personnel. The wages of the quality control personnel were treated as direct-labor. The operating costs of these new computerized devices, including the salaries of the computer specialists, have been included in manufacturing overhead. Hanson presently uses a plantwide manufacturing overhead rate based on direct labor dollars.

The president of Hanson was told how efficiently the new computer devices are working. However, she was surprised to discover that the manufacturing overhead rate had doubled. The president complained, "This information does not make any sense!" The following summarizes the data available:

	After the Devices	Before the Devices
Annual budgeted overhead	$2,700,000	$1,728,000
Annual budgeted direct labor	750,000	960,000
Budgeted overhead rate	360%	180%

Write a brief essay which explains the basis of the dilemma presented in the scenario above and addresses how activity-based costing could help to address the issues and concerns expressed by the president of Hanson.

Exercise 5.4

The Blue Ridge Rehabilitation Center uses activity-based costing. The following data have been budgeted for next year:

Activity	Driver	Cost
House patients	Patient-days	$390,000
Feed patients	Number of meals served	175,500
Therapy care	Number of therapy procedures	88,000
Nursing care	Number of hours worked	296,000

Item	Type of Patient Care Needed Regular	Critical	Total
Meals served	30,000	9,000	39,000
Therapy procedures used	400	700	1,100
Hours of nursing care	7,500	11,000	18,500
Patient-days	10,000	3,000	13,000

(a) Compute the budgeted cost per activity driver unit for each of the four activities.

(b) Using the activity cost per driver unit rates computed in part (a), calculate the cost of each activity that will be assigned to regular patient care and to critical patient care.

(c) Calculate the total annual budgeted cost for each type of patient care.

(d) Assuming that costs are assigned to patients on the basis of patient-days, calculate the budgeted cost per patient-day for each type of patient care.

SOLUTIONS TO SELF-TEST QUESTIONS AND EXERCISES

MATCHING

1. J	6. Y	11. K	16. V	21. P
2. D	7. A	12. B	17. S	22. G
3. N	8. Q	13. M	18. I	23. O
4. X	9. U	14. R	19. L	24. T
5. F	10. E	15. C	20. W	25. H

TRUE-FALSE QUESTIONS

1. T
2. T
3. F   In activity-based costing, each cost pool for manufacturing overhead has its own cost driver.
4. F   It is reasonable to assume that there is a causal relationship between the number of production runs and packing and shipping costs.
5. T
6. T
7. F   An effort is made to account for as many costs as possible as direct costs of production.
8. T
9. F   This is called waiting time.
10. T
11. T
12. F   Labor is now a much smaller portion of total production costs than in the past.
13. T
14. T
15. T
16. F   This is done in stage one of an ABC system.

FILL-IN-THE-BLANK QUESTIONS

1. cost driver
2. Strategic cost analysis
3. process time
4. storage time
5. move time
6. consumption ratio
7. process (or functional) layout
8. product-sustaining level
9. transaction-based costing
10. product diversity
11. Storyboarding
12. value chain
13. the same

MULTIPLE-CHOICE QUESTIONS

1. **(d)** They are all cost drivers as measured in terms of transactions.
2. **(b)** The objective is to eliminate non-value-added costs.
3. **(b)**
4. **(c)** ($120,000 - $36,000)/$120,000 = 70%
5. **(d)** ($600,000/40,000 MH) X 1.5 MH = $22.50/MH

EXERCISES

Exercise 5.1

(a)

$154,000/15,000 DLH = $10.27/DLH

(b)

To product A: 2 DLH x $10.27/DLH = $20.54/unit

To product B.: I DLH x $10.27/DLH = $10.27/unit

(c)

For Department I: $36,000/10,500 DLH = $3.43/DLH

For Department II: $118,000/8,000 MH = $14.75/MH

(d)

To product A: (1.5 DLH x $3.43/DLH) +(0.6 MH x $14.75/MH) = $14.00/unit

To product B: (0.6 DLH x $3.43/DLH) +(1.0 MH x $14.75/MH) = $16.81/unit

(e)

The unit costs of overhead for product A in parts (b) and (d) are different because each is based on a different set of cost drivers. The same statement applies to product B.

Exercise 5.2

Engineering:

To A: $500,000 x .3/12,000 = $12.50
To B: $500,000 x .5/8,000 = $31.25
To C: $500,000 x .2/3,000 = $33.33

Receiving and inspection:

To A: $180,000x.4/12,000=$ 6.00
To B.: $180,000 x .3/8,000 = $ 6.75
To C: $180,000 x .3/3,000 = $18.00

Material handling:

To A: $430,000 x .5/12,000 = $17.92
To B.: $430,000 x .3/8,000 = $16.13
To C: $430,000 x .2/3,000 = $28.67

Machining:

To A: $960,000 x .6/12,000 = $48.00
To B.: $960,000 x .2/8,000 = $24.00
To C: $960,000 x .2/3,000 = $64.00

Packing:

To A: $120,000 x .5/12,000 = $5.00
To B.: $120,000 x .2/8,000 = $3.00
To C: $120,000 x .3/3,000 = $12.00

Total overhead per unit of product A

$12.50 + $6.00 + $17.92 + $48.00 + $5.00 = $89.42

Total overhead per unit of product B

$31.25 + $6.75 + $16.13 + $24.00 + $3.00 = $81.13

Total overhead per unit of product C

$33.33 + $18.00 + $28.67 + $64.00 + $12.00 = $156.00

Exercise 5.3

When computerized devices replaced fifteen direct laborers, the budgeted annual direct labor costs decreased accordingly, and budgeted manufacturing overhead costs increased. Manufacturing overhead increased as a result of additional salaries expense related to the required computer specialists and depreciation expense related to the new devices.

Activity-based costing (ABC) seeks to account for manufacturing overhead costs by forming homogeneous cost pools, and then ascertaining appropriate cost drivers for those cost pools. If the company used this costing approach, it would be able to track its overhead costs with more accurately than with its present plantwide rate method. In addition, activity-based costing would help the company identify those production activities that add no value to the products it makes. By highlighting the non-value-added activities, management will be encouraged to reduce these non-value-added costs of production.

Exercise 5.4

(a)

House patients:	$390,000/13,000 = $30 per patient-day
Feed patients:	$175,500/39,000 = $4.50 per meal served
Therapy care:	$88,000/1,100 = $80 per procedure
Nursing care:	$296,000/18,500 = $16 per hour

(b)

	Regular Care	Critical Care
House patients:	$30 x 10,000 = $300,000	$30 x 3,000 = $90,000
Feed patients:	$4.50 x 30,000 = $135,000	$4.50 x 9,000 = $40,500
Therapy care:	$80 x 400 = $32,000	$80 x 700 = $56,000
Nursing care:	$16 x 7,500 = $120,000	$16 x 11,000 = $176,000

(c)

	Regular Care	Critical Care
Total coat:	$587,000	$362,500

(d)

Regular care:	$587,000/10,000 = $58.70 per patient-day
Critical care:	$362,500/3,000 = $120.83 per patient-day

IDEAS FOR YOUR STUDY TEAM

1.   Rewrite each of the definitions of the key terms that appear at the end of the chapter using your own words. Imagine that you are trying to explain each key term to a friend who has not taken any accounting classes. Then, get together with the other members of your study team and compare your definitions.

Activity-based costing (ABC) system

Activity-based management (ABM)

Activity cost pool

Activity Dictionary

Batch-level activity

Bill of Activities

Consumption ratio

Cost driver

Cost management system (CMS)

Facility (or general operations) level activity

Homogeneous cost pool

Inspection time

Move time

Non-value-added costs

Pool rate

Process (or functional) plant layout

Process time

Product-sustaining-level activity

Storage time

Storyboarding

Strategic cost analysis

Transaction-based costing

Unit-level activity

Volume-based (or throughput-based) costing system

Waiting time

2. Try to predict the types of questions, exercises and problems that you will encounter on the quizzes and exams that cover this chapter. Review the *Read and Recall Questions* and the *Self-Test Questions and Exercises* that are set forth in this Study Guide. Work through the end-of-chapter review problem(s), if applicable, and the end-of-chapter questions, exercises and problems that were assigned by your instructor. As you perform these tasks, identify the terms, concepts, formulas, etc. that you are responsible for knowing. After you develop the list of questions, exercises and problems that you expect to encounter on quizzes and exams, review the learning objectives that appear at the beginning of the chapter in your textbook to ensure that you have not overlooked anything significant. After you have completed your review of your list, get together with the other members of your study team and compare your predictions.

CHAPTER 6
ACTIVITY-BASED MANAGEMENT AND TODAY'S ADVANCED MANUFACTURING ENVIRONMENT

CHAPTER FOCUS SUGGESTIONS

This chapter continues the discussion of activity-based management and today's advanced manufacturing environment. Again, you may find that you are not be familiar with many of the terms used in this chapter. A listing of key terms appears at the end of the chapter. Become familiar with each of them.

You should focus your attention on the following terms and concepts: just-in-time inventory and production management system, two-dimensional activity-based costing, activity-based management, customer profitability analysis, target costing, kaizen costing, continuous improvement, benchmarking, re-engineering, and the theory of constraints.

READ AND RECALL QUESTIONS

LEARNING OBJECTIVES #1 & #2
After studying this section of the chapter, you should be able to:
- Describe the key features of a production facility employing advanced manufacturing technology.
- List and explain eight important features of just-in-time inventory and production management systems.

Just-in-Time Inventory and Production Management

What is a just-in-time (JIT) inventory and production management system? What is the primary goal of a JIT production system?

Why is a smooth, uniform production rate an important goal of a JIT system? What is the "pull method?" Where does the pull method of production begin?

What is a "withdrawal Kanban?" What is a "production Kanban?"

Why would a company purchase materials and manufacture subassemblies and products in small lot sizes? What benefit is realized?

What must a manufacturer be able to do in order to produce in small lot sizes? What are the benefits of purchasing materials and producing goods only as required?

What is a "total quality control" (or TCQ) program? Why does a TCQ program often accompany a just-in-time production environment?

How can a manufacturer avoid costly down time from machine breakdown?

Why is an atmosphere of teamwork required in order to improve the production system?

What two factors can help prevent bottlenecks? What is caused by bottlenecks?

What is "group technology?" What benefit is realized by group technology?

When are materials and parts purchased from outside vendors when a JIT purchasing is used? What are the five key features of JIT purchasing?

Flexible Manufacturing System

What are computer-numerically-controlled (CNC) machines? What is a computer-aided manufacturing (CAM) system? What is a computer-aided design (CAD) system? What are CAD/CAM systems? What is an automated material-handling system (AMHS)?

What is a flexible manufacturing system (FMS)? What is a FMS cell? What is "cellular" manufacturing?

What is the most advanced level of automated manufacturing?

What is "off-line quality control?"

Cost Management System in Bakersfield

What crucial step did Aerotech need to implement in its Phoenix plant in order to achieve a significant reduction in non-value-added costs?

Direct versus Indirect Costs

What are almost all production costs traced to in Aerotech's Bakersfield plant?

What does "capital-intensive" mean? What does "labor-intensive" mean? Which type of plant (capital-intensive or labor-intensive) would have a much larger proportion of fixed costs? Why?

Why does Aerotech's Bakersfield plant assign facilities costs on the basis of machine hours instead of labor hours, as done by its Phoenix plant?

What is "target costing?"

TWO-DIMENSIONAL ABC AND ACTIVITY-BASED MANAGEMENT

LEARNING OBJECTIVES #3 & #4
After studying this section of the chapter, you should be able to: • Explain the concept of activity-based management, and   • Explain the concept of two-dimensional activity-based costing.

What is activity-based management (or ABM)? What is "activity analysis?" What does it involve?

After studying this section of the chapter, you should be able to:
• List and explain the steps in using ABM to eliminate non-value-added costs.

Using ABM to Eliminate Non-Value-Added Activities and Costs

What are "non-valued-added activities?" What are "non-valued-added costs?"

What five steps provide a strategy for eliminating non-value-added costs in both manufacturing and service industry firms?

What is involved in activity analysis? For example, how should the purchasing function be viewed?

What are the three criteria for determining whether an activity adds value?

What is a "process?" What is "process value analysis" (or PVA)?

Achieving Cost Reduction

What are the four techniques that may be used to reduce the resulting non-value-added costs?

CUSTOMER PROFITABILITY ANALYSIS

LEARNING OBJECTIVE #6 *After studying this section of the chapter, you should be able to:* • Explain and execute a customer profitability analysis.

What is customer profitability analysis? Why is it performed?

What factors can result in some customer being more profitable than others?

What is the first step in implementing customer profitability analysis?

What are some examples of customer-related activities?

How can you determine whether or not the customer related costs of certain customers is a recent event, or an ongoing problem?

What is customer profitability analysis? Why is it performed?

What are the best norms to use as a comparison for customer related costs?

What is a customer profitability profile?

TARGET COSTING, KAIZEN COSTING, AND CONTINUOUS IMPROVEMENT

What is "continuous improvement?"

What is the "price down/cost down concept?"

LEARNING OBJECTIVE #7
After studying this section of the chapter, you should be able to:
- Define and give an example of target costing.

Target Costing

What is "target costing?" What is a "target price?" What is a "target profit?" What is a "target cost?"

If the target price of a product is $5,500, and a target profit of $500 is desired, what is the target cost of the product?

What is "value engineering" (or value analysis)?

After studying this section of the chapter, you should be able to:
• Explain the concept of kaizen costing, and prepare a kaizen-costing chart.

Kaizen Costing

What is "kaizen costing?" How can significant reductions in costs be attained over time when kaizen costing is used?

What three steps can be used to meet kaizen costing goals?

Toyota: Target Costing and Kaizen Costing in Action

What is the essence of cost control at Toyota?

What is employee "empowerment?"

LEARNING OBJECTIVE #9

After studying this section of the chapter, you should be able to:
- Briefly explain the concepts of continuous improvement, benchmarking, re-engineering, and the theory of constraints.

Benchmarking

What is benchmarking? What are "best practices?" What is re-engineering?

How did Cummins Engine achieve a forty percent reduction in engine costs and prices and significantly improved product quality? What happened when AMP re-engineered its supplier management practices? What happened when Motorola re-engineered its accounting functions?

What is the "theory of constraints?"

LEARNING OBJECTIVE #10

After studying this section of the chapter, you should be able to:
- List and briefly explain five keys to successfully implementing ABC, ABM, and other cost management systems.

KEYS TO SUCCESSFULLY IMPLEMENTING ABC AND ABM

What are the five key factors that can increase the likelihood of successful implementation of ABC, ABM, and other cost management techniques?

OTHER COST MANAGEMENT ISSUES IN TODAY'S MANUFACTURING ENVIRONMENT

What is "product life-cycle costing?" What are the five stages that follow the inception of a product's life cycle?

MATCHING

Match each of the key terms listed below with the appropriate textbook definition:

____ 1. Activity analysis
____ 2. Activity-based management (ABM)
____ 3. Automated material-handling system (AMHS)
____ 4. Benchmarking (or competitive benchmarking)
____ 5. Best practices
____ 6. CAD/CAM system
____ 7. Capital intensive
____ 8. Cellular manufacturing
____ 9. Change champion
____ 10. Computer-aided design (CAD) system
____ 11. Computer-aided manufacturing (CAM) system
____ 12. Computer-integrated manufacturing (CIM) system
____ 13. Computer-numerically-controlled (CNC) machines
____ 14. Continuous improvement
____ 15. Customer profitability analysis
____ 16. Customer profitability profile
____ 17. Empowerment
____ 18. Flexible manufacturing system (FMS)

____ 19. FMS cell
____ 20. Just-in-time (JIT) inventory and production management system
____ 21. Just-in-time (JIT) purchasing
____ 22. Kaizen costing
____ 23. Labor-intensive
____ 24. Non-value-added activities
____ 25. Non-value-added costs
____ 26. Off-line quality control
____ 27. Organizational culture
____ 28. Process
____ 29. Process value analysis (PVA)
____ 30. Production Kanban
____ 31. Product life-cycle costing
____ 32. Pull method
____ 33. Re-engineering
____ 34. Target costing
____ 35. Theory of constraints
____ 36. Total quality control (TQC)
____ 37. Two-dimensional ABC model
____ 38. Value engineering (or value analysis)
____ 39. Withdrawal Kanban

A. The organization of a production facility into FMS cells.

B. The process of cost reduction during the manufacturing phase of a product. Refers to continual and gradual improvement through small betterment activities.

C. Activities during the product design and engineering phases, which will improve the manufacturability of the product, reduce production costs, and ensure high quality.

D. A group of machines and personnel within a flexible manufacturing system (FMS).

E. A product-quality program in which the objective is complete elimination of product defects.

F. Computer software used by engineers in the design of a product.

G. An approach to purchasing management in which materials and parts are purchased only as they are needed.

H. The continual search for the most effective method of accomplishing a task, by comparing existing methods and performance levels with those of other organizations or with other subunits within the same organization.

I. The accumulation of costs that occur over the entire life cycle of a product.

J. A card sent to the preceding work center indicating the number and type of parts requested from that work center by the next work center.

K. The most effective methods of accomplishing various tasks in a particular industry often discovered through benchmarking.

L. A combination of the cost assignment view of the role of activity-based costing with its process analysis and evaluation role. Two-dimensional ABC is one way of depicting activity-based management.

M. A comprehensive inventory and manufacturing control system in which no materials are purchased and no products are manufactured until they are needed.

N. Stand-alone machines controlled by a computer via a numerical, machine-readable code.

O. Computer-controlled equipment that automatically moves materials, parts, and products from one production stage to another.

P. The constant effort to eliminate waste, reduce response time, simplify the design of both products and processes, and improve quality and customer service.

Q. A set of linked activities.

R. A production process accomplished largely by machinery.

S. A card specifying the number of parts to be manufactured in a particular work center.

T. A cost reduction and process improvement technique that utilizes information collected about a product's design and production processes and then examines various attributes of the design and processes to identify candidates for improvement.

U. Any production process in which computers are used to help control production.

V. The design of a product, and the processes used to produce it, so that ultimately the product can be manufactured at a cost that will enable a firm to make a profit when the product is sold at an estimated market-driven price. This estimated price is called the target price, the desired profit margin is called the target profit, and the cost at which the product must be manufactured is called the target cost.

W. Individuals who recognizes the need for change, and through his or her own efforts seeks to bring it about.

X. The most advanced form of automated manufacturing in which virtually all parts of the production process are accomplished by computer-controlled machines and automated material handling equipment.

Y. The detailed identification and description of the activities conducted in an enterprise.

Z. The concept of encouraging and authorizing workers to take their own initiative to improve operations, reduce costs, and improve product quality and customer service.

AA. Operations that are either (1) unnecessary and dispensable or (2) necessary, but inefficient and improvable.

BB. Using an activity-based costing system to improve the operations of an organization.

CC. The mind-set of employees, including their shared beliefs, values, and goals.

DD. The complete redesign of a process, with an emphasis on finding creative new ways to accomplish an objective.

EE. A series of manufacturing machines controlled and integrated by a computer, which is designed to perform a series of manufacturing operations automatically.

FF. A method of coordinating stages in a production process. Goods are produced in each stage of manufacturing only as they are needed in the next stage.

GG. A production process accomplished largely by manual labor.

HH. A management approach that focuses on identifying and relaxing the constraints that limit an organization's ability to reach a higher level of goal attainment.

II. The costs of activities that can be eliminated without deterioration of product quality, performance, or perceived value.

JJ. Another term for activity analysis, which is the detailed identification and description of the activities conducted in an enterprise.

KK. See computer-aided design and computer-aided manufacturing.

LL. The use of activity-based costing to determine the activities, costs, and profit associated with serving particular customers.

MM. A graphical portrayal of a company's customer profitability analysis.

TRUE-FALSE QUESTIONS

For each of the following statements, enter a T or F in the blank to indicate whether the statement is true or false.

___1. To achieve and maintain a competitive advantage in today's global economy, many companies are investing heavily in new technology.

___2. The goal of JIT production is to build up inventories as much as possible for future use.

___3. Under JIT costing, raw material purchases are recorded directly in the Raw-Materials Inventory account.

___4. In JIT costing, conversion costs are initially applied directly to Cost of Goods Sold.

___5. Any analysis of an investment in advanced manufacturing systems must consider the costs and benefits of the equipment over the entire life of the equipment.

___6. From the cost assignment viewpoint, the ABC system uses two-stage cost allocation to assign the cost of activities to the firm's resources.

___7. Activity analysis involves identifying the root causes of events that trigger activities.

___8. Activity-based management involves activity analysis, but not an evaluation of the activities.

___9. Activity analysis is sometimes referred to as cost object value analysis.

___10. After identifying non-value-added activities, activity sharing is a technique sometimes used to reduce the costs of these non-value-added activities.

___11. One compelling reason for the need for continuous improvement is the price up/cost down concept.

___12. Target costing applies to the production of a new product.

___13. In kaizen costing actual costs are tracked over time and compared to the kaizen goal.

___14. Benchmarking is used in identifying non-value-added activities and pursuing continuous improvement.

___15. Re-engineering involves searching continually for minute improvements in operations.

___16. The key idea in the theory of constraints is to identify the constraints in a system that prevent the firm from achieving a higher level of success.

___17. Introducing significant change in an organization is never easy.

FILL-IN-THE-BLANK QUESTIONS

For each of the following statements, fill in the blank to properly complete the statement.

1. A(n) _____ production system is a comprehensive inventory and manufacturing control system in which no materials are purchased and no products are made until they are needed.

2. The approach of grouping machines into cells that produce a variety of items requiring similar production technology is called _____.

3. A(n) _____ machine is a stand-alone machine controlled by a computer via a numerical, machine-readable code.

4. Any production process in which computers are used to help control production equipment is called a(n) _____ system.

5. If a production process is accomplished largely by machines instead of manual labor, it is said to be _____.

6. Computer software used by engineers in designing a product is called a(n) _____ system.

7. Target price minus target profit equals _____.

8. Computer-controlled equipment that automatically moves materials and products from one production stage to another is called a(n) _____ system.

9. An integrated system of computer-controlled machines and automated material-handling equipment that is capable of making a variety of technologically similar products is called a(n)_____ system.

10. A production process that is accomplished by computer-controlled machines and automated material-handling equipment and in which the entire production system is an integrated network controlled by a central computer is called a(n) _____system.

11. _____costing is the accumulation of costs for activities that occur over the entire life cycle of a product.

12. The constant effort to eliminate waste, reduce response time, simplify product design, and improve quality and customer service is called _____.

13. _____refers to the design of a product and its production so that ultimately the product can be made at a cost that will yield a profit when the product is sold at an estimated market-driven price.

14. Encouraging workers to take their own initiative to improve operations, reduce costs, and improve product quality and customer service is an example of employee _____ _____.

15. _____is a cost-reduction and process-improvement technique that uses information collected about a product's design and production and then examines various attributes of the design and production to identify candidates for improvement efforts.

16. _____is the complete redesign of a process with an emphasis on finding creative new ways to accomplish an objective.

17. The _____is a management approach that seeks to maximize long-run profit through proper management of organizational bottlenecks.

MULTIPLE-CHOICE QUESTIONS

Circle the best answer or response.

1. Consider the following two statements about activity accounting:

   I. It attempts to assign the costs of significant activities to the products that caused those costs to be incurred.
   II. It seeks to identify the costs of activities so that managers can attempt to reduce or eliminate unnecessary costs. Which statement(s) is (are) true?

   (a) Only I
   (b) Only II
   (c) Both I and II
   (d) Neither I nor II

2. Which of the following is *not* a key feature of the JIT philosophy?
   (a) A smooth, uniform production rate
   (b) A "push" method of coordinating the steps of a production process
   (c) The purchase of materials and the making of products in small lot sizes
   (d) High quality levels for materials and products

3. Which of the following is *not* a key characteristic of the JIT philosophy?
   (a) Single-skilled employees and flexible facilities
   (b) Effective preventive maintenance of equipment
   (c) Quick and inexpensive setups of production equipment
   (d) An atmosphere of teamwork to improve the production system

4. The process of cost reduction during the production phase of an existing product while achieving gradual improvement through small betterment activities is called
   (a) target costing.
   (b) re-engineering.
   (c) kaizen costing.
   (d) outsourcing.

5.	Which of the following will *not* contribute to the successful implementation of ABC and ABM?
	(a)	The support of top management
	(b)	The use of a single factory overhead rate
	(c)	A change champion
	(d)	Making employees aware of cost management goals

EXERCISES

Record your answers to each part of the exercises in the space provided. Show your work.

Exercise 6-1

The following costs were incurred in each of two garden tractor-parts factories in January. Complete the table below, by indicating whether each cost would more likely be regarded as a direct cost or an indirect cost in (a) a traditional factory which uses a traditional costing system, or (b) a JIT/FMS factory which uses activity-based costing.

	(a) Traditional Costing System		(b) Activity-Based Costing System	
	Direct	Indirect	Direct	Indirect
Engineering salaries				
Power and heat				
Raw materials				
Maintenance and repairs				
Depreciation, building				
Direct labor				
Factory insurance				
Quality control				
Janitorial wages				
Depreciation, equipment				

Exercise 6.2

The Casey Company has just designed a new product, called a rignot, which they will make and sell. They anticipate the rignot will sell for about $240 in a year or so. The company hopes to make a profit of $35 on each rignot. Let $240 be the target price and $35 be the target profit of one rignot.

(a) What is the target cost of one rignot based on the given data?

(b) Suppose Casey wants to have a target profit of 20 percent of the target cost when the target price is $240. What is the target cost of a rignot in this situation?

SOLUTIONS TO SELF-TEST QUESTIONS AND EXERCISES

MATCHING

1. Y	9. W	17. Z	25. II	33. DD
2. BB	10. F	18. EE	26. C	34. V
3. O	11. U	19. D	27. CC	35. HH
4. H	12. X	20. M	28. Q	36. E
5. K	13. N	21. G	29. JJ	37. L
6. KK	14. P	22. B	30. S	38. T
7. R	15. LL	23. GG	31. I	39. J
8. A	16. MM	24. AA	32. FF	

TRUE-FALSE QUESTIONS

1. **T**
2. **F** Quite the contrary! The goal of JIT is to reduce inventories as much as possible.
3. **F** They are recorded in the Raw and In-Process Inventory account.
4. **T**
5. **T**
6. **F** Resource costs are assigned to the firm's cost objects.
7. **T**
8. **F** ABM also includes the evaluation of activities.
9. **F** It is sometimes referred to as process value analysis.
10. **T**
11. **F** The reason is the price down/cost down concept.
12. **F** It applies to the design of a new product.
13. **T**
14. **T**
15. **F** It involves a radical shift in thinking about how an objective should be met.
16. **T**
17. **T**

FILL-IN-THE-BLANK QUESTIONS

1. just-in-time
2. group technology
3. computer-numerically-controlled
4. computer-aided manufacturing
5. capital-intensive
6. computer-aided design
7. target cost
8. automated material-handling
9. flexible manufacturing system
10. computer-integrated manufacturing
11. Product life-cycle
12. continuous improvement
13. Target costing
14. Empowerment
15. Value engineering (or Value analysis)
16. Re-engineering
17. theory of constraints

MULTIPLE-CHOICE QUESTIONS

1. **(c)**
2. **(b)** The method of coordinating the steps of a production process is a "pull" method.
3. **(a)** Employees need to be multi-skilled.
4. **(c)**
5. **(b)** ABC uses multiple rates for cost assignment.

EXERCISES

Exercise 6.1

	(a) Traditional Costing System		(b) Activity-Based Costing System	
	Direct	Indirect	Direct	Indirect
Engineering salaries		X	X	
Power and heat		X		X
Raw materials	X		X	
Maintenance and repairs		X	X	
Depreciation, building		X		X
Direct labor	X		X	
Factory insurance		X		X
Quality control		X	X	
Janitorial wages		X		X
Depreciation, equipment		x	X	

Exercise 6-2

(a) $240 - $35 = $205

(b) Let C be the target cost, then $C + 0.2 \times C = \$240$, and so $C = \$200$

IDEAS FOR YOUR STUDY TEAM

1. Rewrite each of the definitions of the key terms that appear at the end of the chapter using your own words. Imagine that you are trying to explain each key term to a friend who has not taken any accounting classes. Then, get together with the other members of your study team and compare your definitions.

Activity analysis

Activity-based management (ABM)

Automated material-handling system (AMHS)

Benchmarking (or competitive benchmarking)

● Best practices

CAD/CAM system

Capital-intensive

Cellular manufacturing

Change champion

Computer-aided design (CAD) system

Computer-aided manufacturing (CAM) system

Computer-integrated manufacturing (CIM) system

● Computer-numerically controlled (CNC) machines

Continuous improvement

Customer profitability analysis

Customer profitability profile

Empowerment

Flexible manufacturing system (FMS)

FMS cell

● Just-in-time (JIT) inventory and production management system

Just-in-time (JIT) purchasing

Kaizen costing

Labor-intensive

Non-value-added activities

Non-value added costs

Off-line quality control

Organizational culture

Process

Process value analysis (PVA)

Production Kanban

Product-life cycle costing

Pull method

Re-engineering

Target costing

Theory of constraints

Total quality control

Two-dimensional ABC model

Value engineering (or value analysis)

Withdrawal Kanban

2. Try to predict the types of questions, exercises and problems that you will encounter on the quizzes and exams that cover this chapter. Review the *Read and Recall Questions* and the *Self-Test Questions and Exercises* that are set forth in this Study Guide. Work through the end-of-chapter review problem(s), if applicable, and the end-of-chapter questions, exercises and problems that were assigned by your instructor. As you perform these tasks, identify the terms, concepts, formulas, etc. that you are responsible for knowing. After you develop the list of questions, exercises and problems that you expect to encounter on quizzes and exams, review the learning objectives that appear at the beginning of the chapter in your textbook to ensure that you have not overlooked anything significant. After you have completed your review of your list, get together with the other members of your study team and compare your predictions.

CHAPTER 7
ACTIVITY ANALYSIS, COST BEHAVIOR, AND COST ESTIMATION

CHAPTER FOCUS SUGGESTIONS

After providing an overview of the importance of the analysis of cost behavior, this chapter expands the introduction to the concepts of fixed and variable costs in chapter 2. Discussions of the behavior of six types of costs are provided, and four of the methods of cost estimation are covered. The difficulties encountered when collecting cost data are identified, and information about some of the other approaches to cost estimation is provided.

You should be familiar with the distinguishing characteristics of the six different types of costs: variable, step-variable, fixed, step-fixed, semivariable (or mixed), and curvilinear costs. You should be able to recognize a cost from a graph representing its behavior, and understand the significance of the relevant range when past cost behavior is used to predict future costs. An in-depth understanding of the account-classification, visual-fit, high-low, and least-squares regression methods of cost estimation is required, as is an appreciation for the problems frequently encountered when collecting data for cost-estimation purposes.

READ AND RECALL QUESTIONS

COST BEHAVIOR PATTERNS

LEARNING OBJECTIVE #1
After studying this section of the chapter, you should be able to:
• Explain the relationships between cost estimation, cost behavior, and cost prediction.

What is "cost estimation?" What is "cost behavior?" What is "cost prediction?

LEARNING OBJECTIVE #2
After studying this section of the chapter, you should be able to:
• Define and describe the behavior of the following types of costs: variable, step-variable, fixed, step-fixed, semivariable (or mixed), and curvilinear.

Variable Costs

What is the relationship between a variable cost and a change in activity level? What kinds of variable costs would you expect to find in a business like Tasty Donuts? When activity triples, what happens to the total amount of variable costs? What happens to the variable cost per unit?

Step-Variable Costs

What is a step-variable cost? What kinds of step-variable costs would you expect to find in a business like Tasty Donuts?

Fixed Costs

What is the relationship between a fixed cost and a change in activity level? What kinds of fixed costs would you expect to find in a business like Tasty Donuts?

When the level of activity changes, what happens to the total amount of fixed costs? What happens to the fixed cost per unit?

Step-Fixed Costs

What is a step-fixed cost? What kinds of step-fixed costs would you expect to find in a business like Tasty Donuts?

Semivariable Cost

What is a semivariable (or mixed) cost? What kinds of semivariable costs would you expect to find in a business like Tasty Donuts?

Curvilinear Cost

What is a curvilinear cost? What kinds of curvilinear costs would you expect to find in a business like Tasty Donuts?

LEARNING OBJECTIVE #3
After studying this section of the chapter, you should be able to:
- Explain the importance of the relevant range in using a cost behavior pattern for cost prediction.

What is a company's "relevant range?" What happens to the estimation (or approximation) of a curvilinear cost when the activity level gets further away from the boundary of the relevant range?

When a straight-line is used to approximate a curvilinear cost within a relevant range, what does the slope of the line represent? What does the intersection of the line at the vertical (or y) axis represent?

Using Cost Behavior Patterns to Predict Costs

How can cost behavior patterns be used by a company?

LEARNING OBJECTIVE #4
After studying this section of the chapter, you should be able to:
• Define and give examples of engineered costs, committed costs, and discretionary costs.

Engineered, Committed, and Discretionary Costs

What is an "engineered" cost? What kinds of engineered costs would you expect to find in a business like Tasty Donuts?

What is a "committed" cost? What kinds of committed costs would you expect to find in a business like Tasty Donuts?

What is a "discretionary" cost? What kinds of discretionary costs would you expect to find in a business like Tasty Donuts?

How can committed costs be distinguished from discretionary costs? What types of costs (committed or discretionary) can be changed in the short run much more easily? When might one company consider a cost to be committed while another considers the same cost to be discretionary?

Shifting Cost Structure in the New Manufacturing Environment

What two factors are causing fixed costs to become more prevalent in many industries? In the electronics industry, what costs that once were largely variable have become committed fixed costs?

Would compensation costs for the highly skilled computer experts and equipment operators required for CIM systems and FMS tend to be variable costs or committed fixed costs? Why?

What are some examples of operations-based cost drivers?

Cost Behavior in Other Industries

What are three common cost drivers in manufacturing firms?

What kinds of production costs are variable? What are some examples of fixed overhead costs? What kinds of overhead costs would be semivariable or curvilinear?

What is the activity base used by most merchandising firms?

What kinds of costs incurred by merchandisers are variable? What kinds of costs incurred by merchandisers are fixed or step-fixed?

What cost drivers might be used in the airline industry?

In general, what are the two crucial determinants of the cost behavior for each cost item?

Why might a hospital consider the cost of compensating anesthesiologists a step-fixed cost? Would the labor costs in the dietary department of the hospital be fixed or variable?

COST ESTIMATION

LEARNING OBJECTIVE #5
After studying this section of the chapter, you should be able to:
• Describe and use the following cost-estimation methods: account classification, visual fit, high-low, and least-squares regression.

What is cost estimation? What are the methods of cost estimation used by Tasty Donuts?

Account Classification Method

When the account-classification (or account analysis) method of cost estimation is used, what information is used to classify each cost as variable, fixed or semivariable?

Visual-Fit Method

What is a scatter diagram? How does the cost analyst determine whether a cost is variable, fixed or semivariable when the visual fit method is used? What is one of the limitations of the visual fit method?

What is an "outlier?" What should a cost analyst do when an outlier is identified?

High-Low Method

What is used to approximate the semivariable cost when the high-low method is used? What formula is used to compute the variable cost per unit when the high-low method is used? How is the fixed-cost estimate then made?

Why is the visual fit method superior to the high-low method?

Least-Squares Regression Method

How is the cost line positioned when the least-squares regression method is used? What is a regression line? What is the equation form of a least-squares regression line? What does each letter in the equation represent? Why is the least-squares regression method considered to be an objective method of cost estimation?

What is meant by "economic plausibility?" What is "goodness of fit?"

LEARNING OBJECTIVE #6
After studying this section of the chapter, you should be able to:
- Describe the multiple regression, engineering, work-measurement, and learning curve approaches to cost estimation.

Multiple Regression

What method can be used when there are two or more independent variables that are important predictors of cost behavior? What is multiple regression? How does it differ from single regression?

Engineering Method of Cost Estimation

What is the "engineering method" of cost estimation? What is a time and motion study?

Effect of Learning on Cost Behavior

What is a learning curve? What is an experience curve?

Costs and Benefits of Information

Except for the multiple regression techniques, what is assumed by the other methods for determining cost behavior? What other simplification assumption is usually made in cost estimation?

Work Measurement

What is "work measurement?" What is a "control factor unit?"

LEARNING OBJECTIVE #7
After studying this section of the chapter, you should be able to:
- Describe some problems often encountered in collecting data for cost estimation.

Data Collection Problems

What six problems frequently complicate the process of data collection?

APPENDIX TO CHAPTER 7: FINDING THE LEAST-SQUARES REGRESSION ESTIMATES

LEARNING OBJECTIVE #8
Determine whether or not you are responsible for this appendix. If so, after studying this section of the chapter, you should be able to:
- Estimate a linear cost function using least-squares regression analysis.

What is the coefficient of determination?

SELF-TEST QUESTIONS AND EXERCISES

MATCHING

Match each of the key terms listed below with the appropriate textbook definition:

____ 1. Account-classification method (also called account analysis)
____ 2. Coefficient of determination*
____ 3. Committed cost
____ 4. Control factor unit
____ 5. Cost behavior
____ 6. Cost estimation
____ 7. Cost prediction
____ 8. Curvilinear cost
____ 9. Dependent variable
____ 10. Discretionary cost
____ 11. Engineered cost
____ 12. Engineering method
____ 13. Experience curve
____ 14. Fixed cost
____ 15. Goodness of fit
____ 16. High-low method

____ 22. Independent variable
____ 23. Learning curve
____ 24. Least-squares regression method
____ 25. Multiple regression
____ 26. Normal equations*
____ 27. Outlier
____ 28. Regression line
____ 29. Relevant range
____ 30. Scatter diagram
____ 31. Semivariable (or mixed) cost
____ 32. Simple regression
____ 33. Step-fixed costs
____ 34. Step-variable costs
____ 35. Variable cost
____ 36. Visual-fit method
____ 37. Work measurement

* This key term is included in the appendix to the chapter.

A. The relationship between cost and activity.

B. A graph (or other mathematical representation) that shows how a broad set of costs decline as cumulative production output increases.

C. A set of plotted cost observations at various activity levels.

D. A cost that remains fixed over wide ranges of activity, but jumps to a different amount for activity levels outside that range.

E. A cost-estimation method in which the cost line is fit to the data by statistical analysis. The method minimizes the sum of the squared deviations between the cost line and the data points.

F. A variable whose value depends on other variables, called independent variables.

G. The systematic analysis of a task for the purpose of determining the inputs needed to perform the task.

H. A cost-estimation method involving a careful examination of the ledger accounts for the purpose of classifying each cost as variable, fixed, or semivariable.

I. A cost-estimation method in which a cost line is fit using exactly two data points—the high and low activity levels.

J. A cost-estimation method in which a detailed study is made of the process that results in cost incurrence.

K. The range of activity within which management expects the organization to operate.

L. Forecast of cost at a particular level of activity.

M. A cost with both a fixed and a variable cost.

N. A data point that falls far away from the other points in a scatter diagram and is not representative of the data.

O. A cost that results from an organization's ownership or use of facilities and its basic organization structure.

P. A cost that changes in total in proportion to changes in an organization's activity.

Q. The variable upon which an estimate is based in least-squares regression analysis.

R. A cost that results from a discretionary management decision to spend a particular amount of money.

S. A cost that does not change in total as activity changes.

T. A regression analysis based on a single independent variable.

U. A cost that is nearly variable, but increases in small steps instead of continuously.

V. A cost that results from a definitive physical relationship with the activity measure.

W. A graphical expression of the decline in the average labor time required per unit as cumulative output increases.

X. A method of cost estimation in which a cost line is drawn through a scatter diagram according to the visual perception of the analyst.

Y. A statistical method in which a linear (straight-line) relationship is estimated between a dependent variable and two or more independent variables.

Z. A measure of work or activity used in work measurement.

AA. The closeness with which a regression line fits the data upon which it is based.

BB. The process of determining how a particular cost behaves.

CC. A cost with a curved line for its graph.

DD. A line fit to a set of data points using least-squares regression.

EE. A statistical measure of goodness of fit; a measure of how closely a regression line fits the data on which it is based.

FF. The equations used to solve for the parameters of a regression equation.

TRUE-FALSE QUESTIONS

For each of the following statements, enter a T or F in the blank to indicate whether the statement is true or false.

___**1.** A fixed cost remains unchanged in total as the associated cost-driver level varies.

___**2.** If the steps in a step-variable cost behavior pattern are large enough, this cost can be approximated by a variable cost without much loss in accuracy.

___**3.** A semivariable cost is the same as a step-variable cost.

___**4.** A variable cost per unit changes in direct proportion to a change in the associated cost-driver level.

___**5.** Management is interested in cost behavior that is within the organization's relevant range.

___**6.** Cost behavior is relevant to management functions of planning, control, and decision making.

___**7.** Managerial accountants often use a step-variable cost behavior pattern to approximate a curvilinear cost.

___**8.** Fixed cost per unit does not change as the associated cost-driver level varies.

___**9.** A marginal cost is the cost of making the next unit in a production process.

___**10.** The slope of a total semivariable cost line is the variable cost per unit of activity.

___**11.** Total variable cost remains constant as the associated cost-driver level changes.

___**12.** In any cost analysis, it is preferable to work with total fixed costs rather than fixed cost per unit.

___**13.** Cost prediction is an important part of the planning process.

___**14.** Management can change committed costs only through relatively major decisions that have short-term implications.

___**15.** The primary drawback of the visual-fit method is its lack of objectivity.

___**16.** In any cost-estimation method, the estimate of a cost behavior pattern should be restricted to the relevant range.

___**17.** Both the nature of an organization and the cost driver are crucial determinants of the cost behavior of cost items in the organization.

___**18.** Under the least-squares regression method, the cost line is positioned so as to minimize the sum of the deviations between the cost line and the data points.

___**19.** All cost-estimation methods are usually based on the assumption that cost behavior patterns are linear within the relevant range.

___**20.** As a firm gets experience with a product, estimates of direct labor costs should be adjusted upward.

___**21.** (Appendix) Under the least-squares regression method, the coefficient of determination is a measure of the goodness of fit.

FILL-IN-THE-BLANK QUESTIONS

For each of the following statements, fill in the blank to properly complete the statement.

1. _____is a forecast of a cost at a specific level of activity.

2. Costs that are nearly variable, but increase in small steps, are called _____ ___costs.

3. A(n) _____cost has both fixed and variable elements.

4. A(n) _____cost behavior pattern has a curve for its graph.

5. The range of activity within which the management of an organization expects to operate is called the _____.

6. A cost that bears a definite physical relationship to the activity measure used is called a(n) _____cost.

7. A(n) _____helps the analyst to visualize the relationship between cost and the level of a cost driver.

8. _____is the process of determining how a particular cost behaves.

9. A cost that remains fixed over a wide range of activity, but jumps to a different amount for activity levels outside that range, is called a(n) _____ ___cost.

10. A(n) _____cost results from an organization's ownership or use of facilities and its basic organizational structure.

11. A(n) _____cost comes about as a result of a management decision to spend a certain amount of money for some purpose.

12. A(n) _____is a data point that falls away from other points in a scatter diagram and is not representative of the data.

13. In the _____method of cost estimation, the semivariable cost approximation is computed using exactly two data points.

14. The _____method of cost estimation involves a careful examination of the organization's ledger accounts to determine which costs are variable, fixed, or semivariable.

15. In regression analysis, where the regression line is given by $Y = a + bX$, X is referred to as the _____ and Y is called the _____.

16. Two criteria used to evaluate a particular regression line based on a given data set are _____ and _____.

17. _____is a statistical method that estimates a linear relationship between one dependent variable and two or more independent variables.

18. The _____method of cost estimation is a detailed study of the production technology, materials, and labor used in the manufacturing process.

19. A graphical-expression of the situation where the average labor time needed per unit decreases as cumulative production output increases is called a(n) _____.

20. _____is the systematic analysis of a task for the purpose of determining the inputs needed to perform that task..

21. The measure of work or activity in work measurement is often called a(n) _____.

22.   A graphical expression where the learning-curve concept is applied to costs other than labor is called a(n) _____ .

MULTIPLE-CHOICE QUESTIONS

Circle the best answer or response.

1.   Consider the following statements and determine which statement(s) is (are) true.

   I.   Direct materials and direct labor are usually considered variable costs.
   II. Fixed manufacturing costs are generally the costs of creating production capacity.

   (a) Only I
   (b) Only II
   (c) Both I and II
   (d) Neither I nor II

2.   Which of the following is a *disadvantage* of the visual-fit method of cost estimation?
   (a) The method lacks objectivity.
   (b) The method is difficult to use.
   (c) The method does not give a useful view of the overall cost behavior pattern.
   (d) The method does not provide a means of detecting outliers.

3.   Given the data set forth in the table below, and using the high-low method of cost estimation, the variable cost per hour of activity is:

Activity level	Cost
300 hours	$1,100
500 hours	1,900
400 hours	1,500
200 hours	1,000

   (a) $5
   (b) $3
   (c) $4
   (d) $2

4.   Fixed costs are becoming more prevalent in many industries because:
   (a) Labor unions have been increasingly successful in negotiating agreements that result in a relatively stable work force.
   (b) Labor is replacing automation to an increasing extent.
   (c) Both (a) and (b).
   (d) Neither (a) nor (b).

5.   Which of the following is true?
   (a) Supervisory salaries are usually step-variable costs.
   (b) Depreciation on plant and production equipment is a variable cost.
   (c) In merchandising firms, the cost driver is usually sales revenue.
   (d) In merchandising firms, the cost of merchandise sold is a fixed cost.

6.   A *disadvantage* of the high-low method of cost estimation is that
   (a) only two data points are used and the rest are ignored.
   (b) it is less objective than the visual-fit method.
   (c) the computations involved are complex.
   (d) it is not appropriate for semivariable costs.

7.   Which of the following statements is *not* true about the least-squares regression method?
   (a) It is an objective method of cost estimation.
   (b) It makes use of all available data.
   (c) It requires less computation than does the high-low method.
   (d) It has desirable statistical properties for making cost predictions and inferences about the relationship between cost and activity.

8.   Which of the following are problems in data collection for cost-estimation purposes?
   (a) Misplaced source documents or failure to record a transaction can result in missing data.
   (b) The units of time for which the dependent and independent variables are measured may not match.
   (c) Both (a) and (b).
   (d) Neither (a) or (b).

EXERCISE

Exercise 7.1

You are a management accountant for Hunter Enterprises, Inc. The president of Hunter, John Box, was recently at a conference where he heard the term "mixed cost" used by one of the speakers. The president asked you the meaning of that term, and your immediate response was "Oh! That's the same as a semivariable cost." The president's reply was, "You accountants are forever using jargon.

Write a brief memo to the president that clearly and concisely explains the meaning and significance of the term "mixed or semivariable cost."

INTERNAL MEMORANDUM

To: Mr. John Box, President

From:

Date:

Subject: The Meaning and Significance of the Term "Mixed or Semivariable Cost"

Exercise 7.2

The claims department of the Ebert Insurance Company uses labor hours as the cost driver of the department's costs. The department had the following cost data for May and June:

Month	Fixed Costs	Variable Costs	Total Costs	Labor Hours
May	$7,000	$14,400	$21,400	1,800
June	7,000	12,800	19,800	1,600

(a) Calculate the variable cost per labor hour.

(b) Calculate the fixed cost per labor hour for May and for June.

(c) Calculate the total cost per labor hour for May and for June.

(d) Assume that in July the department expects to use 2,000 labor hours. Estimate the total department cost for July.

Exercise 7.3

The Delaney Company has tracked the cost of material handling for the past two months and has found the following results:

Month	Material Requisitions	Total Cost of Material Handling
February	180	$11,320
March	240	$14,560

The company uses the high-low method of cost estimation.

(a) Calculate the variable cost per unit for material handling.

(b) Calculate the fixed cost per month of material handling.

(c) Assuming that 300 material requisitions are expected to be processed in April, estimate the total cost of material handling for April.

Exercise 7.4

The Honsinger Company makes and sells garden tractors and lawn mowers. A company accountant has recently completed a cost study of the Billing Department in which she used work measurement to quantify the department's activity. The control factor unit in the work measurement was number of invoices processed by the department. The following data were assembled:

Month	Control Factor Units of Activity (in hundreds of invoices processed	Billing Department Costs (in $100 units)
July	20	57
August	23	62
September	25	64
October	21	58
November	19	59
December	15	54

(a) Find a cost-estimation equation for the Billing Department costs as a function of the control factor units (hundreds of invoices processed) using the high-low method.

(b) Use the equation found in part (a) to predict the Billing Department cost for January; 2,200 invoices are expected to be processed in January.

(c) (Appendix) Repeat parts (a) and (b) using the least-squares regression method.

SOLUTIONS TO SELF-TEST QUESTIONS AND EXERCISES

MATCHING

1. H	8. C C	15. AA	22. N	29. U
2. EE	9. F	16. I	23. DD	30. P
3. O	10. R	17. Q	24. K	31. X
4. Z	11. V	18. W	25. C	32. G
5. A	12. J	19. E	26. M	
6. BB	13. B	20. Y	27. T	
7. L	14. S	21. FF	28. D	

True-False Questions

1. T
2. F The steps need to be small enough to approximate the cost by a variable cost.
3. F A semivariable cost has no steps; it is linear, with variable and fixed components.
4. F A variable cost per unit is constant as the associated cost-driver level changes.
5. T
6. T
7. F They often use a semivariable cost to approximate a curvilinear cost.
8. F Fixed cost per unit varies as the associated cost-driver level varies.
9. T
10. T
11. F Total variable cost varies directly as the associated cost-driver level changes.
12. T
13. T
14. F These committed costs can change only through relatively major decisions having long-term implications.
15. T
16. T
17. T
18. F It is positioned so as to minimize the sum of the squares of the deviations between the cost line and the data points.
19. T
20. F They should be adjusted downward to take into account the learning effect.
21. T

FILL-IN-THE-BLANK QUESTIONS

1. Cost prediction
2. step-variable
3. semivariable
4. curvilinear
5. relevant range
6. engineered
7. scatter diagram
8. Cost estimation

9. semifixed
10. committed
11. discretionary
12. outlier
13. high-low
14. account-classification
15. independent variable, dependent variable
16. economic plausibility, goodness of fit
17. Multiple regression
18. engineering
19. learning curve
20. Work measurement
21. control factor unit
22. experience curve

MULTIPLE-CHOICE QUESTIONS

1. **(c)**
2. **(a)** The method is very subjective.
3. **(b)** The variable cost per hour is $(1,900 - 1,000)/(500 - 200) = \$3$.
4. **(a)** Automation is replacing labor to an increasing extent.
5. **(c)** The other statements are false.
6. **(a)** The other statements are false.
7. **(c)** It requires much more computation than does the high-low method.
8. **(c)**

EXERCISES

Exercise 7.1

A mixed or semivariable cost is one that has both variable and fixed components. The variable component changes in direct proportion to changes in the driver of this cost while the fixed component remains constant in the short run with respect to this driver. The fact that cost is a mix of these two components helps to explain why it is sometimes referred to as a "mixed cost.

The idea of a mixed or semivariable cost is significant because this type of cost is common to many different organizations. The costs of maintenance, utilities, and energy are good examples of this type of cost. Consider maintenance cost as an illustration. The fixed component is the cost of having maintenance service available when there is no consumption of the cost driver, and the variable component is the proportional cost of maintenance that results from the usage of that maintenance service in relation to the specified cost driver.

Exercise 7-2

(a)

$14,400/1,800 hr. = $8.00/hr

(b)

$7,000/1,800 hr. = $3.89/hr. in May

$7,000/1,600 hr. = $4.38/hr. in June

(c)

$21,400/1,800 hr. = $11.89/hr in May

$19,800/1,600 hr. = $12.38/hr in June

(d)

$7,000 + ($8 x 2,000) = $23,000

Exercise 7.3

(a)

Variable cost per unit = ($14,560 - $11,320)/(240 -180) = $54

(b)

Fixed cost per month = $ 11,320 - ($54 x 180) = $1,600

(c)

Total cost = $1,600 + ($54 x 300) = $17,800

Exercise 7.4

(a)

The high point occurs in September and the low point in December.

Variable cost per unit = ($64 - $54)/(25 - 15) = $1

Fixed cost per month = 64 – ($1 x 25) = $39 (in $100 units), or $3,900

(b)

For January: $39 + ($1 x 22) = $61 (in $100 units), or $6,100

(c)

X	Y	X x X	X x Y
20	57	400	1,140
23	62	529	1,426
25	64	625	1,600
21	58	441	1,218
19	59	361	1,121
15	54	225	810
123	354	2,581	7,315

$a = [(354 \times 2,581) - (123 \times 7,315)]/[(6 \times 2,581) - (123 \times 123)] = \$39.02$

$b = [(6 \times 7,315) - (123 \times 354)]/[(6 \times 2,581) - (123 \times 123)] = \$0.9748$

Thus, $Y = \$39.02 + \$0.9748 \times X$

If $X = 22$, then $Y = \$39.02 + (\$0.9748 \times 22) = \$60.46$ (in \$100 units), or \$6,046

IDEAS FOR YOUR STUDY TEAM

1. Rewrite each of the definitions of the key terms that appear at the end of the chapter using your own words. Imagine that you are trying to explain each key term to a friend who has not taken any accounting classes. Then, get together with the other members of your study team and compare your definitions.

Account classification method (also called account analysis)

Coefficient of determination

Committed cost

Control factor unit

Cost behavior

Cost estimation

Cost prediction

Curvilinear cost

Dependent variable

Discretionary cost

Engineered cost

Engineering method

Experience curve

Fixed cost

Goodness of fit

High-low method

Independent variable

Learning curve

Least-squares regression method

Multiple regression

Normal equations

Outlier

Regression line

Relevant range

Scatter diagram

Semivariable (or mixed) cost

Simple regression

Step-fixed costs

Step-variable costs

Variable cost

Visual-fit method

Work measurement

2.   Try to predict the types of questions, exercises and problems that you will encounter on the quizzes and exams that cover this chapter. Review the *Read and Recall Questions* and the *Self-Test Questions and Exercises* that are set forth in this Study Guide. Work through the end-of-chapter review problem(s), if applicable, and the end-of-chapter questions, exercises and problems that were assigned by your instructor. As you perform these tasks, identify the terms, concepts, formulas, etc. that you are responsible for knowing. After you develop the list of questions, exercises and problems that you expect to encounter on quizzes and exams, review the learning objectives that appear at the beginning of the chapter in your textbook to ensure that you have not overlooked anything significant. After you have completed your review of your list, get together with the other members of your study team and compare your predictions.

CHAPTER 8
COST-VOLUME-PROFIT ANALYSIS

CHAPTER FOCUS SUGGESTIONS

Analyzing the relationships among cost, volume, and profit is fundamental to providing information to managers to help them make decisions. This chapter provides an in-depth discussion of cost-volume-profit (CVP) analysis, a technique for examining the effects of changes in an organization's volume of activity on its revenues, costs, and profits. The coverage of CVP analysis applies to both manufacturing and service organizations. The effects of advanced technology on and the implications of activity-based costing for CVP analysis are also addressed.

You should be familiar with the concept of contribution margin, and be able to prepare an income statement using the contribution margin format You will need to know how to compute the break-even point using both the contribution-margin approach and the equation approach. You will also need to know how to compute the sales units and sales dollars required to earn a target profit using both approaches. A good understanding of these concepts (which goes beyond just memorizing the formulas and equations) will help you to use CVP analysis in determining the effect on profits of changes in fixed expenses, variable expenses, sales prices and sales volume, and the role of operating leverage in CVP relationships. This understanding will also help you appreciate the key assumptions and limitations of CVP analysis.

READ AND RECALL QUESTIONS

ILLUSTRATION OF COST-VOLUME-PROFIT ANALYSIS

LEARNING OBJECTIVE #1
After studying this section of the chapter, you should be able to:
- Compute a break-even point using the contribution-margin approach and the equation approach.

What is "cost-volume-profit analysis" (or CVP analysis)? What is the first step in cost-volume-profit analysis?

THE BREAK-EVEN POINT

What is the "break-even point?"

What is the formula for the calculation of total contribution margin? What is total contribution margin?

Contribution-Margin Approach

What is the unit contribution margin?

Using the contribution-margin approach, what is the formula for the break-even point (in units)?

Equation Approach

What is the formula for the income (profit) statement? How can the income statement formula be restated using sales volume information? (Let *x* denote the number of units of sales required to break-even.)

LEARNING OBJECTIVE #2

After studying this section of the chapter, you should be able to:
- Compute the contribution-margin ratio and use it to find the break-even point in sales dollars.

How are the contribution-margin ratio and the contribution-margin percentage calculated? Using the contribution margin ratio, what is the general formula for the calculation of the break-even point (in sales dollars)?

GRAPHING COST-VOLUME-PROFIT RELATIONSHIPS

LEARNING OBJECTIVE #3

After studying this section of the chapter, you should be able to:
- Prepare a cost-volume-profit graph and explain how it is used.

What information is shown on a cost-volume-profit (CVP) graph? What are the seven steps for the preparation of a CVP graph? How is the break-even point determined using a CVP graph?

Alternative Format for the CVP Graph

What alternative format of the CVP graph highlights the amount of profit or loss? How does this graph differ from the normal format of the CVP graph? How can the break-even point be determined on a profit-volume graph?

TARGET NET PROFIT

LEARNING OBJECTIVE #4

After studying this section of the chapter, you should be able to:
- Apply CVP analysis to determine the effect on profit of changes in fixed expenses, variable expenses, sales prices, and sales volume.

What is "target net profit?"

Contribution-Margin Approach

Using the contribution-margin approach, what is the formula for the number of sales units required to earn a target net profit? How does this formula differ from that used to compute the number of sales units required to break-even?

Using the contribution margin ratio, what is the general formula for the calculation of the total dollar sales required to earn a target net profit? How does this formula differ from that used to compute the total sales dollar required to break-even?

Equation Approach

How can the income statement formula be restated using sales volume information? (Let *x* denote the number of units of sales required to earn a target net profit.)

Graphical Approach

How is the sales volume required to earn a target net profit determined using a CVP graph?

APPLYING CVP ANALYSIS

Safety Margin

What is "safety margin?"

Changes in Fixed Expenses

What happens to a organization's break-even point in units if its fixed expenses increase? What if its fixed expenses decrease? Is there a relationship between the percentage change in fixed expenses and the percentage change in the break-even point in units?

What is a donation equivalent to for a nonprofit organization? Would the receipt of a donation increase or decrease the nonprofit organization's break-even point (in units)? What is the formula for the break-even point (in units) for a nonprofit organization that receives donations?

Changes in the Unit Contribution Margin

What effect will an increase in variable expenses have on an organization's unit contribution margin? What effect will an increase in variable expenses have on an organization's break-even point (in units)?

What effect will an increase in unit sales price have on an organization's unit contribution margin?

Does a lower break-even point increase or decrease the risk of operations from a loss if sales are sluggish?

Predicting Profit Given Expected Volume

Assuming that fixed expenses do not change, what two factors can cause a difference in expected profit?

What is "incremental analysis?"

Interdependent Changes in Key Variables

What three factors can cause a difference in expected profits?

CVP Information in Published Annual Reports

What does British Airways mean when it refers to its break-even passenger load factor?

CVP ANALYSIS WITH MULTIPLE PRODUCTS

LEARNING OBJECTIVE #5
After studying this section of the chapter, you should be able to:
• Compute the break-even point and prepare a profit-volume graph for a multiproduct enterprise.

What is a company's "sales mix?"

What is the weighted-average unit contribution margin? How is it calculated? Using the contribution-margin approach, what is the formula for the break-even point (in units) when an organization has multiple products?

What is a limitation of the formula used to calculate the break-even point (in units) when a company has multiple products?

ASSUMPTIONS UNDERLYING CVP ANALYSIS

LEARNING OBJECTIVE #6
After studying this section of the chapter, you should be able to:
- List and discuss the key assumptions of CVP analysis.

What are the four important assumptions that must be made for any cost-volume-profit analysis to be valid?

Role of Computerized Planning Models and Electronic Spreadsheets

What is "sensitivity analysis?" What has made sensitivity analysis relatively easy to do?

CVP RELATIONSHIPS AND THE INCOME STATEMENT

LEARNING OBJECTIVE #7
After studying this section of the chapter, you should be able to:
- Prepare and interpret a contribution income statement.

What is the formula for a traditional income statement? What is the formula for a contribution income statement? Which format of the income statement do operating managers frequently prefer? Why?

If contribution margin increases, how is net income affected?

What is the relationship between contribution margin changes and change in sales volume?

COST STRUCTURE AND OPERATING LEVERAGE

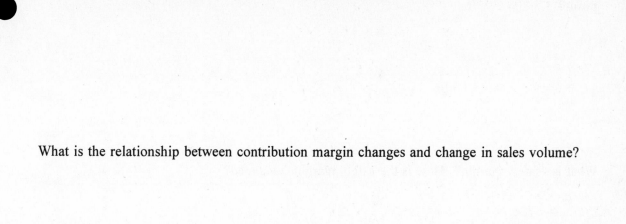

LEARNING OBJECTIVE #8
After studying this section of the chapter, you should be able to:
• Explain the role of cost structure and operating leverage in CVP relationships.

What is the "cost structure" of an organization? As the proportion of fixed costs in a firm's cost structure increases, what is the impact of profit from a given percentage change in sales revenue?

Operating Leverage

What is "operating leverage?" What does the term refer to when a managerial accountant uses it? How is the operating leverage factor calculated? What will you get if you multiply the percentage increase in sales revenue times the operating leverage factor?

Does a firm with relatively high operating leverage have a relatively low or high break-even point?

What is "safety margin?" How is the safety margin calculated?

How does a movement toward an advanced manufacturing environment often affect a company's break-even point? Why? How does a movement toward an advanced manufacturing environment often affect a company's safety margin point? Why? How does a movement toward an advanced manufacturing environment often affect a company's operating leverage? Why?

Why do high-technology manufacturing systems generally allow greater potential for profitability? What might happen to a firm with high-technology manufacturing systems in an economic recession? Why?

Cost Structure and Operating Leverage: A Cost-Benefit Issue

Does a firm with proportionately high fixed costs have relatively low or high operating leverage?

What is the effect on net income when a firm with high operating leverage generates a relatively small percentage increase in sales revenue?

Does a firm with relatively high operating leverage have a relatively low or high break-even point? What is the trade-off that must be considered in determining the optimal cost structure?

CVP ANALYSIS, ACTIVITY-BASED COSTING, AND ADVANCED MANUFACTURING SYSTEMS

> **LEARNING OBJECTIVE #9**
> *After studying this section of the chapter, you should be able to:*
> • Understand the implications of activity-based costing for CVP analysis.

What cost driver is the focus of traditional cost-volume-profit analysis?

LEARNING OBJECTIVE #10
After studying this section of the chapter, you should be able to:
• Be aware of the effects of advanced manufacturing technology on CVP relationships.

A Move toward JIT and Flexible Manufacturing

Assume management is considering the installation of a flexible manufacturing system and a move toward just-in-time production. Would you expect the company's variable costs to increase or decrease? Why? Would you expect general factory overhead costs to increase or decrease? Why?

Are setup, inspection and material handling costs fixed or variable with respect to sales volume? Are setup, inspection and material handling costs fixed or variable with respect to other cost drivers, such as the number of setups, inspections and hours of material handling?

What is the fundamental distinction between a traditional CVP analysis and an activity-based CVP analysis?

When a firm installs an advanced manufacturing system, does the break-even point (in units) typically increase or decrease? Why? When a firm installs an advanced manufacturing system, does the number of units required to earn a target net profit typically increase or decrease? Why?

APPENDIX TO CHAPTER 8: EFFECT OF INCOME TAXES

Determine whether or not you are responsible for this appendix

What is before-tax net income? What is after-tax net income? What is the formula for the calculation of after-tax net income? (Let *t* denote the income tax rate.)

Does the requirement that a firm pay income taxes affect its cost-volume-profit relationships? Why or why not?

What is the formula for the calculation of target before-tax net income? (Let *t* denote the income tax rate.)

Using the equation approach, what is the formula for the number of units that must be sold to achieve the target after-tax net income? (Let *x* denote the number of units that must be sold and *t* denote the income tax rate.)

Using the contribution margin approach, what is the formula for the number of units that must be sold to achieve the target after-tax net income? (Let *x* denote the denote the income tax rate.)

SELF-TEST QUESTIONS AND EXERCISES

MATCHING

Match each of the key terms listed below with the appropriate textbook definition:

___ 1. After-tax net income*
___ 2. Before-tax income*
___ 3. Break-even point
___ 4. Contribution income statement
___ 5. Contribution-margin ratio
___ 6. Contribution margin, total
___ 7. Cost structure
___ 8. Cost-volume-profit (CVP) Analysis
___ 9. Cost-volume-profit graph
___ 10. Operating leverage

___ 11. Operating leverage factor
___ 12. Profit-volume graph
___ 13. Safety margin
___ 14. Sales mix
___ 15. Sensitivity analysis
___ 16. Target net profit (or income)
___ 17. Total contribution margin
___ 18. Unit contribution
___ 19. Weighted-average unit contribution margin

* This key term is included in the appendix to the chapter.

A.   The unit contribution margin divided by the sales price per unit.
B.   The extent to which an organization uses fixed costs in its cost structure. The greater the proportion of fixed costs, the greater the operating leverage.
C.   A study of the relationships between sales volume, expenses, revenue, and profit.
D.   Differences between budgeted sales revenue and break-even sales revenue.
E.   The profit level set as management's objective.
F.   An income statement on which fixed and variable expenses are separated
G.   A measure of operating leverage at a particular sales volume. Computed by dividing an organization's total contribution margin by its net income.
H.   Sales price minus the unit variable cost.
I.   Graphical expression of the relationship between profit and sales volume.
J.   A graphical expression of the relationships between sales volume, expenses, revenue, and profit.
K.   An organization's net income after its income-tax expense is subtracted.
L.   See contribution margin, total.
M.   Average of a firm's several products' unit contribution margins, weighted by the relative sales proportion of each product.
N.   Total sale revenue less total variable expenses.
O.   The relative proportions of an organization's fixed and variable costs.
P.   The volume of activity at which an organization's revenues and expenses are equal. May be measured either in units or in sales dollars.
Q.   Relative proportion of sales of each of an organization's multiple products.
R.   An organization's income before its income-tax expense is subtracted.
S.   A technique for determining what would happen in a decision analysis if a key prediction or assumption proves to be wrong.

TRUE-FALSE QUESTIONS

For each of the following statements, enter a T or F in the blank to indicate whether the statement is true or false.

___1. Cost-volume-profit analysis is *not* used by non-profit organizations.

___2. Analyzing an organization's cost behavior is a necessary first step in any cost-volume-profit analysis.

___3. In a profit-volume graph, the break-even point is where the graph crosses the vertical axis.

___4. If the unit contribution margin is $12 and period fixed expenses are $57,960, then the period break-even units are 4,380.

___5. Total contribution margin for a single product changes in direct proportion to sales revenue from that product.

___6. If a firm sells 2,800 units a month, the unit selling price is $15, the unit variable cost is $5, and monthly fixed costs are $18,000, then monthly profit is $12,000.

___7. Sales revenue equals variable expenses plus fixed expenses plus profit.

___8. The position of the break-even point within an organization's relevant range of activity provides important information to management.

___9. In a cost-volume-profit graph, the break-even point is determined by the intersection of the total-revenue line and the total-variable-expense line.

___10. If the unit-selling price is $20 and the unit variable cost is $12, then the contribution-margin percentage is 60 percent.

___11. Decreasing fixed expenses decreases the break-even point, assuming that the unit contribution margin stays constant.

___12. Sometimes a change in one key variable in the profit formula will cause a change in another key variable.

___13. The break-even point in units in a multi-product firm is the same for every possible sales mix.

___14. In a traditional income statement, the cost of goods sold includes both fixed and variable manufacturing costs.

___15. Increasing the unit variable expense decreases the break-even point, assuming that the fixed expenses and the unit selling price remain unchanged.

___16. Assume that fixed costs remain unchanged. If contribution margin increases by a given amount, then net income will increase by exactly the same amount.

___17. The greater the proportion of fixed costs in a firm's cost structure, the less will be the impact on profit from a given percentage change in sales revenue.

___18. Decreasing the unit sales price will decrease the break-even point, assuming that the fixed expenses and unit variable expense stay constant.

___19. In a contribution income statement, all fixed costs are subtracted from the contribution margin to obtain net income.

___20. If contribution margin is $40,000 and net income is $10,000, then the operating leverage factor is 0.25.

___21. The operating leverage factor is independent of the level of sales.

___22. A movement toward an advanced manufacturing system usually results in a higher operating leverage.

___23. (Appendix) If the target after-tax net income is $42,000 and the tax rate is 30 percent, then the target before-tax income is $60,000.

FILL-IN-THE-BLANK QUESTIONS

For each of the following statements, fill in the blank to properly complete the statement.

1. _____ is a technique that summarizes the effects of changes in an organization's volume of activity on its cost, revenue, and profit.

2. The _____ is the volume of activity where an organization's profit is zero.

3. The difference between the unit sales prices and the unit variable cost is called the _____.

4. Fixed expenses divided by the contribution-margin ratio equals the _____.

5. A(n) _____ graph shows the relationship between profit and volume of activity and crosses the horizontal axis at the break-even point.

6. The difference between the budgeted sales revenue and the break-even sales revenue is called the _____.

7. Increasing fixed expenses causes the break-even point to _____, assuming that the unit contribution margin remains unchanged.

8. _____ is the difference between total sales revenue and total variable expenses.

9. For a multi-product firm, the relative proportion of each type of product sold is called the _____.

10. In performing a CVP analysis, the use of different estimates for prices, unit variable expenses, and fixed expenses to study the impact on profit is called _____.

11. The contribution income statement highlights the distinction between _____ and _____ expenses.

12. Decreasing the unit variable expenses will _____ the break-even point, assuming that the fixed expenses and the unit selling price stay constant.

13. The increase in sales revenue times _____ equals the increase in net income.

14. The _____ of a firm is the relative proportion of its fixed and variable costs.

15. Increasing the unit sales price will _____ the break-even point, assuming that the fixed expenses and unit variable expense do not change.

16. The extent to which an organization uses fixed costs in its cost structure is called _____.

17. A firm with proportionately high fixed costs has relatively _____ operating leverage.

18. A firm with high operating leverage has a relatively _____ break-even point.

19. (Appendix) If the factor 1 minus the tax rate is multiplied by the before-tax income, the result is _____.

MULTIPLE-CHOICE QUESTIONS

Circle the best answer or response.

1. A firm makes and sells a single product. The selling price is $32 and the unit variable cost is $24. Monthly fixed costs are $28,800. Which of the following statements is true?
   (a) The contribution-margin ratio is 0.25.
   (b) The unit contribution margin is $6.
   (c) The monthly break-even point in units is 4,800.
   (d) The monthly break-even sales dollars are $38,400.

2. An organization makes and sells only one product. If the target net profit for the month is $26,000, monthly fixed expenses are $39,000, and the unit contribution margin is $13, then the number of sales units needed to earn the monthly target net profit is
   (a) 2,000
   (b) 3,000
   (c) 4,000
   (d) 5,000

3. In CVP analysis:
   (a) the behavior of total revenue is assumed to be linear.
   (b) the behavior of total expenses is assumed to be linear.
   (c) Both (a) and (b).
   (d) Neither (a) nor (b)

4. A firm makes and sells a single product. If monthly fixed expenses are $19,500, monthly unit sales are 3,000, and the unit contribution margin is $20, then monthly net profit is
   (a) $45,000
   (b) $40,500
   (c) $21,000
   (d) $35,000

5. Suppose that a firm makes two products, A and B. The sales mix in units for the period is 70 percent for A and 30 percent for B. If the unit contribution margin for A is $8 and the unit contribution margin for B is $5, then the weighted-average unit contribution margin is
   (a) $7.10
   (b) $5.90
   (c) $6.20
   (d) $4.80

6. Consider the following statements and determine which statement(s) is (are) true.

   I. In CVP analysis, it is assumed that in multi-product firms the sales mix varies over the relevant range.
   II. In CVP analysis, it is assumed that in manufacturing firms beginning and ending inventory levels are the same.

   (a) Only I
   (b) Only II
   (c) Both I and II
   (d) Neither I nor II

7.   (Appendix)A firm makes and sells a single product. Monthly fixed expenses are $18,000, the unit contribution margin is $10, and the target after-tax monthly net income is $28,000. If the tax rate is 30 percent, the number of sales units needed in one month to achieve the target after-tax monthly net income is:
       (a) 11,133
       (b) 4,600
       (c) 5,800
       (d) 8,250

EXERCISES

Record your answers to each part of the exercises in the space provided. Show your work.

Exercise 8.1

The Robbins Company makes and sells only one product. This product has a unit sales price of $40 and a unit variable cost of $24. Fixed expenses are $32,000 per month.

(a) Calculate the following:

   (1) Unit contribution margin

   (2) Contribution-margin ratio

   (3) Monthly break-even point in units

(4) Monthly break-even points in dollars

(5) The monthly sales units needed to achieve a monthly before-tax income of $28,000

(b) Suppose that during July the company plans to sell 3,500 units. Compute each of the following for July based on planned sales:

(1) Total revenue

(2) Total contribution margin

(3) Before-tax income

(4) Safety margin

(5) Operating leverage factor

Exercise 8.2

The Waldron Company produces a single product for sale. Based on current accounting records, the company's unit sales price is $20, unit variable expense is $12, and monthly fixed costs are $49,600.

(a) Compute the monthly break-even point in units.

Assume it is estimated that monthly fixed costs will increase by 10 percent. (All other factors remain the same.)

(b) Compute the monthly break-even point in units.

Returning to the original data, assume that variable costs decrease by 5 percent. (All other factors remain the same.)

(c) Compute the monthly break-even point in units.

Returning again to the original data, assume that the unit sales price increases by 15 percent while other factors stay the same.

(d) Compute the monthly break-even point in units.

Returning again to the original data, assume that during October the company sold 10,000 units.

(e) Calculate the total sales revenue for October.

(f) Calculate the before-tax income for October.

(g) Use the operating leverage factor for October to compute the dollar increase in before-tax income that would result from selling 11,000 units instead of 10,000.

(h) (Appendix) Assuming that the company's tax rate is 30 percent, calculate October's after-tax net income.

Returning again to the original data, assume that the tax rate is 30 percent.

(i) (Appendix) Compute how many monthly sales units are needed to achieve a target after-tax net income of $42,000.

Exercise 8.3

The Kramer Company manufactures and sells two products, X and Y, in its Huntsville Division. Data concerning these products are as follows:

	Product	
	X	Y
Unit selling price	$200	$160
Unit variable cost	120	112

Monthly fixed costs are $480,000. Of the total units typically sold in one month, 20 percent are product X and 80 percent are product Y.

(a) Calculate the contribution margin per unit for each product.

(b) Calculate the weighted-average unit contribution margin based on the given sales mix.

(c) Calculate the number of units of each product that must be sold in one month in order to break even, assuming the given sales mix.

Exercise 8.4

The Sanders Company makes and sells a board game called Starburst which currently has the following revenue and cost data:

Unit sales price	$30
Unit variable manufacturing cost	$16
Annual fixed selling and administrative cost	$48,000
Unit variable selling cost	$2

Annual fixed manufacturing cost (with respect to sales volume):	
Depreciation	$63,000
Setups (52 setups @ $90 each)	$4,680
Inspections (1,040 inspections @ $18 each)	$18,720
Material handling (1,248 hrs @ $10/hr.)	$12,840

Management is considering the installation of new computer-controlled equipment that will streamline the production process and generate output of higher quality than the present production system. With the new equipment there will be a reduction of direct labor costs, but fixed costs with respect to sales volume will increase; the new revenue and cost data will be as follows:

Unit sales price	$30
Unit variable manufacturing cost	$10
Annual fixed selling and administrative cost	$48,000
Unit variable selling cost	$2

Annual fixed manufacturing cost (with respect to sales volume):	
Depreciation	$195,030
Setups (365 setups @ $32 each)	$11,680
Inspections (365 inspections @ $10 each)	$3,650
Material handling (120 hrs @ $13/hr.)	$1,560

The management of Sanders would like to have a target net profit next year of $198,000.

(a) Calculate the break-even point in annual sales units under the:

(1) Present production system.

(2) New production system, which uses computer-controlled equipment.

(b) Calculate the annual sales units needed to achieve management's desired target net profit for next year under the:

(1) Present production system.

(2) New production system, which uses compute-controlled equipment.

(c) Write a brief essay that explains why the answers in parts (a) and (b) have different break-even points and different sales units needed to achieve the same target net income.

SOLUTIONS TO SELF-TEST QUESTIONS AND EXERCISES

MATCHING

1. K	7. O	13. D	19. M
2. R	8. C	14. Q	
3. P	9. J	15. S	
4. F	10. B	16. E	
5. A	11. G	17. L	
6. N	12. I	18. H	

TRUE-FALSE QUESTIONS

1. F   CVP analysis is used by nonprofit organizations as well as profit oriented firms.
2. T
3. F   It is where the graph crosses the horizontal axis.
4. F   The break-even point is 57,960/12 = 4,830 units.
5. T
6. F   Profit equals [$2,800 x ($15 - $5)] - $18,000 = $10,000
7. T
8. T
9. F   It is determined by the intersection of the total revenue line and the total-expenses line.
10. F   It is 8/20 = 40 percent.
11. T
12. T
13. F   It varies with the sale mix.
14. T
15. F   It increases the break-even point.
16. T
17. F   The impact on profit will be greater in this case.
18. F   It will increase the break-even point.
19. T
20. F   The operating leverage factor is $40,000/$10,000 = $4.
21. F   It does depend on sales, because net income depends on sales.
22. T
23. T

FILL-IN-THE-BLANK QUESTIONS

1. CVP analysis
2. break-even point
3. unit contribution margin
4. break-even point in sales dollars
5. profit-volume
6. safety margin
7. increase
8. Total contribution margin
9. sales mix
10. sensitivity analysis
11. fixed, variable
12. decrease
13. contribution-margin percentage
14. cost structure

15. decrease
16. operating leverage
17. high
18. high
19. after-tax net income

MULTIPLE-CHOICE QUESTIONS

1. **(a)** The contribution-margin ratio is 8/32 = .25. The unit contribution margin is 8. Monthly break-even units are $28,800/$8 = 3,600. Monthly break-even sales dollars are $28,800/.25 = $115,200.
2. **(d)** ($39,000 + $26,000)/$13 = 5,000 units.
3. **(c)**
4. **(b)** (3,000 x $20) - $19,500 = $40,500.
5. **(a)** (.7 x $8) + (.3 x $5) = $7.10.
6. **(b)** It is assumed that the sales mix is constant over the relevant range.
7. **(c)** [$18,000 + ($28,000/.7)]/$10 = 5,800 units.

EXERCISES

Exercise 8-1

(a) (1)

$40 - $24 = $16

(a) (2)

16/40 = 0.4

(a) (3)

$32,000/$16 = 2,000 units

(a) (4)

$32,000/.4 = $80,000

(a) (5)

($32,000 + $28,000)/$16 = 3,750 units

(b) (1)

3,500 x $40 = $140,000

(b) (2)

3,500 x $16 = $56,000

(b) (3)

$56,000 - $32,000 = $24,000

(b) (4)

$140,000- $80,000 = $60,000

(b) (5)

$56,000/$24,000 = 2.33

Exercise 8.2

(a)

$49,600/$(20 − 12) = 6,200 units

(b)

$49,600 x 1.1 = $54,560, then $54,560/$8 = 6,820 (The break-even point went up by 10 percent.)

(c)

$12 x .95 = $11.40, then $49,600/($20 − $11.40) = 5,768 units (The break-even point decreased.)

(d)

$20 x 1.15 = $23, then $49,600/($23 − $12) = 4,510 units (The break-even point decreased.)

(e)

10,000 x $20 = $200,000

(f)

(10,000 x $8) - $49,600 = $30,400

(g)

Operating leverage factor = $80,000/$30,400 = 2.632.

11,000 = 1.1 x 10,000.

If the sales units (and hence sales revenue) increase by 10 percent, then before-tax income will increase by .1 x 2.632, or 26.32 percent. Thus, .2632 x $30,400 = $8,001.

(h)

$30,400 − (.3 x $30,400) = $21,280

(i)

[$49,600 + ($42,000/.7)]/$8 = 13,700 units

Exercise 8.3

(a)

For X: $200 - $120 = $80

For Y: $160 - $112 = $48

(b)

(.2 x $80) + (.8 x $48) = $54.40

(c)

Total break-even units = \$480,000/\$54.40 = 8,824

Units of X needed to break even = .2 x 8,824 = 1,765

Units of Y needed to break even = .8 x 8,824 = 7,059

Exercise 8.4

(a) (1)

Annual fixed costs = \$147,240

Contribution margin per unit = \$12

Break-even sales units = \$147,240/\$12 = 12,270

(a) (2)

Annual fixed costs = \$259,920

Contribution margin per unit = \$18

Break-even sales units = \$259,920/\$18 = 14,440

(b) (1)

Units needed = (\$147,240 + \$198,000)/\$12 = 28,770

(b) (2)

Units needed = (\$259,920 + \$198,000)/\$18 = 25,440

(c)

The cost structure of the new production system with the computer-controlled equipment has a lower proportion of variable cost than the present system because of the reduction in direct labor. Also, the new system has a larger proportion of fixed costs (with respect to sales volume) than the present system, primarily because of the increased depreciation expense on the computer-controlled equipment. This shift in cost structure usually results in different break-even points and different levels of sale units needed to achieve a given target net profit, as is the case in this situation.

IDEAS FOR YOUR STUDY TEAM

1. Rewrite each of the definitions of the key terms that appear at the end of the chapter using your own words. Imagine that you are trying to explain each key term to a friend who has not taken any accounting classes. Then, get together with the other members of your study team and compare your definitions.

After-tax net income

Before-tax income

Break-even point

Contribution income statement

Contribution-margin ratio

Contribution margin, total

Cost structure

Cost-volume-profit (CVP) analysis

Cost-volume-profit graph

Operating leverage

Operating leverage factor

Profit-volume graph

Safety margin

Sales mix

Sensitivity analysis

Target net profit (or income)

Total contribution margin

Unit contribution margin

Weighted-average unit contribution margin

2. Try to predict the types of questions, exercises and problems that you will encounter on the quizzes and exams that cover this chapter. Review the *Read and Recall Questions* and the *Self-Test Questions and Exercises* that are set forth in this Study Guide. Work through the end-of-chapter review problem(s), if applicable, and the end-of-chapter questions, exercises and problems that were assigned by your instructor. As you perform these tasks, identify the terms, concepts, formulas, etc. that you are responsible for knowing. After you develop the list of questions, exercises and problems that you expect to encounter on quizzes and exams, review the learning objectives that appear at the beginning of the chapter in your textbook to ensure that you have not overlooked anything significant. After you have completed your review of your list, get together with the other members of your study team and compare your predictions.

CHAPTER FOCUS SUGGESTIONS

The purposes of budgeting systems, the role of assumptions and predictions in the budgeting process, and the similarities and differences in the operational budgets prepared by manufacturers, service-oriented firms, merchandisers, and nonprofit organizations are set forth in this chapter.

The focus is on the overall master budget prepared using the concepts of activity-based costing. You should carefully follow the logical procedures that are used in developing this budget. Each part of the budget depends on the previous parts that have been constructed.

READ AND RECALL QUESTIONS

PURPOSES OF BUDGETING SYSTEMS

LEARNING OBJECTIVE #1
After studying this section of the chapter, you should be able to:
- List and explain five purposes of budgeting systems.

What is a budget? What is a budgeting system? What are the five primary purposes of budgeting systems?

TYPES OF BUDGETS

What is a master budget? What are pro forma financial statements?

What is a capital budget? What is a financial budget? What are rolling (also revolving or continuous) budgets?

THE MASTER BUDGET: A PLANNING TOOL

Sales of Services or Goods

What is the starting point for any master budget?

Sales Forecasting

What is sales forecasting? What major factors are considered when forecasting sales? What is the starting point in the sales forecasting process?

What is an econometric model?

LEARNING OBJECTIVE #2

After studying this section of the chapter, you should be able to:

- Describe the similarities and differences in the operational budgets prepared by manufacturers, service industry firms, merchandisers, and nonprofit organizations.

Operational Budgets

What budgets comprise the operational portion of the master budget of manufacturing firms? What budgets comprise the operational portion of the master budget of merchandisers? What budgets comprise the operational portion of the master budget of service industry firms?

What types of information are summarized in a cash budget?

Nonprofit Organizations

In what ways do master budgets for nonprofit organizations differ from master budgets of profit-making organizations?

ACTIVITY-BASED BUDGETING

LEARNING OBJECTIVE #3 *After studying this section of the chapter, you should be able to:* • Explain the concept of activity-based budgeting and the benefits it brings to the budgeting process

How many stages are used in activity-based costing (ABC)? What happens in each of these stages?

What is activity-based budgeting (ABB)? What are the three steps in ABB? How does ABB conceptually relate to ABC?

LEARNING OBJECTIVE #4
After studying this section of the chapter, you should be able to:
• Prepare each of the budget schedules that make up the master budget.

What is another name for the master budget?

Sales Budget

What is the purpose of the sales budget? How is sales revenue determined? How is total sales revenue determined?

Production Budget

What is the purpose of a production budget? What is the formula for the calculation of the number of units to be produced?

Direct-Material Budget

What is the purpose of a direct-material budget? What is the formula for the calculation of the amount of raw material to be purchased?

Direct-Labor Budget

What is the purpose of a direct-material budget?

Manufacturing Overhead Budget

What is the purpose of a manufacturing-overhead budget? Why is depreciation given special treatment in this budget?

In Cozycamp.com's cost hierarchy, what are its unit-level costs? Its batch-level costs? Its product-level costs? Its facility (or general-operations) level costs?

What is needed to achieve real, sustainable payoffs from activity-based costing and activity-based management?

Selling, General, and Administrative (SG&A) Expense Budget

What is the purpose of a selling, general, and administrative expense budget?

In Cozycamp.com's cost hierarchy, what are its unit-level expenses? Its customer-level expenses? Its facility (or general-operations) level expenses?

Cash Receipts Budget

What is the purpose of a cash receipts budget? What are the sources of the cash receipts that will be collected during the period?

Cash Disbursements Budget

What is the purpose of a cash disbursements budget? What are the origins of the cash payments for raw materials that will be made during the period?

Cash Budget: Combining Receipts and Disbursements

What is the purpose of a cash budget?

Budgeted Schedule of Cost of Goods Manufactured and Sold

What is the purpose of a budgeted schedule of cost of goods manufactured and sold?

Budgeted Income Statement

What is the purpose of a budgeted income statement?

Budgeted Statement of Cash Flows

What is the purpose of a budgeted statement of cash flows?

Budgeted Balance Sheet

What is the purpose of a budgeted balance sheet?

ASSUMPTIONS AND PREDICTIONS UNDERLYING THE MASTER BUDGET

LEARNING OBJECTIVE #5
After studying this section of the chapter, you should be able to:
- Discuss the role of assumptions and predictions in budgeting.

What types of assumptions and estimates are made during the preparation of a master budget? What is the level of accuracy of these assumptions?

Financial Planning Models

What is a financial planning model? How is it useful in the budgeting process?

BUDGET ADMINISTRATION

LEARNING OBJECTIVE #6
After studying this section of the chapter, you should be able to:
- Describe a typical organization's process of budget administration.

What are the responsibilities of a budget director or chief budget officer? What is the purpose of a budget manual? What are the responsibilities of a budget committee?

E-Budgeting

What is e-budgeting?

Firewalls and Information Security

What is a firewall?

ZERO-BASE BUDGETING

What is zero-based budgeting? What is base budgeting? What is a base package? What is an incremental package?

INTERNATIONAL ASPECTS OF BUDGETING

What additional challenges do firms with international operations face in the budgeting process?

BUDGETING PRODUCT LIFE-CYCLE COSTS

LEARNING OBJECTIVE #7
After studying this section of the chapter, you should be able to:
• Understand the importance of budgeting product life-cycle costs.

What are the five phases of a product's life cycle? What must be considered to justify the introduction of a new product?

BEHAVIORAL IMPACT OF BUDGETS

> **LEARNING OBJECTIVE #8**
> *After studying this section of the chapter, you should be able to:*
> • Discuss the behavioral implications of budgetary slack and participative budgeting.

Budgetary Slack: Padding the Budget

What is the perception of many sales managers in the budgeting process?

What is "padding" the budget? What is budgetary slack? What are the three primary reasons that people pad budgets with budgetary slack? How can an organization solve the problem of budgetary slack?

Participative Budgeting

What is the idea behind participative budgeting? Why are participative approaches to budgeting often successful?

Ethical Issues in Budgeting

What serious ethical issues can arise in situations where a budget is the basis for rewarding managers?

APPENDIX TO CHAPTER 9: INVENTORY MANAGEMENT

LEARNING OBJECTIVE #9

Determine whether or not you are responsible for this appendix. If so, after studying this section of the chapter, you should be able to:

• Understand the differences between the economic-order-quantity and just-in-time approaches to inventory management.

Economic Order Quantity

What is an "economic order quantity?"

What are some examples of ordering costs? What are some examples of holding costs? What are some examples of shortage costs?

How is the total annual cost of ordering and holding inventory determined when the tabular approach is used?

How is the total annual cost of ordering and holding inventory determined when the equation approach is used?

What is the formula for the economic order (or least-cost order) quantity when the equation approach is used?

Timing of Orders

What is lead time? What is safety stock?

JIT INVENTORY MANAGEMENT: IMPLICATIONS FOR EOQ

What is the goal of the JIT philosophy with regards to inventory levels? How are the basic philosophies of JIT and EOQ different?

SELF-TEST QUESTIONS AND EXERCISES

MATCHING

Match each of the key terms listed below with the appropriate textbook definition:

___	1. Activity-based budgeting	___	20. Direct-material budget
___	2. Base budgeting	___	21. Direct-labor budget
___	3. Base package	___	22. e-budgeting
___	4. Budget	___	23. Economic order quantity*
___	5. Budget administration	___	24. Financial budget
___	6. Budget committee	___	25. Financial planning model
___	7. Budget director (or chief budget officer)	___	26. Firewall
___	8. Budget manual	___	27. Incremental package
___	9. Budgetary slack	___	28. Lead time*
___	10. Budgeted balance sheet	___	29. Manufacturing overhead budget
___	11. Budgeted financial statements (or pro forma financial statements)	___	30. Master budget (or profit plan)
___	12. Budgeted income statement	___	31. Operational budgets
___	13. Budgeted schedule of cost of goods manufactured and sold	___	32. Padding the budget
___	14. Budgeted statement of cash flows	___	33. Participative budgeting
___	15. Budgeting system	___	34. Production budget
___	16. Capital budget	___	35. Profit plan (or master budget)
___	17. Cash budget	___	36. Rolling budgets (also revolving or continuous budgets)
___	18. Cash disbursements budget	___	37. Safety stock*
___	19. Cash receipts budget	___	38. Sales budget
		___	39. Sales forecasting
		___	40. Selling, general, and administrative expense budget
		___	41. Zero-base budgeting

* This key term is included in the appendix to the chapter.

A. A set of planned financial statements showing what an organization's overall financial condition is expected to be at the end of the budget period if planned operations are carried out.

B. A schedule showing the number of units and the cost of material to be purchased and used during a budget period.

C. The amount by which the cost of one action exceeds that of another.

D. The individual designated to be in charge of preparing an organization's budget.

E. The set of procedures used to develop a budget.

F. A schedule showing the cost of overhead expected to be incurred in the production process during a budget period.

G. A long-term budget that shows planned acquisition and disposal of capital assets, such as land, buildings, and equipment.

H. The process of involving people throughout an organization in the budgeting process.

I. A set of written instructions that specifies who will provide budgetary data, when and in what form the data will be provided, how the master budget will be prepared and approved, and who should receive the various schedules comprising the budget.

J. A budget that is continually updated by adding another incremental time period and dropping the most recently completed period.

K. The order size that minimizes inventory ordering and holding costs.

L. The difference between the budgetary projection provided by an individual and his or her best estimate of the item being projected. (For example, the difference between a supervisor's expected departmental utility cost and his or her budgetary projection for utilities.)

M. The initial budget set for each of an organization's departments, set in accordance with a base package, under an approach called base budgeting.

N. Extra inventory consumed during periods of above-average usage in a setting with fluctuating demand.

O. The time required to receive inventory after it has been ordered.

P. A schedule that details the expected cash receipts and disbursements during a budget period.

Q. The process of developing a master budget using information obtained from an activity-based costing (ABC) analysis.

R. A schedule detailing the direct material, direct labor, and manufacturing overhead costs to be incurred and showing the cost of goods to be sold during a budget period.

S. The process of building budgetary slack into a budget by overestimating expenses and underestimating revenue.

T. A set of budgets that specifies how operations will be carried out to produce an organization's services or goods.

U. A planned income statement showing the expected revenue and expenses for the budget period, assuming that planned operations are carried out.

V. A schedule showing the planned amounts of selling, general, and administrative expenses during a budget period.

W. A schedule showing the planned amounts of labor required during a budget period.

X. A schedule showing the number of units of services or goods to be produced during a budget period.

Y. An initial budget, which includes that minimal resources needed for a subunit to exist at an absolute minimal level.

Z. A schedule detailing the expected cash collections during the budget period.

AA. The procedures used to prepare a budget, secure its approval, and disseminate it to the people who need to know its contents.

BB. A schedule that outlines how an organization will acquire financial resources during the budget period (for example, through borrowing or sale of capital stock).

CC. A planned balance sheet showing the expected end-of-period balances for the organization's assets, liabilities, and owners' equity, assuming that planned operations are carried out.

DD. A comprehensive set of budgets that covers all phases of an organization's operations for a specified period of time.

EE. A budgeting approach in which the initial budget for each activity in an organization is set to zero. To be allocated resources, an activity's continuing existence must be justified by the appropriate management personnel.

FF. A group of top-management personnel who advise the budget director during the preparation of the budget.

GG. The process of predicting sales or services or goods. The initial step in preparing a master budget.

HH. A schedule detailing expected cash payments during a budget period.

II. A detailed plan, expressed in quantitative terms, that specifies how resources will be acquired and used during a specified period of time.

JJ. Another term used to describe master budget.

KK. A schedule that provides information about the expected sources and uses of cash for operating, investing, and financing activities during a particular period of time.

LL. An electronic and enterprise-wide budgeting process in which employees throughout the organization can submit and retrieve budget information electronically via the Internet.

MM. A set of mathematical relationships that express the interactions among the various operational, financial, and environmental events that determine the overall results of an organization's activities.

NN. A computer or information router that is placed between a company's internal network and the Internet to control and monitor all information between the outside world and the company's local network.

OO. A schedule displaying the projected sales in units and the projected sales revenue.

TRUE-FALSE QUESTIONS

For each of the following statements, enter a T or F in the blank to indicate whether the statement is true or false.

___1. Pro forma financial statements show the financial condition and performance for a period of time that has occurred in the past.

___2. A long-range budget covers a period from 6 months to 1 year.

___3. Developing a budget is a critical step in any economic activity.

___4. The starting point for any master budget is a sales revenue budget.

___5. The selling, general, and administrative expense budget is an example of a budgeted financial statement.

___6. The direct-material budget is developed from the production budget.

___7. Sales forecasting is a useful, but not a critical, step in the budgeting process.

___8. Every business should prepare a cash budget.

___9. Nonprofit organizations begin their budgeting process with a budget that shows the level of services to be provided.

___10. The cash budget is the same as the cash disbursements budget.

___11. The cash budget is an example of an operational budget.

___12. A merchandising firm develops a budget for merchandise purchases instead of a production budget.

___13. Direct labor and overhead budgets are prepared based on the direct-material budget.

___14. If the cash balance on May 1 is $15,000, cash receipts for May are $92,000, and cash disbursements for May are $105,000, then the cash balance on May 31 is $28,000.

___15. The budgeting process is a major activity in every large organization.

___16. The participative budgeting approach is sometimes used so as not to go to the extreme of zero-based budgeting.

___17. Nonprofit organizations do not prepare budgets showing their anticipated funding, because this information is not useful for planning purposes.

___18. Human reactions to the budgeting process have negligible influence on an organization's overall effectiveness.

___19. Budget padding means underestimating costs and overstating revenues.

___20. The planning of life-cycle costs is a crucial step in making a decision about the introduction of a new product.

___21. (Appendix) Inventory decisions involve a delicate balance among ordering costs, holding costs, and shortage costs.

FILL-IN-THE-BLANK QUESTIONS

For each of the following statements, fill in the blank to properly complete the statement.

1. A(n) _____ is a detailed plan in quantitative terms that specifies how resources will be acquired and used in a specific period of time.

2. A(n) _____ budget is a comprehensive set of budgets covering all phases of an organization's operations for a specified period of time.

3. A(n) _____ budget is a plan for the acquisition of capital assets.

4. A(n) _____ budget shows the number of product units to be manufactured.

5. The _____ budget shows expected cash receipts and planned cash disbursements.

6. Budgeted _____ show the overall financial results of the organization's planned operations for the budget period.

7. A(n) _____ budget is continually updated by periodically adding a new incremental time period and dropping the period just covered.

8. The _____ budget shows the dollar amount of materials that need to be purchased during the budget period.

9. In large organizations, the _____ is usually the person who specifies the process by which budget data will be gathered, collects the information, and prepares the master budget.

10. The _____ is the document which says who is responsible for providing various types of information, when the information is required, and what form the information is to take.

11. Often a(n) _____ is appointed to advise the budget director during the preparation of the budget.

12. Under _____ budgeting, the budget for virtually every activity of an organization is initially set to zero.

13. A(n) _____ is a set of mathematical relationships that expresses the interactions among various operational, financial, and environmental events that determine the overall results of an organization's activities.

14. The difference between the revenue or cost projection that a person provides and a realistic estimate of the revenue or cost is called _____

15. The idea of _____ budgeting is to involve employees throughout an organization in the budgetary process.

16. (Appendix) The _____ is the length of time it takes for material to be received after an order is placed.

MULTIPLE-CHOICE QUESTIONS

Circle the best answer or response.

1. Which of the following are major factors when forecasting sales?

    I   Past sales levels and trends
    II.   Economic trends in the company's industry III. Political and legal events

    (a) Only I and II
    (b) Only II and III
    (c) Only I and III
    (d) I, II, and III

2. Which of the following is *not* a primary purpose of budgeting?
   (a) Facilitating communication and coordination throughout the organization
   (b) Providing basic information in determining tax obligations for a previous period's operations
   (c) Controlling profits and operations
   (d) Quantifying a plan of action

3. The March 1 inventory of finished units at the J Company is 3,000. During March the company plans to sell 35,000 units and desires a March 31 inventory of 5,000 units. The number of units that the company should plan on producing in March is:
   (a) 53,000
   (b) 37,000
   (c) 42,000
   (d) 33,000

4. The Jason Company plans to produce 24,000 units during January. Each unit of finished product requires 1.5 direct-labor hours, and each direct-labor hour costs $12. The amount that should be budgeted for direct labor to meet the planned production in January is:
   (a) $288,000
   (b) $36,000
   (c) $432,000
   (d) 360,000

5. The Graham Company plans to sell 20,000 units in April, 30,000 in May, and 25,000 in June. Each unit sells for $25, and sales in any month consist of 80 percent credit sales and 20 percent cash sales. All credit sales are paid for in the month following the month of sale. The cash receipts in May from all planned sales amount to:
   (a) $60,000
   (b) $550,000
   (c) $150,000
   (d) $500,000

6. The Finley Company plans to produce 25,000 units during July. Each unit of finished product requires 2 pounds of direct material X This direct material costs $4 per pound. The July 1 inventory of X is 2,000 pounds, and the desired July 31 inventory of X is 1,000 pounds. The cost of material X purchases in July is planned to be:
   (a) $204,000
   (b) $196,000
   (c) $200,000
   (d) $180,000

7. The Hanover Company sells only one product and plans to sell 80,000 units in November and 120,000 units in December. The unit sales price is $4.80. The sales each month consist of 30 percent cash sales and the rest on credit; however, credit sales are always paid for in the month following the month of sale. The planned accounts receivable balance on November 30 is:
   (a) $268,800
   (b) $56,000
   (c) $384,000
   (d) $403,200

8. (Appendix) The Munson Company needs 12,000 units of material Y annually. This material is ordered periodically from a regular supplier. The cost of placing one order is $60, and the annual holding cost per unit is $.16. For material Y the economic order quantity is:

    (a) 2,000 units

    (b) 3,000 units

    (c) 4,000 units

    (d) 3,280 units

EXERCISES

Record your answers to each part of the exercises in the space provided. Show your work.

Exercise 9.1

The Sharkey Company makes and sells a single product. Forecasted sales of this product for October are 30,000 units; for November, 50,000 units; for December, 45,000 units; and for January, 35,000 units. This product is made from a liquid Z. and one unit of finished product requires 2 gallons of Z. The price of liquid Z is $8 per gallon. Because of the nature of liquid Z. the company wants no ending inventories of Z at all, and they do not have any work-in-process inventories. The company does desire to have an ending inventory of finished product equal to 5 percent of next month's sales in units. On September 30 the inventory of finished product amounted to 1,700 units.

(a) Prepare a production budget for October, November, and December

(b) Prepare a direct-material budget for October, November, and December

Exercise 9.2

General Eye Care, Inc., is a large, all-around eye-care practice which expects 50,400 office visits next year; these visits are spread evenly over the year. Seventy percent of these visits will be for 20-minute appointments, and the rest will be for 40-minute appointments. On average, a 20-minute appointment will generate $80 in revenue and a 40-minute appointment $140 in revenue. Forty percent of the revenue goes for labor. Eighty percent of a month's revenue is collected during the month, and the remainder is collected in the month following the appointment. There are no bad debts.

(a) Prepare a labor budget for February

(b) Determine the cash collections during February for professional eye care

Exercise 9.3

Harwit Nurseries sells a variety of plants, shrubs, and lawn products. It is now February 28. The following data are available:

- Sales are budgeted at $280,000 for March and $340,000 for April. February sales were $250,000
- Collections from the sale of nursery items will be 75 percent in the month of sale and the rest in the month following sale. There are no bad debts.
- The cost of sales is expected to be 70 percent of sales revenue.
- Sixty percent of the nursery products are purchased in the month prior to sale, and 40 percent are bought in the month of sale. Payment for nursery items bought from suppliers is always in the month following the purchase.
- The annual depreciation amounts to $240,000.
- Other monthly expenses amount to $38,000 and are paid for in cash.
- The income tax rate is 30 percent; taxes are paid in cash.

The balance sheet on February 28 was as follows:

HARWIT NURSERIES
Balance Sheet
February 28

Assets

Cash	$ 20,000
Accounts receivable	62,500
Inventory (nursery products)	117,600
Property, plant, and equipment,	
Net of accumulated depreciation of $540,000	660,000
Total assets	$860,100

Liabilities and Equities

Accounts Payable (nursery products)	$187,600
Common Stock	600,000
Retained earnings	72,500
Total liabilities and equity	$860,100

(a) Prepare a cash receipts budget for March

(b) Prepare a budgeted income statement for March

(c) Prepare a cash disbursements budget for March

(d) Prepare a budgeted balance sheet as of March 31

Exercise 9.4

The headmaster of Loudonville Academy told the budget committee, "In preparing next year's budget we would be wise to underestimate our revenues and overstate our expenses." You are a member of this budget committee and are asked by the chairman of the committee to give your views on the statement made by the headmaster.

Write a brief essay that explains the meaning of the headmaster's statement and the reasons why managers often follow this philosophy.

SOLUTIONS TO SELF-TEST QUESTIONS AND EXERCISES

MATCHING

1. Q	9. L	17. P	25. MM	33. H	41. EE
2. M	10. CC	18. HH	26. NN	34. X	
3. Y	11. A	19. Z	27. C	35. JJ	
4. II	12. U	20. B	28. O	36. J	
5. AA	13. R	21. W	29. F	37. N	
6. FF	14. KK	22. LL	30. DD	38. OO	
7. D	15. E	23. K	31. T	39. GG	
8. I	16. G	24. BB	32. S	40. V	

TRUE-FALSE QUESTIONS

1. **F** They show the projected financial condition and performance for a future time period.
2. **F** It covers a period of more than 1 year.
3. **T**
4. **T**
5. **F** It is an example of an operational budget.
6. **T**
7. **F** It is a critical step in the budgeting process.
8. **T**
9. **T**
10. **F** The summary cash budget shows the change that is expected to occur over the budget period.
11. **T**
12. **T**
13. **F** The direct-labor and overhead budgets are based on the production budgets.
14. **F** The ending balance is $15,000 + $92,000 - $105,000 = $2,000.
15. **T**
16. **F** Base budgeting is sometimes used so as to not go to the extreme of zero-based budgeting.
17. **F** These organizations do prepare budgets showing their anticipated funding.
18. **F** It has a significant influence on overall effectiveness.
19. **F** It means underestimating revenues and overstating expenses.
20. **T**
21. **T**

FILL-IN-THE-BLANK QUESTIONS

1. budget
2. master
3. capital
4. production
5. cash
6. financial statements
7. rolling
8. direct-material
9. budget director
10. budget manual

11. budget committee
12. zero-based
13. financial planning model
14. budgetary slack
15. participative
16. lead time

MULTIPLE-CHOICE QUESTIONS

1. **(d)**
2. **(b)** Budgeting pertains to future events, not information on a previous period's tax obligations.
3. **(b)** 35,000 + 5,000 - 3,000 = 37,000 units.
4. **(c)** $12 x 1.5 x 24,000 = $432,000.
5. **(b)** (30,000 x 25 x .2) + (20,000 x 25 x .8) = $550,000.
6. **(b)** [(25,000 x 2) + 1,000 - 2,000] x $4 = $196,000.
7. **(a)** 80,000 x $4.80 x .7 = $268,800.
8. **(b)** $(2 \times 12,000 \times \$60/\$.16)^{1/2}$ = 3,000 units.

EXERCISES

Exercise 9.1

(a)

SHARKEY COMPANY
Production Budget
For the Fourth Quarter

| | Month | | |
	October	November	December
Sales in units	30,000	50,000	45,000
Add: Desired ending inventory	2,500	2,250	1,750
Total units needed	32,500	52,250	46,750
Less: Beginning inventory	1,700	2,500	2,250
Units to be produced	30,800	49,750	44,500

(b)

SHARKEY COMPANY
Direct-Material Budget
For the Fourth Quarter

	October	Month November	December
Units to be produced	30,800	49,750	44,500
Direct material needed per unit (gal)	x 2	x 2	x 2
Direct material needed for production and to be purchased*	61,600	99,500	89,000
Price per gallon	x 8	x $8	x $8
Cost of direct material purchases	$492,800	$796,000	$712,000

*No beginning or ending inventories of material Z are desired.

Exercise 9.2

(a)

GENERAL EYE CARE, INC.
Labor Budget
For the Month of February

20-minute appointments:
    (50,400/12) x 0.7 = 2,940 appointments
    Revenue from appointments = 2,940 x $80 = $235,200
    Direct labor needed = $235,200 x 0.4 = $ 94,080

40-minute appointments:
    (50,400/12) x 0.3 = 1,260 appointments
    Revenue from appointments = 1,260 x $140 = $176,400
    Direct labor needed = $176,400 x 0.4 =   70,560
Total direct labor needed $164,640

(b)

GENERAL EYE CARE, INC.

Schedule of Cash Collections

For the Month of February

Collections from January services ($411,600* x .2)	$ 82,320
Collections from February services ($411,600 x .8)	329,280
Total cash collections in February	$411,600

*(235,200 + 176,400) The revenue is assumed to be the same each month.

Exercise 9.3

(a)

HARWIT NURSERIES

Cash Receipts Budget

For the Month of March

Cash collections from February sales: (.25 x $250,000)	$ 62,500
Cash collections from March sales: (.75 x $280,000)	210,000
Total cash receipts	$272,500

(b)

HARWIT NURSERIES

Budgeted Income Statement

For the Month of March

Sales revenue	$280,000
Cost of goods sold (70% of sales)	196,000
Gross margin	84,000
Less: Operating expenses (besides depreciation)	38,000
Less: Depreciation	20,000
Income before taxes	26,000
Income taxes (30%)	7,800
Net Income after taxes	$ 18,200

(c)

HARWIT NURSERIES
Cash Disbursements Budget
For the Month of March

Cash payments for February purchases	$187,600
Cash payments for other March expenses	38,000
Cash payment for March Income taxes	7,800
Total cash disbursements	$233,400

(d)

HARWIT NURSERIES
Budgeted Balance Sheet
For March 31

Assets

Cash (1)	$59,100
Accounts receivable (2)	70,000
Inventory (3)	142,800
Property, plant, and equipment (net) (4)	640,000
Total assets	$911,900

Liabilities and Equity

Accounts Payable (5)	$221,200
Common stock	600,000
Retained earnings (6)	90,700
Total liabilities and equity	$911,900

Computations:
(1) $20,000 + $272,500 - $233,400
(2) 0.25 x $280,000
(3) $117,600 + (0.4 x 0.7 x $280,000) + (0.6 x 0.7 x $340,000) – (0.7 x $280,000)
(4) $660,000 – ($240,000/12)
(5) (0.4 x 0.7 x $280,000) + (0.6 x 0.7 x $340,000)
(6) $72,500 + $18,200

Exercise 9.4

The statement made by the headmaster is commonly referred to as "budgetary slack" or "padding the budget. It occurs when those preparing the budget intentionally understate anticipated revenues and overstate anticipated expenses. Reasons for padding the budget include:

- A padded budget increases the chances of obtaining favorable budget variances, and this makes performance look better.
- Budgetary slack is a way to help cope with budget uncertainties.
- Budgetary slack is also is a way of dealing with budget cuts made in resource-allocation decisions.

IDEAS FOR YOUR STUDY TEAM

1. Rewrite each of the definitions of the key terms that appear at the end of the chapter using your own words. Imagine that you are trying to explain each key term to a friend who has not taken any accounting classes. Then, get together with the other members of your study team and compare your definitions.

Activity-based budgeting

Base budgeting

Base package

Budget

Budget administration

Budget committee

Budget director (or chief budget officer)

Budget manual

Budgetary slack

Budgeted balance sheet

Budgeted financial statements (or pro forma financial statements)

Budgeted income statement

Budgeted schedule of cost of goods manufactured and sold

Budgeted statement of cash flows

Budgeting system

Capital budget

Cash budget

Cash disbursements budget

Cash receipts budget

Direct-material budget

Direct labor budget

e-budgeting

Economic order quantity

Financial budget

Financial planning model

Firewall

Incremental package

Lead time

Manufacturing overhead budget

Master budget (or profit plan)

Operational budgets

Padding the budget

Participative budgeting

Production budget

Profit plan (or master budget)

Rolling budgets (also revolving or continuous budgets)

Safety stock

Sales budget

Sales forecasting

Selling, general, and administrative expense budget

Zero-base budgeting

2. Try to predict the types of questions, exercises and problems that you will encounter on the quizzes and exams that cover this chapter. Review the *Read and Recall Questions* and the *Self-Test Questions and Exercises* that are set forth in this Study Guide. Work through the end-of-chapter review problem(s), if applicable, and the end-of-chapter questions, exercises and problems that were assigned by your instructor. As you perform these tasks, identify the terms, concepts, formulas, etc. that you are responsible for knowing. After you develop the list of questions, exercises and problems that you expect to encounter on quizzes and exams, review the learning objectives that appear at the beginning of the chapter in your textbook to ensure that you have not overlooked anything significant. After you have completed your review of your list, get together with the other members of your study team and compare your predictions.

CHAPTER 10

STANDARD COSTING AND PERFORMANCE MEASURES FOR TODAY'S MANUFACTURING ENVIRONMENT

CHAPTER FOCUS SUGGESTIONS

This chapter begins the discussion of standard-costing systems. In chapter 3, you learned about the use of predetermined overhead rates based on budgeted data. As explained in this chapter, standard-costing systems extend this same concept to material and labor costs. In addition, this chapter also includes coverage of variance analysis (i.e., the investigation of differences between standard and actual costs) for material and labor costs.

You should be familiar with the use of standard costing for purposes of cost control, the procedures used to set standards, the differences between perfection and practical standards, some behavioral effects of standard costing, and the advantages of standard costing. Practicing the use of both the formula and diagram approaches should help to ensure that you are able to compute: direct-material price, direct-material quantity, direct-labor rate, and direct-labor efficiency variances. You will be also need to know how to investigate these variances. You should also be familiar with the implications of today's manufacturing environment on standard-costing systems.

READ AND RECALL QUESTIONS

MANAGING COSTS

> **LEARNING OBJECTIVE #1**
> *After studying this section of the chapter, you should be able to:*
> • Explain how standard costing is used to help control costs.

What are the three basic parts of any control system?

What is a "standard cost?" What is a "cost variance?"

Management by Exception

What is "management by exception?" What constitutes a significant variance?

SETTING STANDARDS

LEARNING OBJECTIVE #2
After studying this section of the chapter, you should be able to:
• Describe two ways to set standards.

Methods for Setting Standards

In a mature production process, what is one indicator of future costs?

What adjustments might be required when cost predictions are based on historical costs?

What is task analysis? Who does the managerial accountant work with when performing task analysis? What is the primary difference between task analysis and analysis of historical data?

Participation in Setting Standards

Who should determine standards? Why?

LEARNING OBJECTIVE #3
After studying this section of the chapter, you should be able to:
• Distinguish between perfection and practical standards.

Perfection versus Practical Standards: A Behavioral Issue

What is a "perfection standard?" What is another term for perfection standard? What is assumed when a perfection standard is set?

Why do some managers believe that perfection standards motivate employees to achieve the lowest cost possible? Why do other managers believe that perfection standards discourage employees? How might a perfection standard result in lower product quality?

What is a "practical standard?" What is another term for practical standard?

USE OF STANDARDS BY NONMANUFACTURING ORGANIZATIONS

What types of standard do service firms (such as UPS) use?

COST VARIANCE ANALYSIS

LEARNING OBJECTIVE #4
After studying this section of the chapter, you should be able to:
•   Compute and interpret the direct-material price and quantity variances.

Direct-Material Standards

What is the "standard material quantity?" What is the "standard material price?"

Direct-Labor Standards

What is the "standard direct-labor quantity?" What is the "standard labor rate?"

Standard Costs Given Actual Output

What is "actual output?"

How is the total standard (or budgeted costs) for direct material computed? How is the total standard (or budgeted costs) for direct labor computed?

Direct-Material Variances

What is the formula for the direct-material price variance? When would this variance be considered favorable? When would it be considered unfavorable?

What is the formula for the direct-material quantity variance? When would this variance be considered favorable? When would it be considered unfavorable?

When should the direct-material price variance be calculated? Why? When should the direct-material quantity variance be calculated? Why?

Why must the standard quantity of material be based on the actual production output in order for the quantity variance to be meaningful?

Direct-Labor Variances

What is the formula for the direct-labor rate variance? When would this variance be considered favorable? When would it be considered unfavorable?

What is the formula for the direct-labor efficiency variance? When would this variance be considered favorable? When would it be considered unfavorable?

Multiple Types of Direct Material or Direct Labor

If a manufacturing process involves several types of direct material, how should the direct-material price and quantity variances be computed?

If a production process involves several types of direct labor, how should the direct-material price and quantity variances be computed?

Allowing for Spoilage or Defects

Should spoilage or defective production be taken into account when the standard quantity of material is computed? Why or why not?

How should the "input quantity allowed" be computed?

SIGNIFICANCE OF COST VARIANCES

LEARNING OBJECTIVE #5
After studying this section of the chapter, you should be able to:
• Explain several methods for determining the significance of cost variances.

Why do managerial accountants often show the relative magnitude of variances in their cost-variance reports? Is the absolute or relative size of the variance more important? What action would a manager take when a variance, which exceeds the rule of thumb for absolute size or relative magnitude, appears on a cost-variance report?

Assume a manager notes that a variance, which does not exceed the rule of thumb for absolute size or relative magnitude, recurs at a reasonably high level for several consecutive months. What action would the manager take? Why?

Assume that a manager notes an unfavorable trend in a variance month after month, even though the variance does not exceed the rule of thumb for absolute size or relative magnitude. What action would the manager take? Why?

Why is the controllability of the cost item an important consideration in deciding when to look into the causes of a variance?

Why is it just as important to investigate significant favorable variances as significant unfavorable variances?

What factors are considered when a cost-benefit analysis underlies the decision to investigate a cost variance?

A Statistical Approach

What is a "statistical control chart?" What is a statistically determined "critical value?" How is the critical value usually determined? Why wouldn't a manager investigate variances that do not exceed the critical value?

LEARNING OBJECTIVE #6
After studying this section of the chapter, you should be able to:
- Describe some behavioral effects of standard costing.

Suppose a manager earns a bonus when departmental costs are below the budgeted amount, given actual sales. What positive effects might this reward structure have? What negative effects might it have?

CONTROLLABILITY OF VARIANCES

Who is in the best position to influence direct-material price variances? Who is in the best position to influence direct-material quantity variances?

Who is in the best position to influence direct-labor rate variances? Who is in the best position to influence direct-labor efficiency variances?

Interaction among Variances

How might the purchase of off-standard material result in a (an):

(1) Favorable direct-material price variance?

(2) Unfavorable direct-material quantity variance?

(3) Unfavorable direct-labor rate variance?

(4) Unfavorable direct-labor efficiency variance?

Is the decision to purchase off-standard material necessarily a poor one if it resulted in unfavorable direct-material quantity, direct-labor rate, and direct-labor efficiency variances? Why or why not?

STANDARD COSTS AND PRODUCT COSTING

LEARNING OBJECTIVE #7
After studying this section of the chapter, you should be able to:
- Explain how standard costs are used in product costing.

How are the amounts of direct-material and direct-labor that are added to the Work-in-Process Inventory account determined in a standard-costing system?

ADVANTAGES OF STANDARD COSTING

LEARNING OBJECTIVE #8
After studying this section of the chapter, you should be able to:
- Summarize some advantages of standard costing.

What six advantages are traditionally attributed to standard costing?

CHANGING ROLE OF STANDARD-COSTING SYSTEMS IN TODAY'S MANUFACTURING ENVIRONMENT

LEARNING OBJECTIVE #9 *After studying this section of the chapter, you should be able to:* • Describe the changing role of standard-costing systems in today's manufacturing environment.

Criticisms of Standard Costing in Today's Manufacturing Environment

What are several drawbacks attributed to standard costing in an advanced manufacturing setting?

Adapting Standard-Costing Systems

What type of costing (actual or standard) do most manufacturing firms use after adopting advanced manufacturing methods?

Why have the standards and variances used to control labor costs declined in importance in today's manufacturing environment?

What are the key control aspects of the cost management system (CMS) in today's manufacturing environment?

What cost drivers become the focus of the CMS and activity-based costing system in today's manufacturing environment?

Why does the cost structure shift from variable costs toward fixed costs in advanced manufacturing systems?

What three benefits result from the total quality control (TCQ) programs that typically accompany a JIT approach?

What is a key objective of a CMS? Why should standards be revised frequently in a CMS?

What is the effect of shorter product life cycles on the frequency of the standard-setting process?

Why are managers able to eliminate the causes of unfavorable variances more quickly in a CIM system?

What is "benchmarking?"

OPERATIONAL CONTROL MEASURES IN TODAY'S MANUFACTURING ENVIRONMENT

LEARNING OBJECTIVE #10
After studying this section of the chapter, you should be able to:
- Describe the operational performance measures appropriate for today's manufacturing environment.

What is the goal of activity-based management?

Why has purchasing performance become an important area of measurement criteria? What criteria are used to measure purchasing performance? Why is the cost of scrap highlighted as a separate item?

What criteria are used to measure inventory control when a JIT philosophy is employed?

What is "bottleneck machinery?" How does it differ from nonbottleneck machinery?

What is a "bottleneck operation?"

What is the "theory of constraints?"

What are the three measures of product quality when a JIT philosophy is employed?

What is "delivery cycle time?" What is "manufacturing cycle time?" What is "velocity?"

What is the formula for determining manufacturing cycle efficiency (MCE)? What is the value of the MCE measure? What is the level of MCE in many manufacturing companies? Do firms with advanced manufacturing systems strive for a low or high MCE measure?

What is the formula for determining aggregate (or total) productivity? How is a firm's total output measured? How is total input measured?

What is the formula for determining partial (or component) productivity?

What measurement approach is preferable to the productivity measurement approach?

What are some examples of operational (or physical) measures that are also partial productivity measures?

Gain-Sharing Plans

What is a "gain-sharing plan?"

THE BALANCED SCORECARD

How do financial performance measures differ from nonfinancial performance measures?

What is the "balanced scorecard" perspective?

APPENDIX TO CHAPTER 10: USE OF STANDARD COSTS FOR PRODUCT COSTING

LEARNING OBJECTIVE #11
Determine whether or not you are responsible for this appendix. If so, after studying this section of the chapter, you should be able to:
- Prepare journal entries to record and close out cost variances.

What journal entry is used to record the purchase of raw material and the incurrence of an unfavorable price variance? How would this entry change if the variance was favorable?

What journal entry is used to record the use of direct material in production and the incurrence of an unfavorable quantity variance? How would this entry change if the variance was favorable?

What journal entry is used to record the usage of direct labor and the incurrence of unfavorable direct-labor variances? How would this entry change if the variance was favorable?

Are variance accounts permanent or temporary accounts? How do most companies close their variance accounts?

What alternative method do some companies use to close their variance accounts? What is "variance proration?"

What journal entry is used to record the transfer of goods to the finished goods area? How is the dollar amount of the goods that are transferred determined in a standard-costing system?

What journal entry is used to record the sale of goods to customers? How is the dollar amount of the goods that are sold determined in a standard-costing system?

SELF-TEST QUESTIONS AND EXERCISES

MATCHING

Match each of the key terms listed below with the appropriate textbook definition:

___ 1. Aggregate (or total) productivity	___ 16. Manufacturing cycle time
___ 2. Benchmarking	___ 17. Partial (or component) productivity
___ 3. Controllability	
___ 4. Cost variance	___ 18. Perfection (or ideal) standard
___ 5. Critical value	___ 19. Practical (or attainable) standard
___ 6. Customer-acceptance measures	___ 20. Standard cost
___ 7. Delivery cycle time	___ 21. Standard-costing system
___ 8. Direct-labor efficiency variance	___ 22. Standard direct-labor quantity
___ 9. Direct-labor rate variance	___ 23. Standard labor rate
___ 10. Direct-material price variance (or purchase price variance)	___ 24. Standard material price
	___ 25. Standard material quantity
___ 11. Direct-material quantity variance	___ 26. Statistical control chart
___ 12. Gain-sharing plan	___ 27. Task analysis
___ 13. In-process quality controls	___ 28. Velocity
___ 14. Management by exception	
___ 15. Manufacturing cycle efficiency	

A. The average time between the receipt of a customer order and delivery of the goods.

B. Total output divided by total input.

C. The ratio of process time to the sum of processing time, inspection time, waiting time, and move time.

D. A predetermined cost for the production of goods or services, which serves as a benchmark against which to compare the actual cost.

E. The cost expected under perfect or ideal operating conditions.

F. A statistically determined value that triggers an investigation.

G. The cost expected under normal operating conditions.

H. The difference between actual and standard price multiplied by the actual quantity of material purchased.

I. The difference between actual and standard quantity of materials allowed, given actual output, multiplied by the standard price.

J. Total output (in dollars) divided by the cost of a particular input.

K. The total delivered cost, after subtracting any purchase discounts taken.

L. The number of units produced in a given time period.

M. The difference between actual and standard hourly labor rate multiplied by the actual hours of direct labor used.

N. An incentive system that specifies a formula by which the cost savings from productivity gains achieved by a company are shared with the workers who helped accomplish the improvements.

O. The number of hours normally needed to manufacture one unit of product.

P. The total amount of production time (or throughput time) required per unit.

Q. The difference between actual and standard hours of direct labor multiplied by the standard hourly labor rate.

R. The total amount of material normally required to produce a finished product, including allowances for normal waste and inefficiency.

S. The extent to which a firm's customers perceive its product to be of high quality.

T. A plot of cost variances across time, with a comparison to a statistically determined critical value.

U. The continual search for the most effective method of accomplishing a task, by comparing existing methods and performance levels with those of other organizations or with other subunits within the same organization.

V. A managerial technique in which only significant deviations from expected performance are investigated.

W. Total hourly cost of compensation, including fringe benefits.

X. A cost-control and product-costing system in which cost variances are computed and production costs are entered into Work-in-Process Inventory at their standard amounts.

Y. The extent to which managers are able to control or influence a cost or cost variance.

Z. Setting standards by analyzing the production process.

AA. Procedures designed to assess product quality before production is completed.

BB. The difference between actual and standard cost.

TRUE-FALSE QUESTIONS

For each of the following statements, enter a T or F in the blank to indicate whether the statement is true or false.

___1. People will generally be less committed to meeting standards if they are allowed to participate in the process of setting them.

___2. Perfection standards allow for such occurrences as occasional machine breakdowns.

___3. Managers use the budget as a benchmark against which to compare the results of actual operations.

___4. The standard quantity of direct materials allowed for a given budget period depends on the actual production output for that period.

___5. Standard costs are used by manufacturing firms, but not by nonprofit organizations.

___6. The direct-material price variance is unfavorable if actual purchase price exceeds the standard price.

___7. The direct-labor rate variance is unfavorable when the actual labor rate exceeds the standard rate.

___8. The direct-material quantity variance is unfavorable if the actual quantity of direct material used is less than the standard quantity allowed for the output achieved.

___9. Standard costs and variance analysis are useful in diagnosing organizational performance.

___10. The standard hours allowed for a given budget period depend on the actual hours used during that period.

___11. The production manager is generally in the best position to influence material price variances.

___12. The direct-labor efficiency variance is favorable when the actual hours used exceed the standard hours allowed for the output achieved.

___13. The production manager is usually in the best position to influence material quantity variances.

___14. Firms use standard costs for control, but not for product costing

___15. The production supervisor is usually most responsible for the efficient use of employee time.

___16. A consequence of unfavorable cost variances is that they decrease net income.

___17. In the new manufacturing environment there is a reduced emphasis on labor standards and variances.

___18. The emergence of the JIT philosophy has diminished the role of standard costs in product costing.

___**19.** Traditional standard costing focuses more on increasing product quality than cost minimization.

___**20.** (Appendix) The journal entry to record the purchase of raw materials with an unfavorable material price variance in a standard-costing system would include a credit to the Direct-Material Price Variance account.

___**21.** (Appendix) The journal entry to record the usage of direct labor with a favorable labor efficiency variance in a standard-costing system would include a debit to the Direct-Labor Efficiency Variance account.

FILL-IN-THE-BLANK QUESTIONS

For each of the following statements, fill in the blank to properly complete the statement.

1. A(n) _____ is a budget for the production of one unit of product or service.

2. The difference between actual cost and standard cost is called a(n) _____.

3. A(n) _____ standard is one that can be attained only under nearly perfect operating conditions.

4. The _____ is the total amount of material normally required to produce a finished product, including allowances for normal waste or inefficiency.

5. The _____ variance is the difference between the actual material quantity used times the standard price and the standard material quantity allowed for the output achieved times the standard price.

6. The _____ is the number of labor hours normally needed to manufacture one unit of product.

7. The process of following up only on significant cost variances is called _____.

8. The _____ variance is the difference between actual material cost and the actual quantity purchased times the standard price.

9. The _____ of material is the total delivered cost, after subtracting any purchase discounts.

10. _____ standards are standards that are as tight as practical, but still are expected to be attainable.

11. The _____ is the typical total hourly cost of compensation, including fringe benefits.

12. The _____ variance is the difference between actual labor cost and the actual hours used times the standard rate.

13. A(n) _____ plots cost variances over time and compares them with statistically determined critical values.

14. In a(n) _____ costing system the standard costs of direct material and direct labor are entered into Work-in-Process Inventory.

15. The _____ variance is the difference between the actual hours used times the standard rate and the standard hours allowed for the output achieved times the standard rate.

16. _____ is a method of disposing cost variances that apportions them to Work-in-Process Inventory, Finished-Goods Inventory, and Cost of Goods Sold.

17. The _____stresses the importance of identifying and easing the constraints on a firm's operations.

18. Processing time divided by the sum of process time, inspection time, waiting time, and move time is called _____.

19. _____is a productivity measure defined as total output divided by total input.

MULTIPLE-CHOICE QUESTIONS

Circle the best answer or response.

1. Consider the following statements about a control system and determine which statement(s) is (are) true.

    I.   It is a standard performance level.
    II. It has a measure of actual performance.
    III. It compares standard and actual performance.

    (a) Only I and II
    (b) Only I
    (c) Only II
    (d) I, II, and III

2. The direct-material standards for making one unit of output are 4 pounds at $7 per pound. During December, 3,000 units of output were made and 11,500 pounds of direct material were used. The December direct-material quantity variance is
    (a) $500 favorable.
    (b) $500 unfavorable.
    (c) $3,500 favorable
    (d) $3,500 unfavorable.

3. The direct-labor standards for making one chair are 2.5 hours at $14 per hour. During April, 1,800 chairs were made and the actual hours used were 4,800. The April direct-labor efficiency variance is
    (a) $4,200 favorable.
    (b) $4,200 unfavorable.
    (c) $4,500 favorable.
    (d) $4,500 unfavorable.

4. Which of the following are methods used by managerial accountants for setting cost standards?
    (a) Analysis of historical data
    (b) Task analysis
    (c) Both (a) and (b)
    (d) Neither (a) nor (b)

5. The direct-material standards for making one bottle of Wif are 10 ounces at $3 per ounce. During February, 8,000 ounces of direct material were purchased for $26,000. The February direct-material price variance is
    (a) $2,000 unfavorable.
    (b) $2,000 favorable.
    (c) $4,000 unfavorable.
    (d) $4,000 favorable.

6. Which of the following is *not* a guideline factor in determining when a variance should be investigated?
    (a) Size of variance
    (b) Whether or not the variance occurs repeatedly
    (c) The cost-flow assumption used in product costing
    (d) A trend in the variance

7. The direct-labor standards for making one unit of finished product are 3 hours at $12 per hour. During May the company used 9,000 actual direct-labor hours at a cost of $101,070. The May direct-labor rate variance is
    (a) $6,930 unfavorable.
    (b) $6,930 favorable.
    (c) $7,240 unfavorable.
    (d) $7,240 favorable.

8. Which of the following is *not* an advantage of a standard-costing system?
    (a) It enables managers to employ management by exception.
    (b) It provides a means of performance evaluation.
    (c) It eliminates the need to maintain work-in-process inventories.
    (d) It is usually less expensive than actual costing.

EXERCISES

Record your answers to each part of the exercises in the space provided. Show your work.

Exercise 10.1

The Nelson Company makes Product 823 and uses standard costing. Standards for making one unit of this product include the following:

Three quarts of material Q at $2.30 per quart

One-half hour of direct labor at $9.50 per hour

Calculate each of the following:

(a) The standard cost of material Q for one unit of Product 823

(b) The standard cost of direct labor for one unit of Product 823

(c) The number of quarts of material Q that should be used if 2,500 units of Product 823 are made

(d) The number of direct-labor hours that should be used if 2,500 units of Product 823 are made

(e) The number of units of Product 823 that should have been produced if 7,440 quarts of material Q are used

Exercise 10.2

The Schell Company makes nails in batches of 8,000. The standard cost for one batch includes the following:

     Direct material: 300 pounds at $.25 per pound

     Direct labor: 5 hours at $12.50 per hour

During June the following events occurred:

     Two hundred and twenty batches were produced.

     Direct material purchased and used was 62,000 pounds at an actual cost of $17,360.

     Direct labor used was 1,350 hours at an actual cost of $16,335.

(a) Calculate each of the following variances using the formula approach. Indicate whether the variances are favorable or unfavorable.

(1) Direct-material price variances

(2) Direct-material quantity variance

(3) Direct-labor rate variance

(4) Direct-labor efficiency variance

(b) Now, calculate each of the following variances using the diagram approach as in Exhibits 10-2 and 10-3 in the text. Indicate whether the variances are favorable or unfavorable.

(1) Direct-material price variances

(2) Direct-material quantity variance

(3) Direct-labor rate variance

(4) Direct-labor efficiency variance

Exercise 10.3

The Ramsey Company makes baseball bats in its Edaville Plant. The company uses standard costing, with standards for one baseball bat including the following:

Direct material: 3 board-feet at $.60 per board-foot

Direct labor: 0.6 hour at $11.50 per hour

During September the company had the following results at the Edaville Plant:

Direct material purchased and used in production amounted to 11,200 board-feet at a cost of $5,600.

Direct labor used in production was 1,950 hours at a cost of $23,595.

Three thousand bats were produced.

(a) Compute each of the following variances for September using the formula approach. Indicate whether the variances are favorable or unfavorable.

(1) Material price variance

(2) Material quantity variance

(b) Now, calculate each of the material variances using the diagram approach as in Exhibits 10-2 and 10-3 in the text. Indicate whether the variances are favorable or unfavorable.

(c) Compute each of the following variances for September using the formula approach. Indicate whether the variances are favorable or unfavorable.

    (1) Labor rate variance

    (2) Labor efficiency variance

(d) Now, calculate each of the labor variances using the diagram approach as in Exhibits 10-2 and 10-3 in the text. Indicate whether the variances are favorable or unfavorable.

(e) (Appendix) Prepare journal entries to record each of the following for September:

    (1) The purchase of direct materials

    (2) The use of direct materials in production

(3) The use of direct labor in production

Exercise 10.4

The Gates Company makes a certain type of crate and uses standard costing. The following data are available for November:

Material price variance:	$1,200, favorable
Material quantity variance:	$640, unfavorable
Seven thousand crates were finished.	
Direct materials purchased:	60,000 lb.
Standard direct-material pounds per crate:	8 lb.
Standard direct-material cost per pound:	$0.32
Actual direct-labor hours used:	1,600
Standard direct-labor hours per crate:	0.2
Standard direct-labor cost per crate:	$2.40
Labor rate variance:	$800, favorable

There were no inventories of any kind on November 1, and there was no work-in-process on November 30.

Calculate each of the following for November:

(a) Actual cost of direct materials purchased

(b) Actual quantity of direct materials used

(c) Standard direct-labor cost per hour

(d) Labor efficiency variance

(e) Actual cost of direct labor

SOLUTIONS TO SELF-TEST QUESTIONS AND EXERCISES

MATCHING

1.	B	7.	A	13.	AA	19.	G	25.	R
2.	U	8.	Q	14.	V	20.	D	26.	T
3.	Y	9.	M	15.	C	21.	X	27.	Z
4.	BB	10.	H	16.	P	22.	O	28.	L
5.	F	11.	I	17.	J	23.	W		
6.	S	12.	N	18.	E	24.	K		

TRUE-FALSE QUESTIONS

1. **F** They will be more committed.
2. **F** Perfection standards are standards that can be achieved only under nearly perfect operating conditions. Practical standards allow for occasional machine breakdowns.
3. **T**
4. **T**
5. **F** They are also used by nonprofit organizations.
6. **T**
7. **T**
8. **F** This variance is unfavorable when actual quantity used exceeds the standard quantity allowed.
9. **T**
10. **F** The standard hours allowed depend on the actual output achieved.
11. **F** The purchasing manager is generally in the best position to influence this variance.
12. **F** It is favorable when actual hours used are less than standard hours allowed.
13. **T**
14. **F** They also use standard costs for product costing.
15. **T**
16. **T**
17. **T**
18. **F** The role of standard costs has not diminished under the JIT philosophy.
19. **F** Traditional standard costing does focus on cost minimization and not on increasing product quality.
20. **F** It would include a debit to the Direct-Material Price Variance account.
21. **F** It would include a credit to the Direct-Labor Efficiency Variance account.

FILL-IN-THE-BLANK QUESTIONS

1. standard
2. cost variance
3. perfection (ideal)
4. standard quantity of materials
5. direct-material quantity
6. standard quantity of direct labor
7. management by exception
8. direct-material price
9. standard price
10. Practical
11. standard labor rate

12. direct-labor rate
13. statistical control chart
14. standard
15. direct-labor efficiency
16. Variance proration
17. theory of constraints
18. manufacturing-cycle efficiency
19. Aggregate productivity

MULTIPLE-CHOICE QUESTIONS

1. **(d)**
2. **(c)** $[11,500 - (3,000 \times 4)] \times \$7 = (\$3,500)$
3. **(b)** $[4,800 - (1,800 \times 2.5)] \times \$14 = \$4,200$
4. **(c)**
5. **(a)** $(26,000 - (8,000 \times \$3) = \$2,000$
6. **(c)** The cost-flow assumption used in product costing has no bearing on variance investigation.
7. **(b)** $\$101,070 - (9,000 \times \$12) = (\$6,930)$
8. **(c)** Work-in-process inventories are still needed in standard-costing systems.

EXERCISES

Exercise 10.1

(a)

3 qt x $2.30/qt = $6.90

(b)

0.5 hr x $9.50/hr. = $4.75

(c)

2,500 x 3 qt. = 7,500 qt.

(d)

2,500 x 0.5 hr. = 1,250 hr.

(e)

7,440/3 = 2,480 units

Exercise 10.2

Actual purchase price = $17,360/62,000 = $0.28

Actual labor rate = $16,335/1,350 = $12.10

(a)(1)

Material price variance = PQ x (AP - SP) = 62,000 x (.28 - .25) = $1,860 unfavorable

(a)(2)

Material quantity variance = SP x (AQ - SQ) = $.25 x [62,000 – (220 x 300)] = $1,000 favorable

(a)(3)

Labor rate variance = AH x (AR - SR) = 1,350 x (12.10 - 12.50) = $540 favorable

(a)(4)

Labor efficiency variance = SR x (AH - SH) = $12.50 x [1,350 – (220 x 5)] = $3,125 unfavorable

(b)(1) and (2)

Computation of Direct-Material Variances by Diagram Method		
Actual costs	**Actual quantity @ std. price**	**Std. quantity @ std. price**
$17,360	62,000 x $.25 = $15,500	220 x 300 x $.25 = $16,500
$1,820 unfavorable **Material price variance**		$1,000 favorable **Material quantity variance**

(b)(3) and (4)

Computation of Direct-Labor Variances by Diagram Method		
Actual costs	**Actual quantity @ std. price**	**Std. quantity @ std. price**
$16,335	1,350 x $12.50 = $16,875	220 x 5 x $12.50 = $13,750
$540 favorable **Labor rate variance**		$3,125 unfavorable **Labor efficiency variance**

Exercise 10.3

Actual purchase price = $5,600/11,200 = $.50

Actual labor rate = $23,595/1,950 = $12.10

(a)(1)

Material price variance = PQ x (AP - SP) = 11,200 x (.5 - .6) = $1,120 favorable

(a)(2)

Material quantity variance = SP x (AQ - SQ) = $.6 x [11,200 – (3,000 x 3)] = $1,320 unfavorable

(b)

Computation of Direct-Material Variances by Diagram Method

Actual costs	Actual quantity @ std. price	Std. quantity @ std. price
$5,600	11,200 x $.60 = $6,720	3,000 x 3 x $.60 = $5,400

$1,120 favorable	$1,320 unfavorable
Material price variance	**Material quantity variance**

(c)(1)

Labor rate variance = AH x (AR – SR) = 1,950 x (12.10 - 11.50) = $1,170 unfavorable

(c)(2)

Labor efficiency variance = SR x (AH - SH) = 11.50 x [1,950 – (3,000 x 0.6)] = $1,725 unfavorable

(d)

Computation of Direct-Labor Variances by Diagram Method

Actual costs	Actual quantity @ std. price	Std. quantity @ std. price
$23,595	1,950 x $11,50 = $22,425	3,000 x .6 x $11.50 - $20,700

$1,170 unfavorable	$1,725 unfavorable
Labor rate variance	**Labor efficiency variance**

Note that the diagram approach to computing variances makes it convenient for preparing journal entries, because the journal-entry amounts appear in the diagram.

(e) (Appendix)

(1)	Raw-Materials Inventory	6,720	
	Direct-Materials Price Variance		1,120
	Accounts Payable		5,600
(2)	Work-in-Process Inventory	5,400	
	Material Quantity Variance	1,320	
	Raw-Materials Inventory		6,720
(3)	Work-in-Process Inventory	20,700	
	Labor Rate Variance	1,170	
	Labor Efficiency Variance	1,725	
	Wages Payable		23,595

Exercise 10.4

The required items can be computed in the following sequence:

(a)

Actual quantity of direct material at standard price = 60,000 x 0.32 = $19,200

Actual cost of direct material = 19,200 - 1,200 = 18,000

(b)

Standard quantity of direct material at standard price = 7,000 x 8 x 0.32 = $17,920

Actual quantity of direct material used at standard price = 17,920 + 640 = $18,560

Actual quantity of direct material used = 18,560/0.32 = 58,000 lb.

(c)

Standard direct labor cost/hr. = $2.40/0.2 = $12 hr.

(d)

Labor efficiency variance = (1,600 x 12) – (7,000 x 2.40) = $2,400, unfavorable

(e)

Actual cost of direct labor = (1,600 x 12) - 800 = $18,400

IDEAS FOR YOUR STUDY TEAM

1.   Rewrite each of the definitions of the key terms that appear at the end of the chapter using your own words. Imagine that you are trying to explain each key term to a friend who has not taken any accounting classes. Then, get together with the other members of your study team and compare your definitions.

Aggregate (or total) productivity

Benchmarking

Controllability

Cost variance

Critical value

Customer-acceptance measures

Delivery cycle time

Direct-labor efficiency variance

Direct-labor rate variance

Direct-material price variance (or purchase price variance)

Direct-material quantity variance

Gain-sharing plan

In-process quality controls

Management by exception

Manufacturing cycle efficiency (MCE)

Manufacturing cycle time

Partial (or component) productivity

Perfection (or ideal) standard

Practical (or attainable) standard

Standard cost

Standard-costing system

Standard direct-labor quantity

Standard labor rate

Standard material quantity

Statistical control chart

Task analysis

Velocity

2.   Try to predict the types of questions, exercises and problems that you will encounter on the quizzes and exams that cover this chapter. Review the *Read and Recall Questions* and the *Self-Test Questions and Exercises* that are set forth in this Study Guide. Work through the end-of-chapter review problem(s), if applicable, and the end-of-chapter questions, exercises and problems that were assigned by your instructor. As you perform these tasks, identify the terms, concepts, formulas, etc. that you are responsible for knowing. After you develop the list of questions, exercises and problems that you expect to encounter on quizzes and exams, review the learning objectives that appear at the beginning of the chapter in your textbook to ensure that you have not overlooked anything significant. After you have completed your review of your list, get together with the other members of your study team and compare your predictions.

CHAPTER 11

FLEXIBLE BUDGETING AND THE MANAGEMENT OF OVERHEAD AND SUPPORT ACTIVITY COSTS

CHAPTER FOCUS SUGGESTIONS

This chapter continues the discussion of standard-costing systems. Before moving on to the manufacturing-overhead cost component of a standard-costing system, static and flexible budgeting systems are compared and contrasted. This chapter also includes an in-depth discussion of variance analysis for manufacturing-overhead costs. You might want to reacquaint yourself with the manner in which overhead is applied to work-in-process under standard costing before reading this chapter.

You should be familiar with the differences between static and flexible budgets, know the advantages of a flexible overhead budget, and know how to prepare a flexible budget. Practicing the use of both the formula and diagram approaches should help to ensure that you are able to compute the variable-overhead spending and efficiency variances and the fixed-overhead budget and volume variance. You will be also need to know how to investigate these variances.

READ AND RECALL QUESTIONS

OVERHEAD BUDGETS

LEARNING OBJECTIVE #1
After studying this section of the chapter, you should be able to:
- Distinguish between static and flexible budgets, and explain the advantages of a flexible overhead budget.

Can overhead standards be set for products? Explain.

Flexible Budgets

What is a "flexible" budget? How does a firm's relevant range of activity affect the preparation of a flexible budget?

How does a flexible budget differ from a static budget?

Advantages of Flexible Budgets

What is the disadvantage of a static budget? What is the advantage of a flexible budget?

The Activity Measure

Why are the activity levels in a flexible budget based on an input measure rather than an output measure? Is the number of units produced an input or output measure?

How should the amount of standard allowed input (given actual output) be determined?

FLEXIBLE OVERHEAD BUDGET ILLUSTRATED

LEARNING OBJECTIVE #2

After studying this section of the chapter, you should be able to:
- Prepare a flexible overhead budget, using both a formula and a columnar format.

How is a flexible budget prepared when a columnar format is used? What information is listed in the columns under each particular activity level?

When a formula flexible budget is used, what formula is used to calculate total budgeted overhead cost?

Which format (columnar or formula) is more general because it allows the managerial accountant to compute budgeted overhead costs at any activity level?

OVERHEAD APPLICATION IN A STANDARD-COSTING SYSTEM

LEARNING OBJECTIVE #3

After studying this section of the chapter, you should be able to:
- Explain how overhead is applied to Work-in-Process Inventory under standard costing.

What is overhead application?

In a normal-costing system, what is the basis for overhead application (in terms of hours)? In a standard-costing system, what is the basis for overhead application (in terms of hours)?

What is the term used to describe the predetermined overhead rate in a standard-costing system?

CHOICE OF ACTIVITY MEASURE

LEARNING OBJECTIVE #4
After studying this section of the chapter, you should be able to:
- Explain some important issues in choosing an activity measure for overhead budgeting and application.

Why is the choice of an appropriate activity measure for the flexible overhead budget so important?

Criteria for Choosing the Activity Measure

What is the ideal relationship between variable-overhead costs and the activity measure chosen for the flexible overhead budget?

What two activity measures are linked more closely than direct labor to the robotic technology and computer-integrated manufacturing (CIM) systems?

Why are dollar measures, such as direct-labor or raw-material costs, often used as the basis for flexible overhead budgeting? Why should such dollar measures be avoided? What significant drawbacks do these measures have?

COST MANAGEMENT USING OVERHEAD COST VARIANCES

LEARNING OBJECTIVE #5
After studying this section of the chapter, you should be able to:
- Compute and interpret the variable-overhead spending and efficiency variances and the fixed-overhead budget and volume variances.

What is the managerial accountant's primary tool for the control of manufacturing-overhead costs?

VARIABLE OVERHEAD

What is the variable-overhead spending variance? How is it calculated?

What is the variable-overhead efficiency variance? How is it calculated?

The formulas for computing the variable-overhead variances resemble those used to compute the direct-labor variances. As such, is the interpretation of both types of variances the same? Why or why not?

What is the cause of an unfavorable variable-overhead efficiency variance? What is the cause of an favorable variable-overhead efficiency variance?

What does an unfavorable spending variance mean? What factors could cause an unfavorable spending variance?

Does the variable-overhead efficiency variance indicate whether or not variable overhead usage is efficient or inefficient? Explain.

Which is the real control variance for variable overhead?

FIXED OVERHEAD

What is the name of the variance used by managers to control fixed overhead in general?

What is the formula for the fixed-overhead budget variance?

Where is the amount of "budgeted fixed overhead" obtained from when it is used in the calculation of the fixed-overhead budget variance?

What is the formula for calculating the fixed-overhead volume variance?

Where is the amount of "budgeted fixed overhead" obtained from when it is used in the calculation of the fixed-overhead volume variance?

How is the amount of "applied fixed overhead" (or fixed overhead applied to work-in-process) determined?

What is the basis for controlling fixed overhead? Why?

What must take place in order for the amount of budgeted fixed overhead to be equal to the amount of applied fixed overhead?

What is a common, but faulty, interpretation of a positive volume variance?

Why do some firms designate a positive volume variance as unfavorable?

What is the fault with this interpretation of the volume variance? What two matters are ignored?

OVERHEAD COST PERFORMANCE REPORT

LEARNING OBJECTIVE #6
After studying this section of the chapter, you should be able to:
• Prepare an overhead cost performance report.

What information is included in an overhead cost performance report?

ACTIVITY-BASED FLEXIBLE BUDGET

LEARNING OBJECTIVE #7
After studying this section of the chapter, you should be able to:
- Explain how an activity-based flexible budget differs from a conventional flexible budget.

Generally, is a traditional, volume-based product-costing system more or less accurate than an activity-based costing system? Explain.

How does an activity-based flexible budget differ from a conventional flexible budget?

Why does an activity-based flexible budget provide a more accurate prediction (and benchmark) of overhead costs than a conventional flexible budget?

What condition must be present in order for the amount of a budgeted overhead item in a conventional flexible budget to be the same as it is in an activity-based flexible budget?

Why would the amounts of other budgeted overhead items be different in a conventional flexible budget and an activity-based flexible budget?

APPENDIX A TO CHAPTER 11: STANDARD COSTS AND PRODUCT COSTING

LEARNING OBJECTIVE #8
Determine whether or not you are responsible for this appendix. If so, after studying this section of the chapter, you should be able to:
• Prepare journal entries to record manufacturing overhead under standard costing.

What journal entry is used to record the incurrence of actual overhead expenditures (such as the use of indirect-materials and depreciation)?

If the predetermined overhead rate is $7 per machine hour, and 6,000 of standard machine hours are allowed given an actual output of 2,000 units, what is the amount of overhead that is applied?

What entry is used to record the application of overhead to the Work-in-Process Inventory?

If actual overhead exceeds the amount applied during the period, is overhead underapplied or overapplied? Will the overhead account have a debit or credit balance at the end of the period?

If the amount of overhead that is applied during the period exceeds the amount of actual overhead incurred, is overhead underapplied or overapplied? Will the overhead account have a debit or credit balance at the end of the period?

What is the relationship between the total of the four overhead variances during the period and the balance of the overhead account at the end of the period?

What journal entry do most companies use to close the overhead account if overhead was underapplied during the period?

What four accounts are involved in the journal entry when the alternative proration method is used to close the overhead account?

APPENDIX B TO CHAPTER 11: SALES VARIANCES

LEARNING OBJECTIVE #9

Determine whether or not you are responsible for this appendix. If so, after studying this section of the chapter, you should be able to:

- Compute and interpret the sales-price and sales-volume variances.

How is the unit contribution margin determined? What is the unit contribution margin?

How would the amount of the budgeted total contribution margin be determined?

What is the formula for the sales-price variance?

What is the formula for the sales-volume variance?

SELF-TEST QUESTIONS AND EXERCISES

MATCHING

Match each of the key terms listed below with the appropriate textbook definition:

___	1.	Activity-based flexible budget	___	8. Static budget
___	2.	Fixed-overhead budget variance	___	9. Total contribution margin*
___	3.	Fixed-overhead volume variance	___	10. Unit contribution margin*
___	4.	Flexible budget	___	11. Variable-overhead efficiency variance
___	5.	Overhead cost performance report	___	12. Variable-overhead spending variance
___	6.	Sales-price variance*		
___	7.	Sales-volume variance*		

* This key term is included in the appendix to the chapter.

A. A flexible budget based on several cost drivers rather than on a single, volume-based cost driver.

B. A report showing the actual and flexible-budget cost levels for each overhead item, together with variable-overhead spending and efficiency variances and fixed-overhead budget variances.

C. A budget that is valid for a range of activity.

D. The difference between actual and budgeted fixed overhead.

E. A budget that is valid for only one planned activity level.

F. The difference between actual sales volume and budgeted sales volume multiplied by the budgeted unit contribution margin.

G. Sales price minus the unit variable cost.

H. The difference between actual variable-overhead cost and the product of the standard variable-overhead rate and actual hours of an activity base (e.g., machine hours).

I. Total sales revenue less total variable expenses.

J. The difference between budgeted and applied fixed overhead.

K. The difference between actual and expected unit sales price multiplied by the actual quantity of units sold.

L. The difference between actual and standard hours of an activity base (e.g., machine hours) multiplied by the standard variable-overhead rate.

TRUE-FALSE QUESTIONS

For each of the following statements, enter a T or F in the blank to indicate whether the statement is true or false.

___1. A flexible budget is based on only one level of activity.

___2. Units of output is usually not a meaningful measure in a multiproduct firm.

___3. The overhead costs in a flexible overhead budget are divided into fixed and variable costs.

___4. The static budget provides the correct basis for comparison between actual and expected costs, given the actual level of activity.

___5. Total budgeted variable-overhead cost does not change with increasing levels of activity.

___6. A flexible overhead budget should be based on input activity measures instead of output measures.

___7. Manufacturing overhead costs are not traceable to individual products.

___8. If total budgeted fixed overhead is $150,000 at 7,500 machine hours, then the budgeted variable-overhead rate is $20 per machine hour.

___9. Flexible budgeted overhead cost can be used at the end of an accounting period as a benchmark against which actual overhead costs for the period can be compared.

___10. Total budgeted fixed overhead changes with increasing levels of activity.

___11. Both normal- and standard-costing systems use a predetermined overhead rate.

___12. The flexible overhead budget is the chief tool for controlling overhead costs.

___13. As automation increases, more and more firms are switching to labor hours as an activity measure for flexible overhead budgets.

___14. Dollar measures are better than physical measures as cost drivers for flexible overhead budgets.

___15. If actual machine hours exceed standard machine hours allowed for output achieved, then the variable overhead efficiency variance based on machine hours is unfavorable.

___16. Suppose that the activity measure is machine hours. Then the variable-overhead efficiency variance gives a dollar measure of the inefficiencies associated with overhead items such as electricity and indirect materials.

___17. The volume variance is the real control variance for fixed overhead.

___18. The fixed-overhead volume variance does not depend on any actual operating inputs.

___19. If the budgeted activity level at the beginning of the accounting period equals the standard activity level for the output achieved in the period, then the fixed-overhead volume variance is zero.

___20. Nonmanufacturing organizations do not use flexible budgets to control overhead.

___21. An activity-based flexible budget treats inspection and setup costs as fixed costs.

___22. (Appendix) If the actual sales price exceeds the expected sales price, then the sales-price variance is favorable.

FILL-IN-THE-BLANK QUESTIONS

For each of the following statements, fill in the blank to properly complete the statement.

1. A(n) _____budget is a detailed plan for controlling overhead costs that is valid in the firm's relevant range of activity.

2. A(n) _____budget is based on a particular single planned level of activity.

3. In a(n) _____, each budgeted overhead cost item is listed in a column under a particular activity level.

4. Dividing total budgeted variable-overhead cost by the associated activity level yields a(n) _____rate.

5. The activity measure chosen as a basis for the flexible overhead budget should be such that variable-overhead cost and the activity measure move _____ as overall productive activity changes.

6. The difference between total actual overhead cost and total applied overhead cost is called _____.

7. Assume that machine hours is used as the activity measure. The variable-overhead spending variance is unfavorable when actual variable-overhead cost _____ the expected amount, after adjusting that expectation for the actual number of machine hours used.

8. The _____variance is the real control variance for variable overhead.

9. We do not need to specify an activity level to determine budgeted _____ overhead.

10. Actual fixed overhead less budgeted fixed overhead equals the _____ variance.

11. The _____ variance is defined as budgeted fixed overhead minus applied fixed overhead.

12. The _____ variance provides a means of reconciling two different purposes of a cost-accounting system-a control purpose and a product-costing purpose.

13. The _____ variance equals the sum of the variable-overhead spending variance and the fixed-overhead budget variance.

14. When the itemized variances of the combined budget variance are presented along with actual and budgeted costs for each item, the result is a(n) _____ report.

15. The _____ refers to the extent to which a product meets the specifications of its design.

MULTIPLE-CHOICE QUESTIONS

Circle the best answer or response.

1. If the budgeted fixed overhead per month is $18,000 and the budgeted variable-overhead rate is $15.20 per machine hour, then the total budgeted monthly overhead cost corresponding to 1,300 machine hours is
   (a) $37,760.
   (b) $37,500.
   (c) $19,760.
   (d) $18,000

2. Suppose that the standard variable-overhead rate is $12 per machine hour, actual machine hours used in February were 1,800, and the February actual variable-overhead cost was $23,900. The February variable-overhead spending variance is
   (a) $2,300 favorable.
   (b) $2,300 unfavorable.
   (c) $3,600 favorable.
   (d) $3,600 unfavorable.

3. The standard variable-overhead rate is $25 per hour of process time. During May, 840 units of output were produced and 670 hours of process time were actually used. If the standard process time to make one unit is 0.75 hour, the May variable-overhead efficiency variance is
   (a) $4,250 favorable.
   (b) $4,250 unfavorable.
   (c) $1,000 favorable.
   (d) $1,000 unfavorable

4. If actual fixed overhead for June equals $154,000 and the May budgeted fixed overhead is $163,000, then the fixed-overhead budget variance is
   (a) $19,000 favorable.
   (b) $19,000 unfavorable.
   (c) $9,000 favorable.
   (d) $9,000 unfavorable.

5. The Olmstead Company uses process time as the activity measure for its flexible overhead budget. For July the company budgeted fixed overhead at $45,000 and budgeted 20,000 hours of process time. During July, 43,000 units of finished product were made. The standard process time for one unit of product is 0.5 hour. The fixed-overhead volume variance for July is
(a) $3,375 unfavorable.
(b) $3,375 favorable.
(c) $2,000 unfavorable.
(d) $2,000 favorable.

6. The journal entry to record overhead costs applied to production includes a
(a) debit to Manufacturing Overhead.
(b) credit to Work-in-Process Inventory.
(c) credit to Manufacturing Overhead.
(d) credit to Accounts Payable.

7. Consider the following statements and determine which statement(s) is (are) true.

I. Appraisal costs are quality costs.
II. Advertising costs are quality costs.

(a) Only I
(b) Only II
(c) Both I and II
(d) Neither I nor II

8. (Appendix) If the budgeted unit contribution margin is $8, the expected sales price is $23, the budgeted sales volume is 4,000 units, and the actual sales volume is 4,500 units, then the sales-volume variance is
(a) $4,000 unfavorable.
(b) $4,000 favorable.
(c) $11,500 unfavorable.
(d) $11,500 favorable.

EXERCISES

Record your answers to each part of the exercises in the space provided. Show your work.

Exercise 11.1

The Valley View Health Care Center uses a flexible budget to plan and control costs. The accountant at Valley View has assembled the following budget data for one month:

Patient days	6,000
Variable costs:	
Utilities	$ 4,200
Maintenance	2,400
Medical supplies	7,200
Laundry	1,200
Housekeeping	3,000
Fixed costs:	
Health care salaries	$24,000
Administrative salaries	10,000
Depreciation	7,000

(a) Prepare a columnar flexible budget (which is properly labeled) that includes cost categories for 7,000, 7,500, and 8,000 patient days.

(b) Determine the flexible budget formula for Valley View.

Exercise 11.2

The Pitman Company uses standard costing for the product it makes in its Hadley Plant. The standards for one unit of this product include:

Variable overhead   1.5 machine hours at $4 per machine hour
Fixed overhead   1.5 machine hours at $12 per machine hour

During January, 27,000 machine hours were budgeted. The following actual results occurred in January:

- Sixteen thousand units of product were made.
- Variable overhead incurred was $102,000.
- Fixed overhead incurred was $295,000
- Actual machine hours used were 26,000.

(a) Calculate each of the following for the month of January using the formula approach (indicating whether each variance is favorable or unfavorable):

(1) Variable-overhead spending variance

(2) Variable-overhead efficiency variance

(3) Fixed-overhead budget variance

11-19

(4) Fixed-overhead volume variance

(b) Calculate each of the four overhead variances for the month of January using the diagram approach similar to Exhibits 11-6 and 11-8 in the text (indicating whether each variance is favorable or unfavorable)

Exercise 11.3

The Wagner Company makes wibbits in its Bushland Division and uses standard costing. Flexible overhead budget data for one month are as follows:

Budgeted fixed overhead	$80,000
Budgeted process time	3,200 hours
Process time per wibbit	0.8 hours
Standard variable-overhead rate	$4.20 per hour of process time

The actual operating results for March were as follows:

Actual variable overhead	$17,500
Actual wibbits produced	4,200
Actual fixed overhead	$76,800
Actual process time used	3,900 hours

(a) **Calculate each of the following variances for March using the diagram approach similar to Exhibits 11-6 and 11-8 in the text (indicating whether each variance is favorable or unfavorable):**

   (1) Variable-overhead spending variance

   (2) Variable-overhead efficiency variance

   (3) Fixed-overhead budget variance

   (4) Fixed-overhead volume variance

(5) Combined spending variance

(6) Combined budget variance

(7) Under-or overapplied overhead

(b) (Appendix) Prepare journal entries to record the following events for March:

(1) The incurrence of actual overhead costs

(2) The application of overhead to production

(3) The disposition of under- or overapplied overhead to Cost of Goods Sold

SOLUTIONS TO SELF-TEST QUESTIONS AND EXERCISES

MATCHING

1.	A	7.	F
2.	D	8.	E
3.	J	9.	I
4.	C	10.	G
5.	B	11.	L
6.	K	12.	H

TRUE-FALSE QUESTIONS

1. **F** It is based on any given level of activity.
2. **T**
3. **T**
4. **F** The static budget does not provide the correct basis. It is the flexible budget that provides the correct basis.
5. **F** It does change with increasing levels of activity.
6. **T**
7. **T**
8. **F** The $20 is the budgeted fixed-overhead rate.
9. **T**
10. **F** It remains fixed as the level of activity increases.
11. **T**
12. **T**
13. **F** They are moving away from labor hours to other measures of activity as automation increases.
14. **F** Dollar measures are to be avoided as cost drivers if possible, since they tend to fluctuate more than physical measures.
15. **T**
16. **F** This overhead efficiency variance based on machine hours does not reflect the direct inefficiencies associated with items such as electricity and indirect materials.
17. **F** The volume variance is not a measure of control. The real control variance for fixed overhead is the fixed-overhead budget variance.
18. **T**
19. **T**
20. **F** They do use flexible budgets to control overhead.
21. **F** It treats them as variable costs.
22. **T**

FILL-IN-THE-BLANK QUESTIONS

1. flexible overhead
2. static
3. columnar flexible budget
4. budgeted variable-overhead
5. together
6. under or overapplied overhead
7. exceeds
8. variable-overhead spending

9.   fixed
10.   fixed-overhead budget
11.   volume
12.   volume
13.   combined spending
14.   overhead cost performance
15.   quality of conformance

MULTIPLE-CHOICE QUESTIONS

1.   **(a)** $18,000 + ($15.20 \times 1,300) = $37,760.

2.   **(b)** $23,900 − ($12 \times 1,800) = $2,300.

3.   **(d)** $25 \times [670 − (840 \times .75)] = $1,000.

4.   **(c)** $154,000 - $163,000 = ($9,000).

5.   **(b)**   ($45,000/20,000) \times [20,000 − (.5 \times 43,000)] = ($3,375).

6.   **(c)**

7.   **(a)**   Advertising costs are marketing costs, not quality costs.

8.   **(b)** $8 \times (4,500 - 4,000) = $4,000. This is a favorable revenue variance.

EXERCISES

Exercise 11.1

(a)

VALLEY VIEW HEALTH CARE CENTER
Flexible Budget for One Month

	Cost per Patient Day	Patient Days		
		7,000	**7,500**	**8,000**
Variable costs:				
Utilities	$ .70	$ 4,900	$ 5,250	$ 5,600
Maintenance	40	2,800	3,000	3,200
Medical supplies	1.20	8,400	9,000	9,600
Laundry	.20	1,400	1,500	1,600
Housekeeping	.50	3,500	3,750	4,000
Fixed costs:				
Health Care Salaries	--	24,000	24,000	24,000
Administrative services		10,000	10,000	10,000
Depreciation	--	7,000	7,000	7,000
Total		$62,000	$63,500	$65,000

(b)

Total cost = $41,000 + ($3 x number of patient days)

Exercise 11.2

(a)(1)

Variable spending variance = $102,000 – (26,000 x $4) = $2,000 favorable

(a)(2)

Variable efficiency variance = $4 x [26,000 – (16,000 x 1.5)] = $8,000 unfavorable

(a)(3)

Fixed budget variance = $295,000 – (27,000 x $12) = $29,000 favorable

(a)(4)

Fixed volume variance = $12 x [27,000 – (16,000 x 1.5)] = $36,000 unfavorable

(b)

Budgeted fixed overhead = 27,000 x $12 = $324,000

Computation of Variable Overhead Variances by Diagram Method		
Actual costs	**Flex. budget at actual hrs.**	**Flex. budget at std. hrs.**
$102,000	26,000 x $4 = $104,000	16,000 x 1.5 x $4 = $96,000
$2,000 favorable		$8,000 unfavorable
Variable spending variance		**Variable efficiency variance**

Computation of Fixed Overhead Variances by Diagram Method			
			16,000 x 1.5 x $12 =
$295,000	$324,000	$324,000	$288,000
$29,000 favorable		$36,000 unfavorable	
Fixed budget variance		**Fixed volume variance**	

Exercise 11.3

(a)(1) through (a)(4)

Standard fixed-overhead rate = $80,000/3,200 = $25/hr

Computation of Variable Overhead Variances by Diagram Method		
Actual costs	**Flex. budget at actual hrs.**	**Flex. budget at std. hrs.**
$17,500	3,900 x $4.20 = $16,380	4,200 x .8 x $4.20 = $14,112
$1,120 unfavorable		$2,268 unfavorable
Variable spending variance (1)		**Variable efficiency variance (2)**

Computation of Fixed Overhead Variances by Diagram Method			
			4,200 x .8 x $25 =
$76,800	$80,000	$80,000	$84,000
$3,200 favorable		$4,000 favorable	
Fixed budget variance (3)		**Fixed volume variance (4)**	

(a)(5)

Combined spending variance = $1,120 unfavorable + $3,200 favorable = $2,080 favorable

(a)(6)

Combined budget variance = $2,080 favorable + $2,268 unfavorable = $188 unfavorable

(a)(7)

Overapplied overhead = $188 unfavorable + $4,000 favorable = $3,812 favorable

Check: Overapplied overhead = $94,300 - $98,112 = $3,812 favorable

(b)

(1)	Manufacturing Overhead	94,300	
	Various Accounts		94,300
(2)	Work-in-Process Inventory	98,112	
	Manufacturing Overhead		98,112
(3)	Manufacturing Overhead	3,812	
	Cost of Goods Sold		3,812

IDEAS FOR YOUR STUDY TEAM

1. Rewrite each of the definitions of the key terms that appear at the end of the chapter using your own words. Imagine that you are trying to explain each key term to a friend who has not taken any accounting classes. Then, get together with the other members of your study team and compare your definitions.

Activity-based flexible budget

Fixed-overhead budget variance

Fixed-overhead volume variance

Flexible budget

Overhead cost performance report

Sales-price variance

Sales-volume variance

Static budget

Total contribution margin

Unit contribution margin

Variable-overhead efficiency variance

Variable-overhead spending variance

2. Try to predict the types of questions, exercises and problems that you will encounter on the quizzes and exams that cover this chapter. Review the *Read and Recall Questions* and the *Self-Test Questions and Exercises* that are set forth in this Study Guide. Work through the end-of-chapter review problem(s), if applicable, and the end-of-chapter questions, exercises and problems that were assigned by your instructor. As you perform these tasks, identify the terms, concepts, formulas, etc. that you are responsible for knowing. After you develop the list of questions, exercises and problems that you expect to encounter on quizzes and exams, review the learning objectives that appear at the beginning of the chapter in your textbook to ensure that you have not overlooked anything significant. After you have completed your review of your list, get together with the other members of your study team and compare your predictions.

CHAPTER 12
RESPONSIBILITY ACCOUNTING
AND TOTAL QUALITY MANAGEMENT

CHAPTER FOCUS SUGGESTIONS

This chapter covers the topics that relate to reporting income and evaluating performance in segments of an organization.

You should able to identify cost centers, revenue centers, profit centers, and investment centers. You should also know how to prepare a performance report for the various responsibility centers, and understand the relationships among the performance reports for these centers. After becoming familiar with the use of a cost allocation base to allocate costs, you will also need to be able to prepare a segmented income statement.

READ AND RECALL QUESTIONS

LEARNING OBJECTIVE #1
After studying this section of the chapter, you should be able to:
- Explain the role of responsibility accounting in fostering goal congruence.

What is goal congruence?"

What does the term, responsibility accounting, refer to?

RESPONSIBILITY CENTERS

LEARNING OBJECTIVE #2

After studying this section of the chapter, you should be able to:

- Define and give an example of a cost center, a revenue center, a profit center, and an investment center.

What is the basis of a responsibility-accounting system?

What are the four common types of responsibility centers?

What is a "cost center?"

What is a "revenue center?"

What is a profit center?"

What is an "investment center?"

PERFORMANCE REPORTS

LEARNING OBJECTIVE #3
After studying this section of the chapter, you should be able to:
- Prepare a performance report and explain the relationships between the performance reports for various responsibility centers.

What comparison is made on a performance report that is prepared for a particular responsibility center?

How do performance reports enable managers to use "management by exception?"

What is a "hierarchy?"

What information should be summarized on the performance report of a cost center?

What information should be summarized on the performance report of a revenue center?

What information should be included in the performance report of a profit center?

What information should be included in the performance report of an investment center?

Cost Allocation

LEARNING OBJECTIVE #4
After studying this section of the chapter, you should be able to:
- Use a cost allocation base to allocate costs.

What is a "cost pool?"

What are "cost objects?"

Cost Allocation Bases

What is "cost allocation" or "cost distribution?"

What is an "allocation base?" What is another term for allocation base?

What should be reflected in the allocation base chosen for a cost pool?

Allocation Bases Based on Budgets

Should costs be distributed to cost objects on the basis of the *budgeted* amount of the relevant allocation bases or the *actual* amounts? Why?

Activity-Based Responsibility Accounting

What is "activity-based responsibility accounting?" What is management's attention directed to under this approach?

BEHAVIORAL EFFECTS OF RESPONSIBILITY ACCOUNTING

Information versus Blame

What is the proper focus of a responsibility-accounting system?

Should a responsibility-accounting system emphasize blame? Why or why not?

Controllability

What is the benefit of a performance report that distinguishes between the financial results influenced by a manager and those (s)he does not influence?

Motivating Desired Behavior

Why do rush orders typically result in greater costs? As rush orders become more and more frequent, how can a managerial accounting solve the resulting problems that develop between the sales and production manager?

What are the costs of accepting a rush order? What are the benefits of accepting a rush order?

Why should some rush orders be rejected and others accepted?

SEGMENTED REPORTING

LEARNING OBJECTIVE #5
After studying this section of the chapter, you should be able to:
- Prepare a segmented income statement.

What is a "segment?" What is "segmented reporting?"

What are "common costs?" Why do many managerial accountants believe that it is misleading to allocate common costs to an organization's segments?

How does an income statement prepared using the "contribution format" differ from one prepared for external reporting purposes?

Why weren't the $10,000,000 of common fixed expenses in the left-hand column of the segmented income statements in Exhibit 12-7 allocated to the company's two divisions?

Why weren't the $1,000,000 of controllable fixed expenses in the right-hand column of the segmented income statements in Exhibit 12-7 allocated to the division's three hotels?

How can costs that are traceable to segments at one level in an organization (such as the $200,000,000 of traceable fixed expenses in the right-hand column of the segmented income statements in Exhibit 12-7) become common costs at a lower level in the organization?"

Segments versus Segment Managers

What is one advantage of segmented reports like the one in Exhibit 12-7?

Why should property taxes be included in the hotel's costs to properly evaluate the hotel as an investment of the company's resources, but excluded when the performance of the general manager of the hotel is evaluated?

Key Features of Segmented Reporting

What are three important characteristics of segmented reporting?

Customer Profitability Analysis and Activity-Based Costing

Why is customer profitability analysis performed? What concept is used when customer profitability analysis is performed?

What factors can result in some customers being more profitable than others?

TOTAL QUALITY MANAGEMENT

Why is it crucial for organizations to monitor performance in many nonfinancial areas as well as in financial areas?

Measuring and Reporting Quality Costs

What is a product's "grade?" What is a product's "quality of design?" What is the "quality of conformance?"

LEARNING OBJECTIVE #6
After studying this section of the chapter, you should be able to:
• Prepare a quality cost report.

What are four types of costs of ensuring high quality that are monitored by many companies?

Why is quality cost reporting more useful when cost trends are examined over a period of time?

What are "hidden" quality costs? What types of hidden quality costs result when products of inferior quality make it to the market? What opportunity costs result?

LEARNING OBJECTIVE #7
After studying this section of the chapter, you should be able to:
• Discuss the traditional and contemporary views of the optimal level of product quality.

What is the traditional viewpoint with regards to finding the optimal level of product quality?

As the level of product quality (expressed as a percentage of defective products) increases, what happens to the costs of prevention and appraisal?

As the level of product quality (expressed as a percentage of defective products) increases, what happens to the costs of internal and external failure?

How does the contemporary viewpoint with regards to finding the optimal level of product quality differ from the traditional viewpoint?

Under the contemporary viewpoint, when are the total costs of quality minimized?

What is "total quality management" (or TQM)? What would be included in an effective TQM program?

What information is displayed in a "cause and effect" (or Ishikawa or fishbone) diagram?

What information is highlighted on a Pareto diagram? How is a Pareto diagram used by a TQM team?

ISO 9000 STANDARDS

What is the focus of the "ISO 9000 standards?" What are the three objectives of the first standard (ISO 9000)?

What are the five major parts of the ISO 9000 standards?

What are two major implications of the ISO 9000 standards for managerial accountants?

SELF-TEST QUESTIONS AND EXERCISES

MATCHING

Match each of the key terms listed below with the appropriate textbook definition:

___	1.	Activity-based responsibility accounting	___	13. Internal failure costs
___	2.	Allocation base	___	14. Investment center
___	3.	Appraisal costs	___	15. Performance report
___	4.	Common costs	___	16. Prevention costs
___	5.	Cost allocation (or distribution)	___	17. Profit center
___	6.	Cost center	___	18. Quality of conformance
___	7.	Cost objects	___	19. Quality of design
___	8.	Cost pool	___	20. Responsibility accounting
___	9.	Customer profitability analysis	___	21. Responsibility center
___	10.	External failure costs	___	22. Revenue center
___	11.	Goal congruence	___	23. Segmented income statement
___	12.	Grade	___	24. Total quality management (TQM)

A. A responsibility center whose manager is accountable for its costs.

B. Costs of determining whether defective products exist.

C. A responsibility center whose manager is accountable for its revenue.

D. A system for measuring the performance of an organization's people and subunits, which focuses not only on the cost of performing activities but on the activities themselves.

E. Tools and concepts used by managerial accountants to measure the performance of an organization's people and subunits.

F. A meshing of objectives, where managers throughout an organization strive to achieve the goals set by top management.

G. The broad set of management and control processes designed to focus an entire organization and all of its employees on providing products or services that do the best possible job of satisfying the customer.

H. Costs of preventing defective products.

I. A financial statement showing the income for an organization and its major segments (subunits).

J. A measure of activity, physical characteristic, or economic characteristic that is associated with the responsibility centers which are the cost objects in an allocation process.

K. A subunit in an organization whose manager is held accountable for specified financial results of its activities.

L. A report showing the budgeted and actual amounts of key financial results for a person or subunit.

M. Responsibility centers, products, or services to which costs are assigned.

N. Costs of correcting defects found prior to product sale.

O. The process of assigning costs in a cost pool to the appropriate cost objects.

P. A collection of costs to be assigned to a set of cost objects.

Q. The extent of a product's capability in performing its intended purpose, viewed in relation to other products with the same functional use.

R. Using the concepts of activity-based costing to determine how serving particular customers causes activities to be performed and costs to be incurred.

S. The extent to which a product meets the specifications of its design.
T. Costs incurred because defective products have been sold.
U. The extent to which a product is designed to perform well in its intended use.
V. A responsibility center whose manager is accountable for its profit and for the capital invested to generate that profit.
W. A responsibility center whose manager is accountable for its profit.
X. Costs incurred to benefit more than one organizational segment.

TRUE-FALSE QUESTIONS

For each of the following statements, enter a T or F in the blank to indicate whether the statement is true or false.

___1. Most large organizations are centralized.

___2. The data in a performance report do not provide any help for the use of management by exception to control an organization's operations effectively.

___3. The topics of budgeting, variance analysis, and responsibility accounting are closely interrelated.

___4. A division of a large corporation is typically designated as a profit center.

___5. Goal congruence results when the managers of segments throughout an organization strive to achieve the goals set by top management.

___6. A responsibility center is a subunit in an organization, the manager of which is held accountable for specified financial results of the subunit's activities.

___7. The proper focus of a responsibility-accounting system is information.

___8. All costs which are controllable over a long time frame are also controllable within a short time period.

___9. Some organizations use performance reports that distinguish between controllable and uncontrollable costs or revenues.

___10. A cost driver is not the same thing as a cost allocation base.

___11. One function of a responsibility-accounting system is to assign all of an organization's costs to the segments that cause those costs to be incurred.

___12. Managerial accountants often use the responsibility-accounting system to motivate actions considered desirable by upper-level management.

___13. An important use of a responsibility-accounting system is to emphasize the blame for wrong actions on the part of segment managers.

___14. The managerial accountant should design an allocation procedure so that the behavior of one responsibility center does not affect the costs allocated to other responsibility centers.

___15. If sales revenue is to be used as an allocation base, it is better to use actual sales revenue than budgeted sales revenue.

___16. Common costs can be allocated to segments only on some arbitrarily chosen cost allocation base.

___17. Costs that are traceable to segments at one level in an organization will never be common costs at a lower level in the organization.

FILL-IN-THE-BLANK QUESTIONS

For each of the following statements, fill in the blank to properly complete the statement.

1. _____accounting consists of the various concepts and tools used by managerial accountants to measure the performance of people and departments so as to foster goal congruence.

2. A(n) _____center is a segment of an organization in which the manager is held responsible for the revenue attributed to the segment.

3. A(n) _____center is a segment of an organization in which the manager is held accountable for the profit of the segment.

4. A(n) _____shows the budgeted and actual amounts of key financial results appropriate to the type of responsibility center involved.

5. A collection of costs to be assigned is called a(n) _____.

6. A(n) _____is a measure of activity or some physical or economic characteristic associated with the responsibility centers, which are the cost objectives of allocation.

7. _____refers to the preparation of accounting reports by segment and for the organization as a whole.

8. A(n) _____center is a segment of an organization in which the manager is held accountable for the profit of the segment in relation to the capital invested in that segment.

9. The process of assigning costs in a cost pool to cost objects is called _____.

10. Costs of an organization that are incurred to benefit more than one segment are called

_____.

11. A(n) _____center is a segment of an organization in which the manager is held accountable for the costs incurred by the segment.

12. The responsibility centers, products or services to which costs are to be assigned, are called _____.

13. _____is a tool which uses activity-based costing to find out how serving customers.

MULTIPLE-CHOICE QUESTIONS

Circle the best answer or response.

1. Consider the following statements about decentralized organizations:

   I. Managers of the organization's subunits have specialized skills that enable them to manage their departments most effectively.
   II. Managers with some decision-making authority usually exhibit less motivation than those who merely execute the decisions of others. Which is (are) benefits of decentralization?

   (a) Only I
   (b) Only II
   (c) Both I and II
   (d) Neither I nor II

2. Which of the following is *not* a key feature of segmented reporting?

(a) Income statements are in the contribution format.

(b) Income statements highlight costs that can be controlled by segment managers.

(c) Income statements show income for the company as a whole and for its major segments.

(d) Costs are reported by management function with fixed and variable costs not segregated.

EXERCISES

Record your answers to each part of the exercises in the space provided. Show your work.

Exercise 12.1

The Phillips Photocopy Service had the following data for May:

	Flexible Budget	Actual Results
Paper products bought and used	$3,200	$3,492
Revenue from copying government reports	2,800	2,614
Variable overhead	400	238
Fixed overhead	1,200	1,288
Revenue from other copying services	2,300	2,593

Prepare a performance report for May similar to the lower portion of Exhibit 12-4 in the text. Use three columns in your report.

Exercise 12.2

Hill-Top Hospital has two divisions-Health Care and Pharmacy. The hospital accountant has decided to allocate the costs of power and heat to the divisions on the basis of square footage and the cost of business administration to the divisions on the basis of payroll dollars. The following information is available for the month of September:

Division	Budgeted Payroll	Square Footage
Health care	$81,000	15,000
Pharmacy	9,000	1,000

Department	Direct Costs
Power and heat	$ 5,300
Business administration	12,000

Allocate the costs of power and heat and of business administration to the divisions using the cost allocation bases chosen by the hospital accountant.

Exercise 12.3

The Kretser Company sells three products: *X Y*. and *Z*. Data for the last quarter of the year are as follows:

	Products		
	X	**Y**	**Z**
Sales revenue	$150,000	$220,000	$180,000
Contribution margin (%)	45%	55%	40%
Controllable fixed expenses	$ 29,000	$ 54,000	$ 32,000
Fixed expenses controllable by others	$ 16,000	$ 12,000	$ 18,000

Besides the expenses given above, Kretser had $42,000 of common fixed costs. The tax rate is 30 percent.

Prepare a segmented income statement for Kretser for the last quarter of the year. Use the contribution format.

Exercise 12.4

Harold Jameson is the controller of the Southern Division of Artic Products, Inc. The Southern Division had the following divisional income statement data (in $1,000) for 20x2:

	Actual	Budgeted
Sales	$320	$284
Variable expenses	180	159
Variable selling and administrative expenses	26	23
Contribution margin	$114	$102
Fixed overhead expenses	58	49
Fixed selling and administrative expenses	28	23
Net income	$ 28	$ 30

Arctic provides a bonus to each division manager (including the controller) if the division's actual annual net income is at least as large as the budgeted annual income. Before finalizing the actual income statement for 20x2 and sending it to corporate headquarters, Jameson is contemplating deferring those fixed expenses that haven't been paid until the first quarter of 20x3. By doing this, the actual annual net income will exceed the budgeted net income for 20x2.

Write a brief essay that addresses the behavior that Jameson is contemplating.

SOLUTIONS TO SELF-TEST QUESTIONS AND EXERCISES

MATCHING

1.	D	7.	M	13.	N	19.	U
2.	J	8.	P	14.	V	20.	E
3.	B	9.	R	15.	L	21.	K
4.	X	10.	T	16.	H	22.	C
5.	O	11.	F	17.	W	23.	I
6.	A	12.	G	18.	S	24.	G

TRUE-FALSE QUESTIONS

1. F Large organizations are usually decentralized.
2. F The performance report provides very helpful information for the use of management by exception.
3. T
4. F It is typically designated as an investment center.
5. T
6. T
7. T
8. F Some costs, such as a two-year contract to buy merchandise, can be controlled in the long run but not in the short run.
9. T
10. F It is the same thing.
11. T
12. T
13. F Blame should not be emphasized in a responsibility-accounting system. The approach should be constructive, not destructive.
14. T
15. F It is better to use budgeted sales revenue.
16. T
17. F These costs could be common costs at a lower level in the organization.

FILL-IN-THE-BLANK QUESTIONS

1. Responsibility
2. revenue
3. profit
4. performance report
5. cost pool
6. allocation base
7. Segmented reporting
8. Investment
9. cost allocation (cost distribution)
10. common costs
11. cost
12. cost objects
13. Customer profitability analysis

MULTIPLE-CHOICE QUESTIONS

1. **(a)** Managers who have decision-making authority are usually more motivated than those who merely execute the decisions of others

2. **(d)** This choice is not true.

EXERCISES

Exercise 12.1

PHILLIPS PHOTOCOPY SERVICE
Performance Report
For May

	Flexible Budget	Actual Results	Variance
Revenue:			
Copying government reports	$2,800	$2,614	$186 U
Other copy services	2,300	2,593	293 F
Total revenue	5,100	5,207	107 F
Expenses:			
Paper products	3,200	3,492	292 U
Variable overhead	400	238	162 F
Fixed overhead	1,200	1,288	88 U
Total expenses	4,800	5,018	218 U
Profit	$ 300	$ 189	$111 U

Exercise 12.2

Department	Division	Allocation Base	Percent of Total	Cost Allocated
Power and heat	Heath care	15,000 ft.^{2}	93.75%	$ 4,968.75
	Pharmacy	1,000 ft.^{2}	6.25%	331.25
		16,000 ft.^{2}	100.00%	5,300.00
Business	Health care	$ 81,000	90%	$10,800.00
administration	Pharmacy	9,000	10%	1,200.00
		$ 90,000	100%	$12,000.00

Exercise 12.3

KRETSER COMPANY
Segmented Income Statement
For the Last Quarter of the Year

| | | Product Line | | |
	Total	X	Y	Z
Sales revenue	$550,000	$150,000	$220,000	$180,000
Variable expenses	289,500	82,500	99,000	108,000
Contribution margin	260,500	67,500	121,000	72,000
Less: Controllable fixed expenses	115,000	29,000	54,000	32,000
Controllable segment margin	145,500	38,500	67,000	40,000
Less: Fixed expenses controllable				
by others	46,000	16,000	12,000	18,000
Segment margin	99,500	$ 22,500	$ 55,000	$ 22,000
Less: Common fixed costs	42,000			
Income before taxes	57,500			
Less: Income tax expense	17,250			
Net income after taxes	$ 40,250			

12.4

If Jameson carries out his contemplated behavior, he is unethical in several respects. First, he is not performing his professional duties in accord with relevant technical standards. The fixed expenses were incurred in 20x2 and therefore should be reported on the 20x2 income statement. Secondly, he is failing to communicate information fairly and objectively. Finally, he is allowing his own interests to influence the financial reporting and hence is compromising his professional integrity.

IDEAS FOR YOUR STUDY TEAM

1.   Rewrite each of the definitions of the key terms that appear at the end of the chapter using your own words. Imagine that you are trying to explain each key term to a friend who has not taken any accounting classes. Then, get together with the other members of your study team and compare your definitions.

Activity-based responsibility accounting

Allocation base

Appraisal costs

Common costs

Cost allocation (or distribution)

Cost center

Cost objects

Cost pool

Customer profitability

External failure costs

Goal congruence

Grade

Internal failure

Investment center

Performance report

Prevention costs

Profit center

Quality of conformance

Quality of design

Responsibility accounting

Responsibility center

Revenue center

Segmented income statement

Total quality management (TQM)

2.   Try to predict the types of questions, exercises and problems that you will encounter on the quizzes and exams that cover this chapter. Review the *Read and Recall Questions* and the *Self-Test Questions and Exercises* that are set forth in this Study Guide. Work through the end-of-chapter review problem(s), if applicable, and the end-of-chapter questions, exercises and problems that were assigned by your instructor. As you perform these tasks, identify the terms, concepts, formulas, etc. that you are responsible for knowing. After you develop the list of questions, exercises and problems that you expect to encounter on quizzes and exams, review the learning objectives that appear at the beginning of the chapter in your textbook to ensure that you have not overlooked anything significant. After you have completed your review of your list, get together with the other members of your study team and compare your predictions.

CHAPTER 13
INVESTMENT CENTERS AND TRANSFER PRICING

CHAPTER FOCUS SUGGESTIONS

This chapter covers the various methods used by managerial accountants to evaluate investment centers and the performance of investment center managers. In addition, the important issues involved in transfer pricing in decentralized organizations are addressed.

You should understand the concept of goal congruence. You should know how to compute an investment center's return on investment, residual income, and economic value added; understand how an investment center manager can improve these measures; and be familiar with the advantages and disadvantages of these divisional performance measures. You should also know how to determine a division's income and invested capital. In addition to being able to apply the general economic rule for setting optimal transfer prices, you should also know how to base transfer prices on market prices, costs, or negotiations.

READ AND RECALL QUESTIONS

> **LEARNING OBJECTIVE #1**
> *After studying this section of the chapter, you should be able to:*
> Explain the role of managerial accounting in achieving goal congruence.

What is an "investment center?" What is the manager of an investment center responsible for?

What is a "transfer price?" Why is the determination of transfer prices important in a decentralized organization?

DELEGATION OF DECISION MAKING

What are the characteristics of a decentralized organization? What is the biggest challenge in making a decentralized organization function effectively?

Obtaining Goal Congruence: A Behavioral Challenge

What is "goal congruence?"

Why is goal congruence difficult to achieve? What is necessary to obtain goal congruence? What is the managerial accountant's objective in designing a responsibility-accounting system?

What is "management by objective" (or MBO)? Who participates in goal-setting under MBO?

Adaptation of Management Control Systems

What type of decision making process is typical when an organization begins its operations? What changes typically take place as an organization grows?

Measuring Performance In Investment Centers

What responsibility-center designation would be used when each division manager has the authority to make decisions that affect both profits and invested capital?

What are the primary goals of any profit-making enterprise?

What two measures are used to evaluate the performance of investment centers?

LEARNING OBJECTIVE #2
After studying this section of the chapter, you should be able to:
Compute an investment center's return on investment (ROI), residual income (RI), and economic value added (EVA).

Return on Investment

What is the most common investment-center performance measure? How is this performance measure calculated?

How can the ROI formula be rewritten? What information is highlighted when the ROI formula is rewritten this way?

What is "sales margin?" How is sales margin calculated?

What is "capital turnover?" How is capital turnover calculated?

LEARNING OBJECTIVE #3
After studying this section of the chapter, you should be able to:
Explain how a manager can improve ROI by increasing either the sales margin or capital turnover.

How can a manager improve a division's return on investment?

What are two ways in which profit can be increased without changing total sales revenue? How would sales margin be affected?

What are two ways in which a division can increase its capital turnover?

LEARNING OBJECTIVE #2
After studying this section of the chapter, you should be able to:
Compute an investment center's return on investment (ROI), residual income (RI), and economic value added (EVA).

Residual Income

Assume that the return on an investment in new equipment exceeds the company's cost of capital. What should the division manager decide to do in order to achieve goal congruence? Why?

How could the purchase of this new equipment by a division cause a decline in that division's ROI? How might this decline affect the behavior of a division manager who needs to decide whether or not to invest in the new equipment?

What is the major drawback when ROI is used to measure investment-center performance?

What is the "residual income" of an investment center? What is meant by the "imputed" interest rate?

Again, assume that the return on an investment in new equipment exceeds the company's cost of capital. Would the purchase of this new equipment by a division cause an increase or decrease in the division's residual income? How might this information affect the behavior of a division manager who needs to decide whether or not to invest in the new equipment?

LEARNING OBJECTIVE #4
After studying this section of the chapter, you should be able to:
Describe some advantages and disadvantages of both ROI and residual income as divisional performance measures.

Why does residual income facilitate goal congruence while ROI does not?

What is the serious drawback of the use of residual income as a performance measure?

Why do some companies routinely use both measures (ROI and residual income) for divisional performance evaluation?

What is "shareholder value analysis?"

LEARNING OBJECTIVE #2
After studying this section of the chapter, you should be able to:
Compute an investment center's return on investment (ROI), residual income (RI), and economic value added (EVA).

Economic Value Added

What is the most contemporary measure of an investment center's performance? How is this performance measure calculated?

What are the two ways EVA differs from residual income?

What is the formula for the weighted-average cost of capital (WACC)?

What does EVA tell us?

MEASURING INCOME AND INVESTED CAPITAL

LEARNING OBJECTIVE #5
After studying this section of the chapter, you should be able to:
Explain how to measure a division's income and invested capital.

Invested Capital

What are three different ways to measure the amount of a division's invested capital when performing calculations of ROI, residual income, and EVA?

When would the use of total assets be appropriate to measure invested capital?

When would the use of total productive assets be appropriate to measure invested capital?

When would the use of total assets less current liabilities be appropriate to measure invested capital?

What are the advantages and disadvantages of using gross book value (acquisition cost) of long-lived assets when measuring the amount of a division's invested capital?

What are the advantages and disadvantages of using net book value (acquisition cost less accumulated depreciation) of long-lived assets when measuring the amount of a division's invested capital?

Knowing that the tendency for net book value is to produce a misleading increase in ROI over time, would investment centers with old assets show lower or higher ROIs than investment centers with relatively new assets? Why might this have a serious effect on the incentives of investment-center managers? If this behavioral tendency persists, what could happen to the assets of the division over time?

When certain assets are controlled centrally by a company even though these assets are needed to carry on operations in the divisions, how are these assets usually treated when measuring the invested capital of the divisions?

Measuring Investment-Center Income

If top management uses the profit margin controllable by division manager to evaluate the division manager, how should fixed costs traceable to the division be handled?

What terms are used to describe cash bonuses paid to investment-center managers when they meet a predetermined target on a specified performance criterion?

How should the evaluation of the manager's performance differ from the evaluation of the manager's division as a viable economic investment? Why?

Inflation: Historical-Cost versus Current-Value Accounting

Why do some managerial accountants argue that investment-center performance measures that use historical-cost asset values are misleading?

On the other hand, why do most managers indicate that an accounting system based instead on current values would not alter their decisions? What is another reason for using historical-cost accounting for internal purposes?

OTHER ISSUES IN SEGMENT PERFORMANCE EVALUATION

Alternatives to ROI, Residual Income, and Economic Value Added (EVA)

Why are ROI and residual income considered short-run performance measures? Why should a multi-period viewpoint be used? What alternative approaches can be used to avoid this short-term focus?

Importance of Nonfinancial Information

What types of nonfinancial information are used in performance evaluation?

Measuring Performance in Nonprofit Organizations

Why does management control in a nonprofit organization present a special challenge?

Why are the goals of nonprofit organizations often less clear-cut that those of businesses?

TRANSFER PRICING

What is a "transfer price?"

How does a high transfer price affect the profits of the selling (or producing) and buying divisions? How does a low transfer price affect the profits of the selling and buying divisions?

Goal Congruence

What should the goal of the company's controller be when setting transfer prices?

LEARNING OBJECTIVE #6
After studying this section of the chapter, you should be able to:
Use the general economic rule to set an optimal transfer price.

General-Transfer-Pricing Rule

What general rule (or formula) can be used in the setting of a transfer price to ensure goal congruence?

What costs should be included in "additional outlay costs?"

Generally, what is an "opportunity cost?" Assuming that the selling division does not have any excess capacity, why does an opportunity cost arise when goods are transferred to another division? How should this opportunity cost be measured?

How should the opportunity cost be measured if the selling division has excess capacity when it transfers goods to another division?

Assume that a division has to make a decision to accept or reject a special order. To fill the order, the division will have to purchase the goods internally from another division. Should the general rule for setting a transfer price be used in this situation? Will the general rule still promote goal congruence?

Why should the general transfer-pricing rule be viewed as providing a lower bound on the transfer price?

What is "perfect competition?" How does it differ from "imperfect competition?"

Why is it impossible to measure accurately the opportunity cost caused by a product transfer under imperfect competition? What are some of the other reasons that make it difficult or impossible to implement the general transfer-pricing rule?

LEARNING OBJECTIVE #7
After studying this section of the chapter, you should be able to:
Explain how to base a transfer price on market prices, costs, or negotiations.

Transfers Based on the External Market Price

What is the relationship between the general transfer-pricing rule and the external market price when the producing division has no excess capacity and perfect competition prevails? Why?

On the other hand, what is the relationship between the general transfer-pricing rule and the external market price when the producing division does have excess capacity or the external market is imperfectly competitive?

In this situation, would a transfer price based on market price be consistent with responsibility-accounting concepts of profit centers and investment centers? Why or why not?

What are "distress market prices?" What might happen if transfer prices are based on distress market prices? Why do some companies set the transfer price equal to the long-run average external market price?

Negotiated Transfer Prices

Why do many companies use negotiated transfer prices? What are the two drawbacks that sometimes characterize negotiated transfer prices?

Cost-Based Transfer Prices

What is the problem with setting the transfer price equal to the standard variable cost?

What is "full (or absorption) cost?" What formula can be used to calculate the full cost of the transferred product or service?

Why does basing transfer prices on full cost entail a serious risk of causing dysfunctional decision-making behavior?

Standard versus Actual Costs

Why shouldn't transfer prices be based on actual costs?

What impact might differing domestic and foreign income-tax rates have on a transfer price? What have some countries done in response?

BEHAVIORAL ISSUES: RISK AVERSION AND INCENTIVES

Why does the use of common performance measures, such as divisional income, ROI, residual income, and economic value added impose risk on a manager? What is "risk aversion?"

What two factors should be considered in the design of a managerial performance evaluation and reward system?

GOAL CONGRUENCE AND INTERNAL CONTROL SYSTEMS

What is an "internal control system?" What four major lapses in responsible behavior should be prevented by internal control procedures?

SELF-TEST QUESTIONS AND EXERCISES

MATCHING

Match each of the key terms listed below with the appropriate textbook definition.

___ 1. Capital turnover
___ 2. Cash bonus
___ 3. Distress market price
___ 4. Economic value added
___ 5. Full (or absorption) cost
___ 6. Goal congruence
___ 7. Imperfect competition
___ 8. Incentive compensation
___ 9. Internal control system
___ 10. Investment centers
___ 11. Management by objectives (MBO)

___ 12. Merit pay
___ 13. Pay for performance
___ 14. Perfect competition
___ 15. Residual income
___ 16. Return on investment (ROI)
___ 17. Sales margin
___ 18. Shareholder value analysis
___ 19. Transfer price
___ 20. Weighted-average cost of capital

A. A meshing of objectives, where managers throughout an organization strive to achieve the goals set by top management.

B. Sales revenue divided by invested capital.

C. Profit minus an imputed interest charge, which is equal to the invested capital times an imputed interest rate.

D. A responsibility center whose manager is accountable for its profit and for the capital invested to generate that profit.

E. The price at which products or services are transferred between two divisions in an organization.

F. A market in which the price does not depend on the quantity sold by any one producer.

G. After-tax operating income minus the investment center's total assets (net of its current liabilities) times the company's weighted-average cost of capital.

H. A cash bonus awarded to an investment-center manager who meets a predetermined target on a specified performance criterion, such as residual income or ROI. Also known as pay for performance or merit pay.

I. Calculation of the residual income associated with a major product line, with the objective of determining how the product line affects a firm's value to its shareholders.

J. A market in which a single producer can affect the market price.

K. A payment to an investment-center manager who meets a predetermined target on a specified performance criterion, such as residual income or ROI. Also known as incentive compensation, merit pay, or pay for performance.

L. The set of procedures designed to ensure that an organization's employees act in a legal, ethical, and responsible manner.

M. A one-time cash payment to an investment center manager as a reward for meeting a predetermined criterion on a specified performance measure.

N. A product's variable cost plus an allocated portion of fixed overhead.

O. Income divided by invested capital.

P. Income divided by sales revenue.

Q. An artificially low price in a depressed market.

R. The process of designating the objectives of each subunit in an organization and planning for the achievement of those objectives. Managers at all levels participate in setting goals, which they then will strive to achieve.

S. A cash bonus awarded to an investment-center manager who meets a predetermined target on a specified performance criterion, such as residual income or ROI. Also known as pay for performance or incentive pay.

T. [(After-tax cost of debt capital)(market value of debt) + (cost of equity capital)(market value of equity)] / (market value of debt + market value of equity)

TRUE-FALSE QUESTIONS

For each of the following statements, enter a T or F in the blank to indicate whether the statement is true or false.

___**1.** The greatest challenge in making a decentralized organization function effectively is to obtain goal congruence among the organization's autonomous managers.

___**2.** As an organization grows, it is crucial that decision making become more centralized.

___**3.** Return on investment equals invested capital divided by income.

___**4.** Most large organizations are centralized.

___**5.** ROI can be improved by increasing sales margin and holding capital turnover constant.

___**6.** A primary goal of a profit-making enterprise is to use its invested capital as effectively as possible.

___**7.** It is impossible to increase profit without increasing total sales revenue.

___**8.** The key factor in deciding how well a responsibility-accounting system works is the extent to which it directs managers' efforts toward organizational goals.

___**9.** The ROI measure ignores the firm's cost of raising investment capital.

___**10.** Sales margin can never be greater than 100 percent.

___**11.** Capital turnover can never be greater than 100 percent.

___**12.** As an organization grows, its accounting and managerial control system usually becomes more complex.

___**13.** Sales margin can never be greater than the contribution-margin ratio.

___**14.** Residual income is a percentage amount.

___**15.** Residual income is a good measure to use in comparing the performance of different-sized investment centers

___**16.** ROI, residual income, and EVA are computed for a period of time.

___**17.** During periods of inflation, historical-cost asset values soon cease to reflect the cost of replacing those assets.

___**18.** ROI, residual income, and EVA are long-run performance measures.

___**19.** In performance evaluation, nonfinancial measures are not important.

___**20.** Transfer prices affect the profit measurement of the buying division, the selling division, and the organization as a whole.

___**21.** Application of the general transfer-pricing formula results in goal-congruent decision making.

___**22.** If a producing division has excess capacity and the external market is imperfectly competitive, the general-formula transfer price and the external market price will be the same.

___**23.** Basing transfer prices on full costs can cause dysfunctional decision-making behavior.

___**24.** Transfer prices should be based on actual costs.

FILL-IN-THE-BLANK QUESTIONS

For each of the following statements, fill in the blank to properly complete the statement.

1. The price at which products or services are transferred between two divisions in an organization is called a(n) _____.

2. _____ is obtained when the managers of divisions throughout an organization strive to achieve the goals set up by top management.

3. _____ is an approach where managers participate in setting goals which they then strive to achieve.

4. _____ is defined as the difference between income and the product of invested capital times the imputed interest rate.

5. In measuring an investment center's income, the key issue is _____ _____.

6. The overall objective of performance measures in decentralized organizations is to provide incentives for _____ behavior.

7. Sales revenue divided by invested capital is called the _____ _____.

8. ROI can be increased by holding sales margin and sales revenue constant and decreasing _____.

9. _____ exists only when more goods can be produced than the producer is able to sell, due to low demand for the product.

10. Income divided by sales revenue is called the _____.

11. When excess capacity exists, the opportunity-cost component of the transfer price in the general transfer-pricing formula is _____.

12. The amount determined by the general transfer-pricing formula generally provides a(n) _____ bound on the transfer price that should be realized.

13. A(n) _____ system is the set of procedures designed to ensure that an organization's employees act in a legal, ethical, and responsible manner.

MULTIPLE-CHOICE QUESTIONS

Circle the best answer or response.

1. A division of the Wimple Company had a return on investment of 6 percent and a capital turnover of 30 percent last year. The sales margin last year was
    (a) 18 percent.
    (b) 20 percent.
    (c) 25 percent.
    (d) 30 percent.

2. Consider the following statements and determine which statement is (are) true.

    I. Capital turnover can be improved by increasing invested capital and holding sales revenue constant.
    II. Sales margin can be increased by decreasing expenses and holding sales revenue constant.

    (a) Only I
    (b) Only II
    (c) Both I and II
    (d) Neither I nor II

3. Which of the following is *not* a reason for difficulty in measuring opportunity costs for transfer-pricing purposes?
   (a) External markets may have perfect competition.
   (b) The goods being transferred may be unique.
   (c) Special equipment may be needed to make the transferred goods.
   (d) There may be interdependencies among several products being transferred.

4. Consider the following statements and determine which statement(s) is (are) true.

   I. ROI can undermine goal congruence.
   II. Residual income distorts comparisons between investment centers of different sizes.

   (a) Only I
   (b) Only II
   (c) Both I and II
   (d) Neither I nor II

5. Which of the following would *not* be a plausible measure of a division's invested capital?
   (a) Bonds payable
   (b) Total assets less current liabilities
   (c) Total productive assets
   (d) Total assets

6. Suppose that Division A is planning to transfer 3,000 units of a product to Division B. The outlay costs of Division A due to the transfer are $8.50 per unit. The opportunity costs to the organization because of the transfer are $11,490. The transfer price per unit according to the general transfer-pricing formula is
   (a) $8.50.
   (b) $12.33.
   (c) $15.80.
   (d) $19.99.

7. Consider the following statements and determine which statement(s) is (are) true.

   I. Using gross book value to measure invested capital is more consistent with the definition of income than is net book value.
   II. When long-lived assets are depreciated, their gross book value declines over time.

   (a) Only I
   (b) Only II
   (c) Both I and II
   (d) Neither I nor II

EXERCISES

Exercise 13.1

The Wheeler Company has two divisions, X and Y. The company's cost of acquiring capital is 8 percent. The following data are available:

	Division X	Division Y
Sales revenue	(a)	(e)
Income	$ 270,000	(f)
Average investment	$3,000,000	(g)
Sales margin	18%	(h)
Capital turnover	(b)	3
ROI	(c)	17%
Residual income	(d)	$72,000

Determine the unknown amounts:

(a)

(b)

(c)

(d)

(e)

(f)

(g)

(h)

Exercise 13.2

Whitworth Construction has two divisions, the Texas Division and the California Division. Whitworth is publicly traded and has a market value of $500 million. It has $150 million of long term debt with an interest rate of 9%. Whitworth's cost of capital is 12% and its tax rate is 30%.

Before-tax operating income, total assets, and current liabilities for the most recent period for the divisions are as follows:

	Before-Tax Operating Income	Total Assets	Current Liabilities
Texas Division	$38,000,000	$195,000,000	$25,000,000
California Division	17,000,000	80,000,000	20,000,000

(a) Calculate Whitworth's weighted-average cost of capital

(b) Calculate the economic value added for each of Whitworth's divisions.

Exercise 13.3

The Corley Company has two divisions, A and B. Division A makes and sells a product having the following data, which are expected to hold for next year:

Unit selling price	$20
Variable cost per unit	$12
Annual fixed cost	$150,000

The maximum capacity at Division A is 50,000 units. This past year Division B bought 10,000 units of this same product from an outside supplier at $18 per unit. Division B is contemplating the possibility of buying 10,000 units next year from Division A; it could buy these units from the outside supplier at $18 each.

(a) According to the general transfer-pricing formula, what price should Division A charge Division B under each of the following conditions:

(1) Division A can sell only 38,000 units to the outside market next year.

(2) Division A can sell 50,000 units to the outside market next year.

(b) If Division A insists on the price determined in part (a)(2), will a transfer take place? Why or why not?

Exercise 13.4

Redride Products, Inc., has two divisions: North and South. The following data are available for the South Division and the single product it makes:

Unit selling price	$20
Variable cost per unit	$12
Annual fixed cost	$280,000
Investment in South	$1,500,000

Assume that each of the following questions is independent of the others, unless otherwise stated.

(a) How many units must South sell each year to have an ROI of 16 percent?

(b) If South wants an ROI of 20 percent and wishes to sell 50,000 units, what price must be charged instead of the given selling price?

(c) If South wants a residual income of $45,000 and the cost of acquiring capital is 10 percent, what value will the annual capital turnover have to be?

(d) Next year South has a budgeted volume of 80,000 units, of which 10,000 units are expected to be bought by North Division. However, North Division has received an offer from an outside firm to supply the 10,000 units at $18 each. If South fails to meet the $18 price, North will buy from the outside; in such a case South could save $40,000 in fixed costs if its volume dropped to 70,000 units. Assuming that South meets the $ 18 price, what would South's annual profit be?

(e) Assume the same information as in part (d) except that South does not meet the $18 price. How does this assumption impact total profit of Redride?

Exercise 13.5

The Scott Company has two divisions—the Eastern Division and the Western Division. Data for these two divisions for 20x3 are as follows:

Division	Invested Capital	Income
Eastern	$940,000	$75,200
Western	188,000	20,680

Scott uses an imputed interest rate of 4 percent in computing residual income. The president of Scott believes that the best way to compare the performance of the two divisions is to measure performance by residual income because dollar amounts are both easy to understand and concrete.

Write a brief essay commenting on the president's view of comparing the performance of the two divisions. Discuss any weaknesses in his views by using the numerical data for 20x3.

SOLUTIONS TO SELF-TEST QUESTIONS AND EXERCISES

MATCHING

1.	B	7.	J	13.	M	19.	E
2.	K	8.	H	14.	F	20.	T
3.	Q	9.	L	15.	C		
4.	G	10.	D	16.	O		
5.	N	11.	R	17.	P		
6.	A	12.	S	18.	I		

TRUE-FALSE QUESTIONS

1. **T**
2. **F** It is crucial that decision making become more decentralized.
3. **F** Return on investment equals income divided by invested capital.
4. **F** Most large organizations are decentralized.
5. **T**
6. **T**
7. **F** Profit can be increased, for example, by keeping revenue constant and decreasing expenses.
8. **T**
9. **T**
10. **T**
11. **F** It is very possible that annual sales will exceed invested capital, thus making capital turnover exceed 100 percent.
12. **T**
13. **T**
14. **F** Residual income is a dollar amount.
15. **F** It is a poor measure for comparing performance of investment centers, because it is a dollar measure rather than a percentage measure.
16. **T**
17. **T**
18. **F** They are short-run performance measures.
19. **F** Nonfinancial measures are also important.
20. **F** They affect profit measurement in the buying and selling divisions, but not in the organization as a whole.
21. **T**
22. **F** The external market must be perfectly competitive to ensure that the general-formula transfer price and the external market price will be the same.
23. **T**
24. **F** They should be based on budgeted or standard costs.

FILL-IN-THE-BLANK QUESTIONS

1. transfer price
2. Goal congruence
3. Management by objectives
4. Residual income
5. controllability
6. goal-congruent

7.   capital turnover
8.   invested capital
9.   Excess capacity
10. sales margin
11. zero
12. lower
13. internal control

MULTIPLE-CHOICE QUESTIONS

1.   **(b)**   .06/.3 = .2 or 20 percent.
2.   **(b)**   When sales revenue is constant and invested capital increases, capital turnover goes down.
3.   **(a)**   Difficulty in measuring opportunity costs results when external markets are imperfectly competitive.
4.   **(c)**
5.   **(a)**   Bonds payable is a long-term debt; it is not used to measure invested capital.
6.   **(b)** $8.50 + ($11,490/3,000) = $12.33.
7.   **(d)**   Both statements are false.

EXERCISES

Exercise 13.1

For Division X

(a)

Sales revenue = $270,000/.18 = $1,500,000

(b)

Capital turnover = $1,500,000/$3,000,000 = 0.5

(c)

ROI = $270,000/$3,000,000 = 9%

(d)

Residual income = $270,000 – ($3,000,000 x .08) = $30,000

For Division Y

(g)

Average investment = $72,000/(.17 - .08) = $800,000

(e)

Sales revenue = $800,000 x 3 = $2,400,000

(f)

Income = $800,000 x .17 = $136,000

(h)

Sales margin = $136,000/$2,400,000 = 5.67%

Exercise 13.2

(a)

Weighted-average cost of capital:

$[((.09 \text{ x } (1 - .3)) * 150,000,000) + ((.12) \text{ x } (500,000,000))] / (150,000,000 + 500,000,000)$

= .10685

(b)

Economic value added:

Texas Division: $(38,000,000 \text{ x } (1 - .3)) - ((195,000,000 - 25,000,000) \text{ x } .10685) = \$8,435,000$

California Division: $(17,000,000 \text{ x } (1 - .3)) - ((80,000,000 - 20,000,000) \text{ x } .10685) = \$5,489,000$

Exercise 13.3

(a)(1)

Transfer price = $12 + 0 = $12

(a) (2)

Transfer price = $12 + (20 − 12) = $20

(b)

No: Division B can buy the 10,000 units from the outside market at $18 each.

Exercise 13.4

(a)

Income = .16 x $1,500,000 = $240,000

Units needed to be sold = (280,000 + 240,000)/(20 - 12) = 65,000

(b)

Income = .2 x $1,500,000 = $300,000

Let P be the needed sales price.

Then $300,000 = ($P$ x 50,000) - ($12 x 50,000) - ($280,000), and so P = $23.60

(c)

$45,000 = income - (\$1,500,000 \times .10)$

Income = $195,000

ROI = $195,000/$1,500,000 = 13\%$

$195,000 = [(\$20 - \$12) \times Q] - 280,000$

$Q = 475,000/8 = 59,375$

Sales revenue = $\$20 \times 59,375 = \$1,187,500$

Capital turnover = $\$1,187,500/\$1,500,000 = .792$

(d)

Revenue from outside market: 70,000 x $20 =		$1,400,000
Revenue from North Division: 10,000 x $18 =		180,000
		1,580,000
Total revenue		
Variable costs: 80,000 x $12 =	$960,000	
Fixed costs	$280,000	
Total costs		1,240,000
Profit		$ 340,000

(e)

For Redride as a whole:	
Cost saving: $40,000 + (10,000 x $12) =	$160,000
Extra cost: 10,000 x $18 =	180,000
Decrease in annual profit	$ 20,000

Exercise 13.5

The view of the president is misdirected. First of all, residual income which is measured in dollars, is an absolute amount; that is, it is a number that stands alone, unrelated to any base amount. For 20x3 the residual income of Eastern is

$\$75,200 - \$940,000 \times 0.04 = \$37,600$

and for Western is

$\$20,680 - \$188,000 \times 0.04 = \$13,160$

According to the president's view, Eastern had the best performance since it had the largest residual income. In order to have a plausible comparison of divisional performance. the measure should reflect income on a relative basis, and the ROI computation does just that—it compares income to the invested capital in the form of a percentage. Thus, for 20x3 Eastern's ROI is

$75,200/$940,000 = 8\%$, whereas Western's ROI is $20,680/$188,000 = 11\%$. This measure says that Western's performance in 20x3 was better than Eastern's, just the opposite result from the residual income measure. The ROI measure is much better for comparing divisional performance because it puts the divisions onto a comparable footing.

IDEAS FOR YOUR STUDY TEAM

1.   Rewrite each of the definitions of the key terms that appear at the end of the chapter using your own words. Imagine that you are trying to explain each key term to a friend who has not taken any accounting classes. Then, get together with the other members of your study team and compare your definitions.

Capital turnover

Cash bonus

Distress market price

Economic value added

Full (or absorption) cost

Goal congruence

Imperfect competition

Incentive compensation

Internal control system

Investment centers

Management by objectives (MBO)

Merit pay

Pay for performance

Perfect competition

Residual income

Return on investment (ROI)

Sales margin

Shareholder value analysis

Transfer price

Weighted-average cost of capital

2. Try to predict the types of questions, exercises and problems that you will encounter on the quizzes and exams that cover this chapter. Review the *Read and Recall Questions* and the *Self-Test Questions and Exercises* that are set forth in this Study Guide. Work through the end-of-chapter review problem(s), if applicable, and the end-of-chapter questions, exercises and problems that were assigned by your instructor. As you perform these tasks, identify the terms, concepts, formulas, etc. that you are responsible for knowing. After you develop the list of questions, exercises and problems that you expect to encounter on quizzes and exams, review the learning objectives that appear at the beginning of the chapter in your textbook to ensure that you have not overlooked anything significant. After you have completed your review of your list, get together with the other members of your study team and compare your predictions.

CHAPTER 14

DECISION-MAKING: RELEVANT COSTS AND BENEFITS

CHAPTER FOCUS SUGGESTIONS

Some of the accounting procedures used in evaluating managerial performance were covered in previous chapters of the text. The main focus of this chapter is how to decide what information is relevant to various common decision problems faced by managers.

You should be familiar with the steps in the decision-making process, and the relationship between quantitative and qualitative analyses in decision making. You will need to know how to identify relevant costs and benefits, and prepare analyses of various decision problems. You should also recognize the impact of an advanced manufacturing environment and activity-based costing of the decision-making process.

READ AND RECALL QUESTIONS

THE MANAGERIAL ACCOUNTANT'S ROLE IN DECISION MAKING

LEARNING OBJECTIVE #1
After studying this section of the chapter, you should be able to:
• Describe six steps in the decision-making process and the managerial accountant's role in that process.

What is the managerial accountant's role in the decision-making process?

Steps in the Decision-Making Process

What are the six steps that characterize the decision-making process?

Quantitative versus Qualitative Analysis

LEARNING OBJECTIVE #2

After studying this section of the chapter, you should be able to:

• Explain the relationship between quantitative and qualitative analyses in decision making.

Why can qualitative characteristics be just as important as the quantitative measures when a manager makes a final decision?

Obtaining Information: Relevance, Accuracy, and Timeliness

What is the primary characteristic of information that is relevant?

Why must information pertinent to a decision problem be accurate?

Why are highly accurate but irrelevant data of no value to a decision-maker?

Why is timeliness the third important criterion for determining the usefulness of information?

RELEVANT INFORMATION

LEARNING OBJECTIVE #3

After studying this section of the chapter, you should be able to:
- List and explain two criteria that must be satisfied by relevant information.

What two criteria makes information relevant to a decision problem?

Unique versus Repetitive Decisions

What is the difference between unique and repetitive decisions?

Importance of Identifying Relevant Costs and Benefits

What are the two reasons that it is important for the managerial accountant to isolate the relevant costs and benefits in a decision analysis? What is information overload?

IDENTIFYING RELEVANT COSTS AND BENEFITS

LEARNING OBJECTIVE #4

After studying this section of the chapter, you should be able to:
- Identify relevant costs and benefits, giving proper treatment to sunk costs, opportunity costs, and unit costs.

Sunk Costs

What is a "sunk cost?" Why are sunk costs irrelevant to decisions?

What sunk cost might inadvertently be considered when deciding whether or not to replace a piece of equipment? What sunk cost might inadvertently be considered when deciding whether or not to dispose of obsolete inventory?

Irrelevant Future Costs and Benefits

Are the cargo revenue (item 2) and the aircraft maintenance cost (item 8) relevant to the decision analysis that appears in Exhibit 14-4? Would the same decision be reached if these two items were excluded from the analysis?

Opportunity Costs

What is an "opportunity cost?" Are opportunity costs relevant in evaluating decision alternatives?

Summary

What are the two criteria that must be satisfied for costs and benefits to be considered relevant? Are sunk costs relevant? Why or why not? Are opportunity costs relevant? Why or why not?

ANALYSIS OF SPECIAL DECISIONS

LEARNING OBJECTIVE #5

After studying this section of the chapter, you should be able to:

- Prepare analyses of various special decisions, properly identifying the relevant costs and benefits.

Accept or Reject a Special Order

Assuming that the company has excess capacity, are fixed costs typically relevant to a decision to accept or reject a special order? Why or why not? Are variable costs relevant to this type of decision? Why or why not?

Assuming that the company does not have any excess capacity, what other cost must be considered when deciding whether to accept or reject a special order? How should this cost be measured?

Outsource a Product or Service

What is involved in an "outsourcing" decision? What is another term that is used to describe this type of decision problem?

Are variable costs relevant to an outsourcing decision? Why or why not? Are fixed costs relevant to this type of decision? Why or why not?

Fixed costs often are allocated to individual units of product or service for product-costing purposes. What is the downside of this allocation process in many decision problems?

Add or Drop a Service, Product, or Department

What is the difference between "unavoidable" and "avoidable" expenses?

Generally, should a service, product, or department be dropped if it has a positive contribution margin? Why or why not?

SPECIAL DECISIONS IN MANUFACTURING FIRMS

LEARNING OBJECTIVE #6
After studying this section of the chapter, you should be able to:
* Analyze manufacturing decisions involving joint products and limited resources.

Joint Products: Sell or Process Further

What is a "joint production process?" What is the "split-off point?"

What is the "joint cost?" Is the joint cost a relevant cost in a sell or process further decision problem?

What is the "relative sales value method?" How are joint costs allocated when this method is used? If the joint cost has been allocated to the joint products that are in production, is it now relevant to the decision problem? Why or why not?

What is the "separable processing cost?" Using the shortcut method, what should the separable processing cost be compared to when deciding whether to sell or process further?

Decisions Involving Limited Resources

What types of resources might be limited in an organization?

If an organization has a limited resource, how should this information be considered in a decision involving the use of that limited resource? What is the basis that should be used to make a decision about the best use of a limited resource?

What is a "bottleneck operation?" What is the "theory of constraints" (or TOC)? What other name is used for this management approach?

What are five methods that can be used to relax a constraint by expanding the capacity of a bottleneck operation?

Uncertainty

What is "sensitivity analysis?" Why is sensitivity analysis necessary?

What is the "expected value?"

ACTIVITY-BASED COSTING AND THE NEW MANUFACTURING ENVIRONMENT

> **LEARNING OBJECTIVE #7**
> *After studying this section of the chapter, you should be able to:*
> - Explain the impact of an advanced manufacturing environment and activity-based costing on a relevant-cost analysis.

Activity-Based Costing Analysis of the Outsourcing Decision

Why is the amount of "total costs to be avoided" line on Exhibit 14-20 (the ABC analysis) different than that included on Exhibit 14-19 (the conventional analysis)?

Are the concepts underlying relevant-costing analysis valid when activity-based costing is used?

OTHER ISSUES IN DECISION MAKING

Incentives for Decision Makers

What is needed in order for managers to make optimal decisions by properly evaluating the relevant costs and benefits?

Short-Run versus Long-Run Decisions

What time period is affected by a "short-run" decision? What is one important factor that changes in a long-run analysis?

Pitfalls to Avoid

What are the four common mistakes to avoid in decision making?

APPENDIX TO CHAPTER 14: LINEAR PROGRAMMING

LEARNING OBJECTIVE #8
Determine whether or not you are responsible for this appendix. If so, after studying this section of the chapter, you should be able to:
- Formulate a linear program to solve a product-mix problem with multiple constraints.

What are the three steps in constructing a linear program?

What is a "decision variable"

How is the "objective function" written?

What are "constraints?"

What does the "feasible region" represent when a graphical solution approach is used?

SELF-TEST QUESTIONS AND EXERCISES

MATCHING

Match each of the key terms listed below with the appropriate textbook definition:

___	1.	Accurate information	13.	Opportunity cost
___	2.	Avoidable expenses	14.	Outsourcing decision
___	3.	Constraints*	15.	Qualitative characteristics
___	4.	Decision variables*	16.	Relative sales value method
___	5.	Differential cost	17.	Relevant information
___	6.	Expected value	18.	Sensitivity analysis
___	7.	Feasible region*	19.	Separable processing cost
___	8.	Information overload	20.	Split-off point
___	9.	Joint cost	21.	Sunk costs
___	10.	Joint production process	22.	Timely information
___	11.	Make-or-buy decision	23.	Unavoidable expenses
___	12.	Objective function*		

* This key term is included in the appendix to the chapter.

A. The sum of the possible values for a random variable, each weighted by its probability.

B. Algebraic expressions of limitations faced by a firm, such as those limiting its productive resources.

C. Expenses that will continue to be incurred even if a subunit or activity is eliminated.

D. Data that is pertinent to a decision.

E. Another term used to describe a make-or-buy decision.

F. Cost incurred on a joint product after the split-off point of a joint production process.

G. Precise and correct data.

H. A decision as to whether a product or service should be produced in-house or purchased from an outside supplier.

I. The cost incurred in a joint production process before the joint products become identifiable as separate products.

J. Expenses that will no longer be incurred if a particular action is taken.

K. The potential benefit given up when the choice of one action precludes selection of a different action.

L. A method in which joint costs are allocated to the joint products in proportion to their total sales values at the split-off point.

M. An algebraic expression of the firm's goal.

N. The variables in a linear program about which a decision is made.

O. A technique for determining what would happen in a decision analysis if a key prediction or assumption proves to be wrong.

P. The point in a joint production process at which the joint products become identifiable as separate products.

Q. The possible values for decision variables that are not ruled out by constraints.

R. The difference in a cost item under two decision alternatives.

S. Factors in a decision analysis that cannot be expressed easily in numerical terms.

T. The provision of so much information that, due to human limitations in processing information, managers cannot effectively uses it.

U. Data that are available in time for use in a decision analysis.
V. A production process that results in two or more joint products.
W. Costs that were incurred in the past and cannot be altered by any current or future decision.

TRUE-FALSE QUESTIONS

For each of the following statements, enter a T or F in the blank to indicate whether the statement is true or false.

___1. Defining a managerial decision problem is a straightforward matter requiring little or no managerial skill.

___2. Relevant and accurate data are of value in decision making regardless of when these data are made available.

___3. A decision problem involves selecting from among more than two alternatives.

___4. The managerial accountant's role in the decision-making process is to provide relevant information to the managers who make the decisions.

___5. The managerial accountant's role in the decision-making process is primarily to be responsible for the collection of data.

___6. Decision problems involving accounting data are typically specified in qualitative terms.

___7. A decision model is a simplified representation of the issues involved in making choices in a decision problem.

___8. To be relevant to a decision, cost or benefit information must involve a future event.

___9. Information relevant to unique decisions is easier to generate than information relevant to repetitive decisions.

___10. The book value of old equipment is a sunk cost.

___11. In relevant costing problems it is more important to consider out-of-pocket expenditures than it is to consider opportunity costs.

___12. Fixed costs are irrelevant costs.

___13. Costs or benefits that are the same across all alternatives in a decision problem have a definite bearing on the choice of action to be made.

___14. The book value of obsolete inventory is a sunk cost.

___15. In the decision-making process, people seldom overlook or underweight opportunity costs.

___16. Variable costs are sometimes irrelevant costs.

___17. In a joint production process, the joint cost of production is not relevant to the decision problem of selling products at split-off or processing those products further.

___18. In the decision problem of which products to make when resources are scarce or limited, the important question to ask is, "Which products have the largest contribution margin per unit of product?"

___19. Managers typically make decisions that maximize their perceived performance evaluations and rewards.

___20. ABC is superior to traditional product costing in identifying avoidable costs.

FILL-IN-THE-BLANK QUESTIONS

For each of the following statements, fill in the blank to properly complete the statement.

1. _____ are the factors in a decision problem that cannot be expressed effectively in numerical terms.

2. Information is _____ if it is pertinent to a decision problem.

3. Relevant information in decision making must involve costs or benefits that _____ among the possible alternative choices of action.

4. _____ are decisions that arise essentially only once.

5. Costs that have occurred in the past are _____ to a decision problem that is at hand.

6. Relevant information must involve costs and benefits to be realized in the _____; however, the accountant's predictions of those costs and benefits are often based on data from the _____.

7. _____ are decisions that are made over and over again, at regular or irregular intervals.

8. _____ refers to the precision of data.

9. _____ consists of receiving more information than can effectively be used in the decision-making process.

10. _____ are costs that have already been incurred.

11. The computation of _____ costs is a convenient way of summarizing the relative advantage of one alternative over another in a decision problem.

12. A(n) _____ cost is the potential benefit given up when the choice of one action precludes a different action.

13. When there is _____ capacity, the opportunity cost of using a firm's facilities for a special-order decision problem is relevant to the decision.

14. For purposes of decision making, _____ fixed costs can be misleading.

15. Expenses that a manager can escape incurring by taking a certain course of action are called _____ expenses.

16. The point in a production process at which joint products become identifiable is called a(n) _____ point.

17. _____ is a technique for determining what would happen in a decision analysis if a key prediction or assumption proves to be wrong.

18. An important factor that should be considered in long-run decision problems, and which is not considered in short-run decision problems, is the _____.

19. (Appendix) _____ is a mathematical tool to solve the problem of optimizing a linear function subject to linear constraints.

MULTIPLE-CHOICE QUESTIONS

Circle the best answer or response.

1. Which of the following is *not* a key characteristic of information in determining its usefulness for decision making?
   (a) Accuracy
   (b) Scope
   (c) Relevance
   (d) Timeliness

2. The Gleason Company bought a small computer two years ago; its book value is now $2,000, and it has one more year of useful life. The company could buy a new computer now with a useful life of one year (because in one year it will be obsolete) for $1,500. The new computer would result in a cost saving over the next year of $1,800. The change in the company's net income for next year resulting from buying the new computer would be:
    (a) $200 decrease.
    (b) $500 increase.
    (c) $300 increase.
    (d) $400 decrease.

3. Consider the following statements about relevant costing problems and determine which statement(s) is (are) true.

    I. Future costs or benefits that are identical across all decision alternatives are relevant.
    II. Opportunity costs are relevant costs.

    (a) Only I
    (b) Only II
    (c) Both I and II
    (d) Neither I nor II

4. The Thomas Company now has $12,000 of obsolete inventory in stock. This inventory could be sold for $5,000, or modified for $6,000 and sold for $15,000. The change in the company's net income resulting from modifying the inventory and then selling it as opposed to selling it as is would be:
    (a) $3,000 decrease.
    (b) $4,000 increase.
    (c) $7,000 increase.
    (d) $9,000 increase.

5. Of the following steps in the decision-making process, the one that is primarily the responsibility of the managerial accountant is
    (a) Collecting the data.
    (b) Specifying the criterion.
    (c) Developing the decision model.
    (d) Clarifying the decision problem.

6. One of the products made and sold by the Sandier Company is a warble. The contribution margin per warble is $7.80. It takes 0.5 machine hour to make one warble. The contribution margin per machine hour in making warbles is:
    (a) $3.90
    (b) $8.30.
    (c) $15.60.
    (d) $10.40

7. The Rowe Company makes products X and Y in a joint production process. The joint cost of production is $7,000. Product X can be sold for $12 per unit at split-off and for $18 per unit after further processing. The separable cost of producing X is $11 per unit. The change in the company's net income as a result of selling 1,200 units of X at split-off instead of processing these units further is:
   (a) $6,000 increase.
   (b) $3,400 decrease.
   (c) $14,400 increase.
   (d) $7,200 decrease

EXERCISES

Record your answers to each part of the exercises in the space provided. Show your work.

Exercise 14.1

When Hazel Cooper, president of Ripton Enterprises, Inc., saw the annual income statement showing a loss for Product Line X-50, she quickly asserted, "This is first-class evidence that we should discontinue making Product X-50." As controller of Ripton, you believe it would be helpful for Hazel to know some of the issues and factors that should be considered when contemplating dropping a product line that shows a loss on the income statement.

Draft a brief memo to Hazel Cooper that discusses the issues and factors that should be considered when pondering the discontinuance of a product line that shows a loss on the income statement.

RIPTON ENTERPRISES, INC.
MEMORANDUM

Date: _____

To: Ms. Hazel Cooper

From: _____

Subject: _____

Exercise 14.2

The Monroe Company owns a machine that produces a component for the products the company makes and sells. Presently, the company uses 18,000 units of this component in production each year. The costs of making one unit of this component are

Direct material	$ 7
Variable conversion	10
Fixed conversion	5

The fixed conversion costs are unavoidable, and the unit cost is based on the present annual usage of 18,000 units of the component. An outside supplier has offered to sell Monroe this component for $20 per unit and can supply all the units it needs.

(a) Determine the change in net income per year that would result if Monroe buys the component from the outside supplier instead of making the component.

(b) Determine the change in net income per year that would result if Monroe buys the component from the outside supplier instead of making the component *and* is able to rent the machine to another organization for $62,000 per year.

Exercise 14.3

The Hinkell Company makes and sells 32,000 pairs of bowling shoes each year. The cost of making one pair of these shoes is

Direct material	$7
Variable conversion	5
Fixed conversion	6

The fixed conversion costs are unavoidable, and the unit fixed conversion cost is based on the annual capacity of 42,000 pairs of bowling shoes that Hinkell can make. The company has recently received an offer from a company (not a regular customer) that has offered to buy 6,000 pairs of shoes at $16 per pair. Regular customers buy shoes from Hinkell at $22 per pair.

(a) Determine the amount of the change in annual net income that would result if this special order is accepted.

(b) Assume that the special order is for 12,000 pairs of shoes instead of 6,000 pairs. All other conditions stay the same. Determine the amount of the change in annual net income that would result if this special order is accepted.

Exercise 14.4

The Fisher Company makes and sells two products, H and K. The income statement for last year was as follows:

	Product H	Product K
Sales	$160,000	$240,000
Variable cost of goods sold	60,000	100,000
Manufacturing contribution margin	$100,000	$140,000
Expenses:		
Fixed production	50,000	75,000
Variable selling and administration	18,000	50,000
Fixed selling and administration	14,000	21,000
Net income	$ 18,000	$ (6,000)

At Fisher, fixed costs are unavoidable and are allocated to products on the basis of sales revenue. When the president of Fisher saw this income statement, he immediately concluded that product K should be dropped. If product K is dropped, sales of product H are expected to increase by 10 percent next year; the company's cost structure will remain the same.

Determine the amount of the change in annual net income if product K is discontinued and only product H is sold.

Exercise 14.5 (Appendix)

The Hornick Company makes and sells two products, X and Y in its Jacksonville plant. Product X requires 2 hours in the Machining Department and 0.25 hour in the Packing Department. Product Y requires 4 hours in the Machining Department and 0.2 hour in the Packing Department. In any given week there are available at most 16,000 hours in the Machining Department and at most 1,250 hours in the Packing Department. The contribution margin from selling one unit of X is $18 and that of Y is $15. The decision problem at Hornick is how many units of each product should be made each week in order to maximize the total weekly contribution margin.

Formulate the given decision problem as a linear programming problem. Let x be the number of units of X made and sold each week, and let y be the number of units of Y made and sold each week.

SOLUTIONS TO SELF-TEST QUESTIONS AND EXERCISES
MATCHING

1.	G	7.	Q	13.	K	19.	F
2.	J	8.	T	14.	E	20.	P
3.	B	9.	I	15.	S	21.	W
4.	N	10.	V	16.	L	22.	U
5.	R	11.	H	17.	D	23.	C
6.	A	12.	M	18.	O		

TRUE-FALSE QUESTIONS

1. F Defining a managerial decision problem requires considerable managerial skill.
2. F These data must also be available in a timely manner.
3. F There can also be only two alternatives in a decision problem.
4. T
5. T
6. F These problems are specified in quantitative terms.
7. T
8. T
9. F It is harder to generate.
10. T
11. F Opportunity costs are just as important to consider as out-of-pocket costs.
12. F Fixed costs may be relevant; it depends on whether they make a difference when considering alternative possible actions in a decision problem.
13. F They have no bearing on the choice of action to be made.
14. T
15. F They often overlook or underweight opportunity costs.
16. T
17. T
18. F The question should be: "Which product gives the greatest contribution margin per unit of scarce resource?"
19. T
20. T

FILL-IN-THE-BLANK QUESTIONS

1. Qualitative characteristics
2. relevant
3. differ
4. Unique decisions
5. irrelevant
6. future, past
7. Repetitive decisions
8. Accuracy
9. Information overload
10. Sunk costs
11. differential
12. opportunity
13. no excess
14. unitized

15. avoidable
16. split-off
17. Sensitivity analysis
18. time value of money
19. Linear programming

MULTIPLE-CHOICE QUESTIONS

1. **(b)** The scope of information is not a key characteristic in determining its usefulness for decision making.
2. **(c)** $1,800 - $1,500 = $300; the $2,000 book value of the old computer is irrelevant.
3. **(b)** Future costs or benefits that are identical across all decision alternatives are irrelevant.
4. **(b)** ($15,000 - $6,000) - $5,000 = $4,000 increase. The $12,000 book value of obsolete inventory is irrelevant.
5. **(a)**
6. **(c)** $7.80/.5 = $15.60.
7. **(a)** [$12 - ($18 - $11)] x 1,200 = $6,000 increase.

EXERCISES

Exercise 14.1

The decision to drop Product Line X-50 will ultimately relate to the impact it will have on profitability, but only the costs that are relevant to this decision should be considered in evaluating this impact. By dropping Product X-50, it may be possible to avoid some fixed costs. For sake of discussion, suppose X-50 is dropped; if the fixed costs avoided exceed the loss in contribution margin from X-50, dropping the product line is the right decision. Alternatively, if the loss in contribution margin from X-50 is greater than the avoidable fixed costs associated with X-50, dropping the product line is the wrong decision. Thus, it is important to look beyond the bottom line of the income statement and make a careful analysis of the costs that relate to this decision. Additionally, the impact of dropping Product Line X-50 on other product lines should be considered.

Exercise 14.2

(a)

Annual cost saving from not making component (18,000 x $17)		$306,000
Annual cost of buying component on the outside (18,000 x $20)		360,000
Annual decrease in net income due to buying component outside		$(54,000)

(b)

Annual cost saving from not making component (18,000 x $17)	$306,000	
Annual rent from machine	62,000	$368,000
Annual cost of buying component on the outside (18,000 x $20)		360,000
Annual increase in net income due to buying component outside		$ 8,000

Exercise 14.3

(a)

Revenue from special order (6,000 x $16)	$ 96,000
Incremental cost to fill special order [6,000 x ($7 + $5)]	72,000
Increase in net income from accepting special order	$ 24,000

(b)

Revenue from special order (12,000 x $16)		$192,000
Incremental cost to fill special order [12,000 x ($7 + $5)]	$144,000	
Opportunity loss from not selling 2,000 pairs to regular customers [2,000 x ($22 – 12)]	20,000	164,000
Increase in net income from accepting special offer		$ 28,000

Exercise 14.4

Product H

Last year's contribution margin = $160,000 - $60,000 - $18,000 = $82,000
Last year's contribution-margin ratio = $82,000/$160,000 = 51.25%

Product K:

Last year's contribution margin = $240,000 - $100,000 - $50,000 = $90,000
Last year's contribution-margin ratio = $90,000/$240,000 = 37.5%

Incremental contribution margin from *Product H* if *Product K* is dropped ($82,000 x .01)	$ 8,200
Opportunity cost due to contribution margin forgone by dropping *Product K* ($240,000 x .375)	90,000
Decrease in annual net income due to dropping *Product K*	$(81,800)

Exercise 14.5

Maximize $18x + 15y$ subject to:

$2x + 4y = 16,000$ (machining)

$.25x + .2y < 1,250$ (packing)

$x, y > 0$

IDEAS FOR YOUR STUDY TEAM

1.   Rewrite each of the definitions of the key terms that appear at the end of the chapter using your own words. Imagine that you are trying to explain each key term to a friend who has not taken any accounting classes. Then, get together with the other members of your study team and compare your definitions.

Accurate information

Avoidable expenses

Constraints

Decision variables

Differential cost

Expected value

Feasible region

Information overload

Joint cost

Joint production process

Make-or-buy decision

Objective function

Opportunity cost

Outsourcing decision

Qualitative characteristics

Relative sales value method

Relevant information

Sensitivity analysis

Separable processing cost

Split-off point

Sunk costs

Timely information

Unavoidable expenses

2.   Try to predict the types of questions, exercises and problems that you will encounter on the quizzes and exams that cover this chapter. Review the *Read and Recall Questions* and the *Self-Test Questions and Exercises* that are set forth in this Study Guide. Work through the end-of-chapter review problem(s), if applicable, and the end-of-chapter questions, exercises and problems that were assigned by your instructor. As you perform these tasks, identify the terms, concepts, formulas, etc. that you are responsible for knowing. After you develop the list of questions, exercises and problems that you expect to encounter on quizzes and exams, review the learning objectives that appear at the beginning of the chapter in your textbook to ensure that you have not overlooked anything significant. After you have completed your review of your list, get together with the other members of your study team and compare your predictions.

CHAPTER FOCUS SUGGESTIONS

The main focus of this chapter is the managerial decision problem of pricing the products or services that an organization offers for sale.

You should be familiar with the major influences that govern the setting of prices and the profit-maximization pricing model. You will need to know how to set prices using the cost-plus pricing formula and the time and material pricing method. You should be able to discuss the issues involved in the strategic pricing of new products, the key principles of target costing, and the role of value engineering in target costing. Finally, you should be able to determine the relevant information in special-order and competitive-bidding situations and be aware of the implications of activity-based costing.

READ AND RECALL QUESTIONS

MAJOR INFLUENCES ON PRICING DECISIONS

LEARNING OBJECTIVE #1
After studying this section of the chapter, you should be able to:
- List and describe the four major influences on pricing decisions.

What are four major influences that govern the prices that are set by a company?

Customer Demand

Why are product-design issues and pricing considerations interrelated? How can information relating to customer demand be obtained?

Actions of Competitors

Why must a company keep a watchful eye on the firm's competition?

Costs

How does the role of costs in price setting vary widely among industries?

What two factors heavily influence prices in most industries?

Political, Legal, and Image-Related Issues

What are some of the legal issues related to price setting?

What political considerations are sometimes relevant to price setting?

In terms of public image, what is the relationship between quality and price?

ECONOMIC PROFIT-MAXIMIZING PRICING

LEARNING OBJECTIVE #2

After studying this section of the chapter, you should be able to:
- Explain and use the economic profit-maximizing pricing model.

What does it mean if a company is a "price taker?"

Total Revenue, Demand, and Marginal Revenue Curves

What is a "total revenue curve?" What trade-off is shown by a total revenue curve? Does a total revenue curve decrease or increase throughout its range? Why?

What is a "demand curve?" Does a total demand curve decrease or increase throughout its range? Why? What is another term for a demand curve? Why does this term make sense?

What is a "marginal revenue curve?" Does a marginal revenue curve decrease or increase throughout its range? Why?

Total Cost and Marginal Cost Curves

What is a "total cost curve?" Does a total cost curve decrease or increase throughout its range? Why?

What is a "marginal cost curve?" Does a marginal cost curve decrease or increase throughout its range? Why?

Profit-Maximizing Price and Quantity

What information can be determined by examining the total revenue and total cost curves?

Price Elasticity

What is "price elasticity?" When is demand elastic? When is it inelastic? What is "cross-elasticity?"

Limitations of the Profit-Maximizing Model

What are the three major limitations of the economic model of the pricing decision?

What is an "oligopolistic market?"

Costs and Benefits of Information

What combination of factors do most managers base pricing decisions on?

ROLE OF ACCOUNTING PRODUCT COSTS IN PRICING

What are three reasons that managers base prices on accounting product costs, at least to some extent?

LEARNING OBJECTIVE #3
After studying this section of the chapter, you should be able to:
- Set prices using cost-plus pricing formulas.

Cost-Plus Pricing

What is the general form of most cost-based pricing formulas? Why is such a pricing approach called "cost-plus pricing?"

What are the four definitions of "cost" that are used in the various cost-plus pricing formulas?

Absorption-Cost Pricing Formulas

What is the disadvantage of using a variable cost-pricing formula?

Why do absorption-cost or total-cost pricing formulas seem reasonable to buyers?

Why would a company want to use cost-plus pricing based on full costs?

Why is it cost-effective to use absorption-cost information for pricing?

What is the primary disadvantage of absorption-cost or total-cost pricing formulas?

Variable-Cost Pricing Formulas

What are the three advantages attributed to the use of cost-plus pricing based on either variable manufacturing costs or total variable costs? What is the primary disadvantage?

Determining the Markup

If management uses a variable-cost pricing formula, what must be covered by the markup? Alternatively, if management uses a absorption-costing formula, what must be covered by the markup?

What is a common approach to determining the profit margin in cost-plus pricing? What is the formula for determining the amount of the target profit?

What is the formula for computing the markup percentage on total cost when cost-plus pricing is based on total costs?

What is the formula for computing the markup percentage on total variable cost when cost-plus pricing is based on total variable costs?

What is the general formula for computing the markup percentage in cost-plus pricing to achieve a target ROI?

Cost-Plus Pricing: Summary and Evaluation

What must price-setting managers ultimately understand? What other factors must be considered once a starting point in setting prices has been established?

STRATEGIC PRICING OF NEW PRODUCTS

LEARNING OBJECTIVE #4
After studying this section of the chapter, you should be able to:
• Discuss the issues involved in the strategic pricing of new products.

Why is the pricing of a new product an especially challenging decision problem? What are two common uncertainties that exist in these decision problems?

What is "skimming pricing?" When this pricing approach is used, how large will the initial market be? When is this approach used? What changes would subsequently be made to the product's price? Why?

What is "penetration pricing?" What is expected to occur as a result of the price that is set? When is this approach used?

TARGET COSTING

LEARNING OBJECTIVE #5
After studying this section of the chapter, you should be able to:
• List and discuss the key principles of target costing.

What is "target costing?" What types of companies use this process? What is a new product's target cost?

A Strategic Profit and Cost Management Process

What are the seven key principles of target costing? What are life-cycle costs? What is value-chain orientation?

LEARNING OBJECTIVE #6
After studying this section of the chapter, you should be able to:
•   Explain the role of activity-based costing in setting a target cost.

Activity-Based Costing and Target Costing

How can an activity-based costing (ABC) system be helpful to product design engineers?

How can a computer-integrated manufacturing (CIM) system be helpful to the engineer?

LEARNING OBJECTIVE #7
After studying this section of the chapter, you should be able to:
•   Explain how product-cost distortion can undermine a firm's pricing strategy.

Product-Cost Distortion and Pricing: The Role of Activity-Based Costing

What is the relationship between the volume and complexity of products and the amount of activity per unit required for various manufacturing-support activities?

Why can't a traditional product-costing system capture the cost implications of product diversity?

LEARNING OBJECTIVE #8
After studying this section of the chapter, you should be able to:
• Explain the process of value engineering and its role in target costing.

Value Engineering and Target Costing

What is value engineering?

What three value engineering stages does Isuzu use in the design phase of its new products?

What is meant by "tear-down?" What are the eight tear-down methods Isuzu uses?

What four additional value engineering methods does Isuzu use?

TIME AND MATERIAL PRICING

LEARNING OBJECTIVE #9
After studying this section of the chapter, you should be able to:
• Determine prices using the time and material pricing approach.

What charges are determined when the "time and material pricing" cost-based approach to pricing is used? What types of firms would use time and material pricing?

What does the labor charge typically include? What does the material charge generally include?

What is the formula for computing the time charges?

What is the formula for computing the material charges?

COMPETITIVE BIDDING

> **LEARNING OBJECTIVE #10**
> *After studying this section of the chapter, you should be able to:*
> • Set prices in special-order or competitive-bidding situations by analyzing the relevant costs.

What happens in a competitive bidding situation? Why does competitive bidding complicate a manager's pricing problem? Why is there a trade-off between bidding too high and bidding too low?

What is the typical approach to setting prices for special jobs and competitively bid contracts? When should an opportunity cost be considered in a competitive bidding situation?

What qualitative factors might affect the price set in a competitive bidding situation? How should the perceived qualitative benefits affect the bid price?

EFFECT OF ANTITRUST LAWS ON PRICING

> **LEARNING OBJECTIVE #11**
> *After studying this section of the chapter, you should be able to:*
> • Describe the legal restrictions on setting prices.

What is "price discrimination?" What laws prohibit price discrimination?

What is "predatory pricing?" When is a price deemed to be predatory?

SELF-TEST QUESTIONS AND EXERCISES

MATCHING

Match each of the key terms listed below with the appropriate textbook definition:

___ 1. Average revenue curve	___ 11. Price discrimination
___ 2. Competitive bidding	___ 12. Price elasticity
___ 3. Cost-plus pricing	___ 13. Price taker
___ 4. Cross-elasticity	___ 14. Return-on-investment
___ 5. Demand curve (average revenue curve)	___ 15. Skimming pricing
	___ 16. Target cost
___ 6. Marginal cost curve	___ 17. Target costing
___ 7. Marginal revenue curve	___ 18. Time and material pricing
___ 8. Oligopolistic market	___ 19. Total cost curve
___ 9. Penetration pricing	___ 20. Total revenue curve
___ 10. Predatory pricing	___ 21. Value engineering

A. A graph of the relationship between the change in total cost and the quantity produced and sold.

B. Another term for demand curve.

C. A graph of the relationship between the change in total revenue and the quantity sold.

D. The projected long-run product cost that will enable a firm to enter and remain in the market for the product and compete successfully with the firm's competitors.

E. Income divided by invested capital.

F. A firm whose product or service is determined totally by the market.

G. The extent to which a change in a product's price affects the demand for substitute products.

H. A graph of the relationship between total sales revenue and quantity sold.

I. A pricing approach in which the price is equal to cost plus a markup.

J. Setting a high initial price for a new product in order to reap short-run profits. Over time, the price is reduced gradually.

K. An illegal practice in which the price of a product is set low temporarily to broaden demand. Then the product's supply is restricted and the price is raised.

L. A graph of the relationship between sales price and the quantity of units sold.

M. A graph of the relationship between total cost and the quantity produced and sold.

N. A situation where two or more companies submit bids (prices) for a product, service, or project to a potential buyer.

O. A market with a small number of sellers competing among themselves.

P. The design of a product, and the processes used to produce it, so that ultimately the product can be manufactured at a cost that will enable a firm to make a profit when the product is sold at an estimated market-driven price. This estimated price is called the target price, the desired profit margin is called the target profit, and the cost at which the product must be manufactured is called the target cost.

Q. The illegal practice of quoting different prices for the same product or service to different buyers, when the price differences are not justified by cost differences.

R. A cost-plus pricing approach that includes components for labor cost and material cost, plus markups on either or both of these cost components.

S. Setting a low initial price for a new product in order to penetrate the market deeply and gain a large and broad market share.

T. The impact of price changes on sales volume.

U. A cost-reduction and process-improvement technique that utilizes information collected about a product's design and production processes and then examines various attributes of the design and processes to identify candidates for improvement efforts.

TRUE-FALSE QUESTIONS

For each of the following statements, enter a T or F in the blank to indicate whether the statement is true or false.

___1. Discerning customer demand is very important in setting prices of products.

___2. Political considerations are never relevant in setting prices.

___3. As the price of a product or service increases, demand increases, generally speaking.

___4. The demand curve is the same as the average revenue curve.

___5. The law does not prohibit companies from discriminating among their customers in setting prices.

___6. Understanding cost behavior is important in pricing decisions.

___7. In setting the price of a product, managers must be very concerned about the prices that competitors charge for the same type of product.

___8. The total revenue curve gives total sales revenue as a function of price.

___9. In the profit-maximizing price model, the profit-maximizing price corresponds to the demand level where the marginal cost curve intersects the marginal revenue curve.

___10. Measuring price elasticity is important in economics, but not in market research.

___11. In most industries, both market forces and cost considerations heavily influence prices.

___12. In the long run, price must cover all costs and a normal profit margin.

___13. A disadvantage of variable-cost pricing is that it does not require the allocation of common fixed costs to individual product lines.

___14. The profit-maximizing pricing model is not valid for all forms of market organization.

___15. Consideration of a company's public image is not relevant in setting prices.

___16. Demand is elastic if a price increase has a positive impact on sales volume, and vice versa.

___17. In time and material pricing the material charge does not include any cost for material handling and storage.

___18. When a firm has no excess capacity, the bid amount in competitive bidding should include both the incremental costs of the job and a charge that reflects the opportunity cost of using limited excess capacity on that job.

___19. Traditional product costing is effective in capturing the cost implications of product diversity.

FILL-IN-THE-BLANK QUESTIONS

For each of the following statements, fill in the blank to properly complete the statement.

1. If a company's prices are totally determined by the market, the company is known as a(n)_____.

2. The _____curve shows the relationship between sales price and the quantity of units sold.

3. The _____curve shows the change in total revenue that accompanies a change in quantity sold.

4. The _____curve shows the relationship between total cost and quantity produced and sold each month.

5. The_____curve depicts the change in total cost that accompanies a change in quantity produced and sold.

6. In the profit-maximizing pricing model, profit is maximized when _____ equals _____.

7. The impact of price changes on sales volume is called _____.

8. In _____ pricing, price equals the sum of cost and a markup.

9. _____ refers to the extent to which a change in a product's price affects the demand for other substitute products.

10. A common approach to determining the profit margin in cost-plus pricing is to base profit on the firm's target _____.

11. _____ pricing involves determining a charge for labor used on a job and a charge for the materials used on that job.

12. Demand is _____ if price changes have little or no impact on sales quantity.

13. In _____, at least two companies submit sealed bids for a product or service to a potential buyer.

14. _____ pricing involves setting the initial price of a new product high, so as to reap good short-term profits from that product.

15. _____ pricing involves setting an initial price low in order to gain a large market share quickly.

16. Basing a product cost on a price determined by market research and then trying to make the product at that cost is called _____ costing.

17. U.S. antitrust laws prohibit price _____.

18. Cutting prices to broaden demand with the intention of subsequently restricting supply and raising these prices is called the illegal practice of _____ pricing.

MULTIPLE-CHOICE QUESTIONS

Circle the best answer or response.

1. Consider the following statements about the profit-maximizing pricing model and determine which statement(s) is (are) true.

    I. Demand and marginal revenue curves are difficult to discern with precision, generally speaking.
    II. Marginal cost is usually difficult to measure from data available in a firm's cost accounting system.

    (a) Only I
    (b) Only II
    (c) Both I and II
    (d) Neither I nor II

2. Most managers base prices on product costs to some extent because
    (a) most companies sell only one product.
    (b) cost provides the final word in setting prices.
    (c) the cost of a product is a floor below which prices cannot be set in the long run.
    (d) methods of computing cost-based prices require much effort and time, so it is important to use the output of this work.

3. A firm makes and sells only one product, and its annual target ROI is 25 percent. The average invested capital is $400,000. The total cost of one unit of product is $1,250, and the firm expects to sell 500 units next year. The markup percentage of this unit next year, based on total cost and target ROI, should be:
   (a) 16.00 percent.
   (b) 20.00 percent.
   (c) 18.00 percent.
   (d) 17.58 percent.

4. Which of the following would *not* typically be used as a cost base in cost-plus pricing techniques?
   (a) Variable manufacturing cost
   (b) Variable selling and administrative cost
   (c) Total cost
   (d) Absorption manufacturing cost

5. Consider the following statements about absorption-cost pricing and determine which statement(s) is (are) true.

   I. The main disadvantage is that it obscures the cost-behavior pattern of the firm.
   II. The information needed for this pricing method is not readily available from a firm's cost-accounting system.

   (a) Only I
   (b) Only II
   (c) Both I and II
   (d) Neither I nor II

6. The Whitney Company uses time and material pricing. Based on the following data for the Repair Department, the time charge per hour should be:

Labor rate per hour including benefits	$25,000
Annual labor hours	12,000
Annual overhead costs:	
Material handling and storage	$48,000
Other overhead costs	$240,000
Cost of materials used per year	$800,000
Hourly charge to cover profit margin	$10.00

   (a) $59.
   (b) $55.
   (c) $35
   (d) $25

7. Refer again to the Whitney Company in Question 6. The amount needed to be added to each dollar of material cost to obtain the material charge is
   (a) $.06.
   (b) $.20.
   (c) $.24.
   (d) $.32.

EXERCISES

Record your answers to each part of the exercises in the space provided. Show your work.

Exercise 15.1

The Pinkerton Company sells a unique product in the northeastern United States. The marketing and accounting departments have assembled the following data:

Case	Monthly Sales Demand	Unit Sales Price	Average Cost
1	50	$800	$600
2	100	700	550
3	150	600	525
4	200	500	575

(a) For each case, compute the monthly profit from this product. Base your calculations on the method used in panel (c) of Exhibits 15-1, 15-2, and 15-3 in the text.

Case	Sales Demand	Unit Sales Price	Average Cost	Total Revenue	Total Cost	Profit
1						
2						
3						
4						
5						

(b) Suppose that the price of this product is to be based on the profit-maximization pricing model and only one of the four given prices is to be chosen. Which one should be selected? Why?

Exercise 15.2

The Ostrander Company has the following data concerning a deluxe computer table that it manufactures:

Variable manufacturing cost	$40
Applied fixed manufacturing cost	15
Variable selling and administrative cost	7
Allocated fixed selling and administrative cost	12

The president complained, "This information is absurd, and something must be done about it!"

Develop a cost-plus pricing formula that will yield a price of $100 for this computer table for each of the following cost bases:

(a) Variable manufacturing cost

(b) Absorption manufacturing cost

(c) Total variable cost

(d)Total cost

Exercise 15.3

The McClure Company has the following annual budget data for a product called a hipple that it makes and sells at its Hinesville plant:

Units sold	600
Variable costs	$186,000
Fixed costs	$174,000

The invested capital at Hinesville is $500,000. Management desires an annual ROI from the production and sale of hipples to be 15 percent.

Compute the markup percentage using each of the following cost bases in order to reflect management's desired ROI

(a) Total cost

(b) Total variable cost

Exercise 15.4

Clark's Computer Repairs is a small firm that repairs microcomputers and minicomputers. The firm uses time and material pricing. The following data have been assembled for 19x8:

Labor rate per hour including benefits	$20
Annual labor hours	8,200 hours
Yearly overhead costs:	
Material handling and storage	$30,000
Other overhead costs	$125,000
Yearly cost of materials used	$200,000
Hourly charge to cover profit margin	$8

(a) Find the formulas for Clark's:

(1) Time charges

(2) Material charges

(b) Suppose Clark's receives a request for computer repair that requires an estimated 120 hours of labor and $8,000 of material cost. What price should be assigned to this job?

Exercise 15.5

Reddy Industries has just received a special request from the Dolby Company in France for 5,000 gearboxes at a price of $45 each, FOB shipping point. Ordinarily, Reddy sells these gearboxes through its regular channels at $58 each. The managerial accountant at Reddy has done a careful relevant costing analysis of this situation and has found that Reddy can afford to sell these gearboxes at a unit price of $53.20 and still break even. Also, she has learned that there is sufficient production capacity to provide these 5,000 gearboxes to Dolby without interfering with production for regular customers.

Write a brief essay that identifies the factors, besides price, that Reddy should consider before offering to fill the special order for Dolby.

SOLUTIONS TO SELF-TEST QUESTIONS AND EXERCISES

MATCHING

1.	B	7.	C	13.	F	19.	M
2.	N	8.	O	14.	E	20.	H
3.	I	9.	S	15.	J	21.	U
4.	G	10.	K	16.	D		
5.	L	11.	Q	17.	P		
6.	A	12.	T	18.	R		

True-False Questions

1. **T**
2. **F** Sometimes political considerations have a bearing on thrice setting.
3. **F** Generally, as the price increases, demand will decrease.
4. **T**
5. **F** Laws do prohibit price discrimination; the Robinson-Patman Act is an example of such a law.
6. **T**
7. **T**
8. **F** This curve gives total sales revenue as a function of quantity sold.
9. **T**
10. **F** It is also important in market research.
11. **T**
12. **T**
13. **F** This is an advantage since individual product lines are not charged with arbitrarily allocated common costs.
14. **T**
15. **F** A consideration of a company's public image is very relevant in price setting.
16. **F** Demand is elastic if a price increase has a negative impact on sales volume.
17. **F** It does include a charge for material handling and storage.
18. **T**
19. **F** It fails to capture the cost implications of product diversity.

FILL-IN-THE-BLANK QUESTIONS

1. price taker
2. demand
3. marginal revenue
4. total cost
5. marginal cost
6. marginal revenue, marginal cost
7. price elasticity
8. cost-plus
9. Cross-elasticity
10. return on investment
11. Time-and-material
12. inelastic
13. competitive bidding

14. skimming
15. penetration
16. target
17. Discrimination
18. Predatory

MULTIPLE-CHOICE QUESTIONS

1. **(c)**
2. **(c)** Answers (a), (b), and (d) are untrue.
3. **(a)** $100,000/(500 x $1,250) = 16%.
4. **(b)** The answers in the other choices are all used as a cost base.
5. **(a)** Absorption-cost pricing data are readily available from a firm's cost-accounting system.
6. **(b)** $25 + ($240,000/12,000) + $10 = $55.
7. **(a)** $48,000/$800,000= $.06.

EXERCISES

Exercise 15.1

(a)

Case	Sales Demand	Unit Sales Price	Average Cost	Total Revenue	Total Cost	Profit
1	50	$800	$600	$ 40,000	$ 40,000	$ 10,000
2	100	700	550	70,000	55,000	15,000
3	150	600	525	90,000	78,750	11,250
4	200	500	575	100,000	115,000	(15,000)

(b)

The price should be $700, because profit is maximized at that price.

Exercise 15.2

In order to yield a price of $100, we must find the markup percentage corresponding to each cost base. Since Price = Cost + Markup percentage x Cost, Markup percentage = (Price - Cost)/Cost.

(a)

Variable manufacturing cost per unit = $40

Markup percentage = ($100 - $40)/40 = 150%

(b)

Absorption manufacturing cost per unit = $55

Markup percentage = ($100 - $55)/55 = 81.8%

(c)

Total variable cost per unit = $47

Markup percentage = ($100 - $47)/47 = 112.8%

(d)

Total cost per unit = $74

Markup percentage = ($100 - $74)/74 = 35.1%

Exercise 15.3

Target profit = .15 x $500,000 = $75,000

(a)

 Markup percentage = $75,000/(600 x $600) = 20.83%

(b)

 Markup percentage = ($75,000 + $174,000)/(600 x $310) = 133.87%

Exercise 15.4

(a)(1)

Time charge = $20 + ($125,000/8,000) + $8 = $43.63/hour

(a)(2)

Material charge = Material cost for job + (Material cost for job x $30,000/$200,000)

Material charge = Material cost for job + (Material cost for job x 15%)

(b)

Price = (120 x $43.63) + ($8,000 x $1.15) = $14,435.60

Exercise 15.5

Before agreeing to fill Dolby's special request, the management of Reddy should consider the possible impact that this sale will have on future sales to Dolby and how it might affect Reddy's future involvement in the international marketplace. Reddy should also be cognizant of the effect this special sale would have on sales to its regular customers. In addition, the management of Reddy ought to consider the possible tax implications of this sale. Since there is enough extra productive capacity for this special order, Reddy should analyze the effect of this special order on equipment maintenance.

IDEAS FOR YOUR STUDY TEAM

1.   Rewrite each of the definitions of the key terms that appear at the end of the chapter using your own words. Imagine that you are trying to explain each key term to a friend who has not taken any accounting classes. Then, get together with the other members of your study team and compare your definitions.

Average revenue curve

Competitive bidding

Cost-plus pricing

Cross-elasticity

Demand curve (average revenue curve)

Marginal cost curve

Marginal revenue curve

Oligopolistic market

Penetration pricing

Predatory pricing

Price discrimination

Price elasticity

Price taker

Return-on-investment pricing

Skimming pricing

Target cost

Target costing

Time and material pricing

Total cost curve

Total revenue curve

Value engineering

2. Try to predict the types of questions, exercises and problems that you will encounter on the quizzes and exams that cover this chapter. Review the *Read and Recall Questions* and the *Self-Test Questions and Exercises* that are set forth in this Study Guide. Work through the end-of-chapter review problem(s), if applicable, and the end-of-chapter questions, exercises and problems that were assigned by your instructor. As you perform these tasks, identify the terms, concepts, formulas, etc. that you are responsible for knowing. After you develop the list of questions, exercises and problems that you expect to encounter on quizzes and exams, review the learning objectives that appear at the beginning of the chapter in your textbook to ensure that you have not overlooked anything significant. After you have completed your review of your list, get together with the other members of your study team and compare your predictions.

CHAPTER 16
CAPITAL EXPENDITURE DECISIONS:
AN INTRODUCTION

CHAPTER FOCUS SUGGESTIONS

This chapter introduces a class of managerial decision-making problems called capital-budgeting problems. These problems involve the analysis of long-term investments (i.e., expenditures of capital for assets having lives of more than one year).

You should be familiar with concepts relating to the time value of money, and know how to compute both the future and present values of cash flows occurring over time. You will need to be able to use the net-present-value and internal-rate of return methods, and should understand the assumptions that underlie each method. In addition, you will need to know how to use the total-cost and incremental-cost approaches to evaluate investment proposals. The implications of advanced manufacturing technology on capital-budget problems are also addressed.

READ AND RECALL QUESTIONS

What are two types of capital-budgeting decisions encountered by managers?

What are the two alternative courses of action in an "acceptance-or-rejection" decision?

What choice must be made in a capital-rationing decision?

CONCEPT OF PRESENT VALUE

LEARNING OBJECTIVE #1

After studying this section of the chapter, you should be able to:
- Explain the importance of the time value of money in capital-budgeting decisions.

What is the fundamental concept in a capital-budgeting decision analysis?

LEARNING OBJECTIVE #2

After studying this section of the chapter, you should be able to:
- Compute the future value and present value of cash flows occurring over several time periods.

What is meant by the "future value" of an initial investment? What is the simple formula that may be used to compute the future value of any investment?

Which part of the formula is called the "accumulation factor?" How have accumulation factors been simplified?

What is meant by "present value?" What is the simple formula that may be used to compute the present value of any investment?

Which part of the formula is called the "discount factor?" How have discount factors been simplified?

What is an "annuity?" How have annuity discount and annuity accumulation factors been simplified?

DISCOUNTED-CASH-FLOW ANALYSIS

> **LEARNING OBJECTIVE #3**
> *After studying this section of the chapter, you should be able to:*
> • Use the net-present-value method and the internal-rate-of-return method to evaluate an investment proposal.

What is discounted-cash-flow-analysis?

Net-Present-Value Method

What are the four steps comprising a net-present-value analysis of an investment proposal?

Why should the investment proposal be accepted if the net present value (NPV) is positive?

Internal-Rate-of-Return Method

What is an asset's "internal rate or return?"

How could you find the internal rate of return (IRR) using trial and error? How would you know which discount rate is correct?

When the series of cash flows is identical throughout the project's life (that is, when there is an annuity or series of equal payments), what approach can be used (rather than trial and error) to determine the internal rate of return? What is the formula for the annuity discount factor? How would you then use that factor to determine the discount rate?

What are the three steps comprising an internal rate of return analysis of an investment proposal?

What is "interpolation?" What is the formula for determining the true internal rate of return when interpolation is used?

When the cash-flow pattern is uneven, what approach must be used to find the internal rate of return?

LEARNING OBJECTIVE #4

After studying this section of the chapter, you should be able to:

• Compare the net-present-value and internal-rate-of-return methods, and state the assumptions underlying each method.

Comparing the NPV and IRR Methods

What is computed when the net-present-value method is used? What rate should be used as the discount rate? How would you determine whether or not the investment proposal should be accepted under this approach?

What is computed when the internal-rate-of-return method is used? How would you determine whether or not the investment proposal should be accepted under this approach?

What two potential advantages does the net-present-value method exhibit over the internal-rate-of-return method?

Assumptions Underlying Discounted-Cash-Flow Analysis

What four assumptions underlie the NPV and IRR methods of investment analysis?

Choosing the Hurdle Rate

What should the hurdle rate be based on? What should the relationship be between the project's risk and the hurdle rate used to evaluate the project?

Should the investment decision be performed concurrently with the financing decision in a capital-expenditure decision?

How do organizations generate investment capital?

Depreciable Assets

Why aren't depreciation charges included in the discounted-cash-flow analysis?

How does depreciation affect the cash flows of a profit-seeking enterprise?

COMPARING TWO INVESTMENT PROJECTS

> **LEARNING OBJECTIVE #5**
> *After studying this section of the chapter, you should be able to:*
> - Use both the total-cost approach and the incremental-cost approach to evaluate an investment proposal.

What is the "total cost approach?" What information would be included in an analysis of two projects when this approach is used?

What is the "incremental-cost approach?" How would a decision be made between two investment projects when this approach is used?

MANAGERIAL ACCOUNTANT'S ROLE

What information does the managerial accountant draw upon to help in making cost predictions? What other factors should be considered?

Sensitivity Analysis

How can a project analyst determine how much the projections would have to change in order for a different decision to be indicated?

CAPITAL BUDGET ADMINISTRATION

LEARNING OBJECTIVE #6
After studying this section of the chapter, you should be able to:
- Describe a typical capital-budgeting approval process, and explain the concept of a postaudit.

Why do most organizations have an elaborate approval process for proposed investment projects? What is the relationship between the cost of a proposal and the level of authority needed for final approval?

Postaudit

What is a "postaudit" procedure? What are the benefits of performing this procedure?

PERFORMANCE EVALUATION: A BEHAVIORAL ISSUE

LEARNING OBJECTIVE #7
After studying this section of the chapter, you should be able to:
• Explain the potential conflict between using discounted-cash-flow analysis for approving capital projects and accrual accounting for periodic performance evaluation.

Why does a conflict exist between discounted-cash-flow decision methods and accrual-accounting performance-evaluation methods? What is a possible result of this conflict? How can this problem be solved?

JUSTIFICATION OF INVESTMENTS IN ADVANCED MANUFACTURING SYSTEMS

LEARNING OBJECTIVE #8
After studying this section of the chapter, you should be able to:
• Describe the process of justifying investments in advanced manufacturing technology.

What are the difficulties in applying the NPV approach in a CIM investment decision with regards to:

Hurdle rates?

Time horizons?

Level of authority required?

Operating cash flows?

Benefits that are difficult to quantify?

How can the intangible benefits be handled in a NPV analysis?

SELF-TEST QUESTIONS AND EXERCISES

MATCHING

Match each of the key terms listed below with the appropriate textbook definition:

___ 1. Acceptance-or-rejection decision
___ 2. Accumulation factor
___ 3. Annuity
___ 4. Capital-budgeting decision
___ 5. Capital-rationing decision
___ 6. Compound interest
___ 7. Discounted-cash-flow analysis
___ 8. Discount rate
___ 9. Future value
___ 10. Hurdle rate (or minimum desired rate of return)

___ 11. Incremental-cost approach
___ 12. Internal rate of return (or time-adjusted rate of return)
___ 13. Investment opportunity rate
___ 14. Net present value
___ 15. Postaudit (or reappraisal)
___ 16. Present value
___ 17. Principal

A. A decision as to whether or not a particular capital investment proposal should be accepted.

B. The minimum desired rate of return used in a discounted-cash-flow analysis.

C. The rate of return an organization can earn on its best alternative investments that are of equivalent risk.

D. The phenomenon in which interest is earned on prior periods' interest.

E. A given amount that is invested.

F. The discount rate required for an asset's net present value to be zero.

G. A series of equivalent cash flows.

H. An analysis of an investment proposal that takes into account the time value of money.

I. A systematic follow-up of a capital-budgeting decision to see how the project turned out.

J. An approach which considers the difference in the cost of each relevant item under the two alternative proposals.

K. The interest rate used in computing the present value of a cash flow.

L. The value of $(1 + r)^n$, in a future value calculation, where r denotes the interest rate per year and n denotes the number of years.

M. The present value of a project's future cash flows less the cost of the initial investment.

N. A decision in which management chooses which of several investment proposals to accept to make the best use of limited investment funds.

O. The economic value now of a cash flow that will occur in the future.

P. A decision involving cash flows beyond the current year.

Q. The amount to which invested funds accumulate over a specified period of time.

TRUE-FALSE QUESTIONS

For each of the following statements, enter a T or F in the blank to indicate whether the statement is true or false.

___1. It is worth more to a manager to have a dollar one year from now than it is to have it now.

___2. If $2,000 is invested for 5 years at the annual compound interest rate of 10 percent, then at the end of 5 years this investment will be worth $3,222.

___3. If the net present value of a single investment proposal is negative, then the investment should be accepted.

___4. The internal rate of return is the same as the hurdle rate.

___5. The reason for purchasing an asset is an expectation that it will provide benefits in the future.

___6. If the cash flows from an investment are uneven, it is not possible to calculate the investment's internal rate of return.

___7. If an investment analysis is carried out by hand, it is easier to compute a project's NPV than its IRR.

___8. Capital-budgeting problems tend to focus on specific projects or programs.

___9. If $4,000 is to be received at the end of 5 years from now and money is worth 10 percent per year, compounded annually, the present value of this payment is $2,843.60.

___10. If the internal rate of return of an investment exceeds the organization's cost of capital, then the investment should be rejected.

___11. An advantage of the IRR method is that the analyst can adjust for risk considerations.

___12. Discounted-cash-flow analyses treat cash flows of an investment project as though they were known with certainty.

___13. The internal rate of return for an investment is the interest rate that makes the net present value of the investment equal to zero.

___14. Periodic depreciation charges are cash flows.

___15. Both the NPV method and the IRR method make use of a hurdle rate.

___16. Discounted-cash-flow analysis assumes an imperfect capital market.

___17. Most organizations have an elaborate approval process for proposed investment projects.

FILL-IN-THE-BLANK QUESTIONS

For each of the following statements, fill in the blank to properly complete the statement.

1. Decisions involving cash flows beyond the current year are called _____decisions.

2. The fundamental concept in a capital-budgeting decision analysis is the _____.

3. _____is money paid for the use of an invested sum of money and previously earned interest.

4. Decisions where managers must decide which of several worthwhile projects should be adopted in the face of limited funds are called _____decisions.

5. If money is worth 12 percent per year, compounded annually, then $800 now is equivalent economically to the amount _____two years from now.

6. A series of payments is called a(n) _____.

7. Decisions that occur when managers must decide whether or not they should undertake a given investment project are called _____decisions.

8. The interest rate that makes the net present value of an investment zero is called the _____.

9. The hurdle rate used in discounted-cash-flow analysis is determined by management based on the _____rate.

10. The first step in any investment analysis is to determine the cash flows that are _____to the analysis.

11. The total-cost approach and the incremental-cost approach to comparing two competing investment proposals using discounted-cash-flow analysis yield _____ conclusions.

12. The systematic follow-up on accepted projects to see how they turn out in the capital budgeting process is called a(n) _____.

13. Discounted-cash-flow methods of investment decision making put the focus on _____.

14. Accrual accounting methods of evaluating periodic performance put the focus on _____.

MULTIPLE-CHOICE QUESTIONS

Circle the best answer or response.

1. John Harris received four annual payments of $3,000 each from an investment that was made 4 years ago. The interest rate was 18 percent. The original investment 4 years ago was
   (a) $8,070.
   (b) $ 12,000.
   (c) $9,810.
   (d) $2,154

2. Which of the following is *not* a name for the interest rate used in the net-present-value method?
   (a) Hurdle rate
   (b) External rate of return
   (c) Discount rate
   (d) Cost of capital

3. Mary Jackson invested $6,000 at the end of each year for the past 7 years, the last payment being made today. Her money earned compound interest at 14 percent per year. The value of her investment today is
   (a) $25,728.
   (b) $64,380.
   (c) $59,640.
   (d) $42,000.

4. If $16,980 is invested now and returns annual payments of $3,000 for each of the next 12 years, the internal rate of return of this investment is
   (a) 10 percent
   (b) 12 percent.
   (c) 14 percent.
   (d) 16 percent.

5. Which option(s) make(s) the following statement true? For a capital investment proposal to be accepted, the expected future benefits must be sufficient for the purchaser to: I. recover the investment. II. earn a return on the investment which is at least the cost of acquiring capital.
   (a) Only I
   (b) Only II
   (c) Both I and II
   (d) Neither I nor II

6. Which option(s) make(s) the following statement true? Techniques used in practice to analyze investment proposals for which the cash-flow projections are very uncertain are:

I. increasing the hurdle rate.
II. using sensitivity analysis.

(a) Only I
(b) Only II
(c) Both I and II
(d) Neither I nor II

7. A cost performance reporting system used to help control projects would *not* collect information on
(a) the actual cost incurred on the project to date.
(b) the actual cost of work scheduled to date.
(c) the budgeted cost of work scheduled to date.
(d) the budgeted cost of work actually performed to date.

8. Which of the following is *not* a difficulty in applying the net-present-value approach in a computer-integrated manufacturing investment decision?
(a) Hurdle rates may be set too low.
(b) Time horizons may be too short.
(c) There is greater uncertainty about operating cash flows.
(d) Benefits that are difficult to quantify are excluded.

EXERCISES

Record your answers to each part of the exercises in the space provided. Show your work.

Exercise 16.1

Given the following three independent sets of data:

	Set 1	Set 2	Set 3
Initial investment	$80,000	?	$22,918
Yearly cash inflow	$25,000	$14,000	$7,000
Hurdle rate	12%	20%	?
Net present value	?	$8,718	0
Life of investment in years	6	8	5

(a) Determine the missing items in each data set.

(1) Data Set 1:

(2) Data Set 2:

(3) Data Set 3:

(b) What special name is given to the interest rate found in part (a) for data set 3?

Exercise 16.2

The Clifton Springs Landfill is interested in buying a new bulldozer. Two models are available that would adequately meet the needs of the landfill. Model A would cost $75,000 and have annual operating costs of $6,000. Model B would cost $90,000 and have annual operating costs of $4,000. Both models would have a useful life of 10 years and no salvage value at the end of the useful life. The landfill has an 8 percent cost of capital. An existing old bulldozer can be traded in on either model for $3,000.

Employ the net-present-value method to find out which bulldozer model should be bought using:

(a) the total-cost approach.

(b) the incremental-cost approach.

Exercise 16.3

The Board of Education of the Summersville Central School has been told by its insurance company that the school's fire insurance premium will increase to $45,000 annually unless it replaces its existing sprinkler system, which is inadequate and not repairable. The board has ascertained that if it installs a new sprinkler system, which costs $135,600 and has a useful life of 10 years with no salvage value, the school will have to pay an annual fire insurance premium of only $21,000. The school's cost of capital is 10 percent.

(a) Determine whether the board should invest in the new sprinkler system using the internal-rate-of-return method.

(b) Compute the unrecovered investment amount at the end of the first, second, and third years of this investment. Make your calculations similar to those used in Exhibit 16-7 in the text and use the internal rate of return in your calculations.

Exercise 16.4

Christopher Smallen is the director of grants at the National Ecological Foundation (NEF). In this position he is responsible for the final choices of grant proposals that have been submitted to him from an Awards Committee. There are currently two proposals, *A* and *B*, of essentially equal merit relative to all of the qualitative factors of concern. However, the net present value (NPV) of the cost of Proposal *A* is $385,000 while that of Proposal *B* is $349,000.

Only one of these proposals can be funded by the NEF. It is customarily the case that in a situation like this, the proposal having the smaller NPV would be selected. However, several of the costs used in developing the NPV of Proposal *A* are for expenses most likely to be paid to the Hemingway Construction Company, which is owned by Smallen's father-in-law. Smallen's father-in-law has told him, "Anytime I get business from one of your grant recipients, I want you to share in my good fortune." Smallen reasoned that since he knows that Hemingway will do "first-class" construction work, Proposal *A* will be funded.

Write a brief essay that addresses the ethics of Christopher Smallen's behavior in this situation.

SOLUTIONS TO SELF-TEST QUESTIONS AND EXERCISES

MATCHING

1.	A	7.	H	13.	C
2.	L	8.	K	14.	M
3.	G	9.	Q	15.	I
4.	P	10.	B	16.	O
5.	N	11.	J	17.	E
6.	D	12.	F		

TRUE-FALSE QUESTIONS

1. F   Quite the contrary! It is worth more to have a dollar now than one year from now, simply because money can earn interest over time.
2. T   2,000 x 1.611.
3. F   It should be rejected.
4. F   The hurdle rate is the same as the minimum required rate of return or the cost of capital. The internal rate of return is that rate which makes the net present value equal to zero.
5. T
6. F   A trial-and-error method can be used in this situation to calculate the internal rate of return.
7. T
8. T
9. F $4,000 x .621 = $2,484.
10. F   The investment should be accepted.
11. F   This is a direct advantage of the net-present-value method, not the IRR method.
12. T
13. T
14. F   Depreciation charges themselves are not cash flows.
15. T
16. F   It assumes a perfect capital market.
17. T

FILL-IN-THE-BLANK QUESTIONS

1. capital-budgeting
2. time value of money
3. Compound interest
4. Capital-rationing
5. $1,003.20 = $800 x 1.254
6. annuity
7. acceptance-or-rejection
8. internal rate of return (time-adjusted rate of return)
9. investment opportunity
10. relevant
11. equivalent
12. postaudit (reappraisal)
13. cash flows
14. accounting revenues and expenses

MULTIPLE-CHOICE QUESTIONS

1. **(a)** $3,000 x 2.69 = $8,070.
2. **(b)**
3. **(b)** $6,000 x 10.73 = $64,380.
4. **(c)** $16,980/$3,000 = 5.66. From Table IV in Chapter 16 in the text, we see that the appropriate interest rate is 14 percent.
5. **(c)**
6. **(c)**
7. **(b)**
8. **(a)** The difficulty is that hurdle rates may be set too high.

EXERCISES

Exercise 16.1

(a)(1) Data Set 1

$n = 6$ and $r = 12$ percent; from Table IV we obtain the annuity discount factor of 4.111. The net present value = $25,000 x 4.111 - $80,000 = $22,775.

(a)(2) Data Set 2

$n = 8$ and $r = 20$ percent; from Table IV the annuity discount factor is 3.837. Let P be the initial investment amount. Then $14,000 x 3.837 - $P = $8,718$, and so $P = 45,000$.

(a)(3) Data Set 3

$n = 5$ and r is to be determined. The annuity discount factor = 22,918/7,000 = 3.274. From Table IV with $n = 5$, we see that an annuity discount factor of 3.274 corresponds to $r = 16$ percent. No interpolation is needed in this case.

(b)

Internal rate of return or time-adjusted rate of return.

Exercise 16.2

(a)

Total-cost approach:

	Model A	Model B
Trade-in value of old bulldozer now	$ 3,000	$ 3,000
Cost of new bulldozer now	(75,000)	(90,000)
Annual operating cost for 10 years	(6,000)	(4,000)

For this application $n = 10$ and $r = 8$ percent; from Table IV the annuity discount factor is 6.710.

Model A: NPV = -$6,000 x 6.710 - ($75,000 - $3,000) = $(112,260)

Model B: NPV = -$4,000 x 6.710 – ($90,000 - $3,000) = $(113,840)

Model A should be chosen on economic grounds. (Note that the $3,000 salvage value of the old bulldozer can be considered irrelevant.)

(b)

Incremental-cost approach:

Differences will be in the form: Model B less Model A.

	Difference
Trade-in value of old bulldozer now	$ 0
Cost of new bulldozer now	(15,000)
Annual operating cost for 10 years	2,000

As in part (a), the annuity discount factor is 6.710.

NPV of differences: $2,000 x 6.710 - $15,000 = $(1,580)

Hence, Model A should be chosen on economic grounds. Notice that $(113,840) - $(112,260) = $(1,580), showing that the total-cost approach and the incremental-cost approach give equivalent results.

Exercise 16.3

(a)

Here $n = 10$ and the annuity discount factor based on the given data is $135,600/($45,000 - $21,000) = 5.65. From Table IV with $n = 10$, this annuity discount factor corresponds to $r = 12$ percent (no interpolation needed), which is the internal rate of return. Since 12% > 10% (the cost of capital), the sprinkler system should be installed.

(b)

	Year 1	**Year 2**	**Year 3**
Unrecovered investment at the beginning of the year	$135,600	$127,872	$119,217
Cost savings during the year	24,000	24,000	24,000
Return on unrecovered investment	16,272	15,345	14,306
Recovery of investment during the year	7,728	8,655	9,694
Unrecovered investment ache end of the year	127,872	119,217	109,523

Note: For $r = 12\%$ and $n = 3$, the Table III factor is .712 and the Table IV factor is 2.402. As a check, observe that ($109,523 x .712) + ($24,000 x 2.402) = $135,628 (not equal to $135,600 due to rounding).

Exercise 16.4

Smallen is digressing from the customary procedure in granting awards for reasons that are suspect. His professional behavior is unethical because he is not avoiding an actual or apparent conflict of interest. In addition, it is reprehensible that Smallen should be influenced by the potential "kickbacks" he might receive from grant recipients' business received by Hemingway. This behavior this violates the Standards of Ethical Conduct for Managerial Accountants, which asserts that "management accountants have a responsibility to refuse any gift, favor or hospitality that would influence or would appear to influence their actions."

IDEAS FOR YOUR STUDY TEAM

1. Rewrite each of the definitions of the key terms that appear at the end of the chapter using your own words. Imagine that you are trying to explain each key term to a friend who has not taken any accounting classes. Then, get together with the other members of your study team and compare your definitions.

Acceptance-or-rejection decision

Accumulation factor

Annuity

Capital-budgeting decision

Capital-rationing decision

Compound interest

Discounted-cash-flow analysis

Discount rate

Future value

Hurdle rate (or minimum desired rate of return)

Incremental-cost approach

Internal rate of return (or time-adjusted rate of return)

Investment opportunity rate

Net present value

Postaudit (or reappraisal)

Present value

Principal

2.   Try to predict the types of questions, exercises and problems that you will encounter on the quizzes and exams that cover this chapter. Review the *Read and Recall Questions* and the *Self-Test Questions and Exercises* that are set forth in this Study Guide. Work through the end-of-chapter review problem(s), if applicable, and the end-of-chapter questions, exercises and problems that were assigned by your instructor. As you perform these tasks, identify the terms, concepts, formulas, etc. that you are responsible for knowing. After you develop the list of questions, exercises and problems that you expect to encounter on quizzes and exams, review the learning objectives that appear at the beginning of the chapter in your textbook to ensure that you have not overlooked anything significant. After you have completed your review of your list, get together with the other members of your study team and compare your predictions.

CHAPTER FOCUS SUGGESTIONS

This chapter extends the discounted-cash-flow analysis discussed in the previous chapter by considering the tax implications of capital expenditure decisions. In addition, the pros and cons of some other criteria used in capital-budgeting decisions are presented.

READ AND RECALL QUESTIONS

INCOME TAXES AND CAPITAL BUDGETING

LEARNING OBJECTIVE #1

After studying this section of the chapter, you should be able to:
- Discuss the impact of income taxes on capital-budgeting decisions in profit-seeking enterprises.

How might the various aspects of an investment project affect the company's income tax payments?

LEARNING OBJECTIVE #2

After studying this section of the chapter, you should be able to:
- Determine the after-tax cash flows in an investment analysis.

After-Tax Cash Flows

What is "after-tax cash flow?"

Will the amount of incremental sales revenue, net of cost of goods sold, that is generated by a project be less than or greater than the after-tax cash flow of the project? Why? What is the formula for computing the after-tax cash inflow from incremental sales?

Will the amount of incremental expense that is generated by a project be less than or greater than the after-tax cash flow of the project? Why? What is the formula for computing the after-tax cash outflow from incremental expenses?

LEARNING OBJECTIVE #3
After studying this section of the chapter, you should be able to:
- Compute an asset's depreciation tax shield.

What is a "depreciation tax shield?" How does depreciation, which is a noncash expense, result in a reduced cash outflow?

What are some examples of cash flows that do not appear on the income statement but still need to be considered in a capital-budget analysis?

Is it reasonable to assume that the cash flows resulting from income taxes occur during the same year as the related before-tax cash flows? Why or why not?

Accelerated Depreciation

Why is it advantageous for a business to take tax deductions as early as allowable under the tax law?

Why do both the 200% declining-balance and sum-of-the-years' digits methods result in greater present values for the depreciation tax shield than the straight-line method?

Does current tax law require the use of the same depreciation method for both tax and external-reporting purposes?

Modified Accelerated Cost Recovery System (MACRS)

What is the "Modified Accelerated Cost Recovery System" (or MACRS)? When is the use of this method required to determine the amount of depreciation for tax purposes?

What is the asset's useful life used for when MACRS is used? What method is used to depreciate assets in the 3-year, 5-year, 7-year and 10-year MACRS property classes? What method is used for assets in the 15-year and 20-year MACRS property classes? What method is used for assets in the 27.5-year and 31.5-year MACRS property classes?

How much depreciation for tax purposes is allowed during the tax year in which an asset is placed in service? How is salvage value considered when determining the asset's depreciation basis?

When does tax law permit the use of the straight-line method to depreciate an asset? When might a business prefer this approach? What life should be used to determine the depreciation for tax purposes? Is the half-year convention still applicable?

Why should a manager have a managerial accountant on one side and a tax accountant on the other when making an important investment decision?

LEARNING OBJECTIVE #5

After studying this section of the chapter, you should be able to:

- Evaluate an investment proposal using a discounted-cash-flow analysis, giving full consideration to income-tax issues.

Gains and Losses on Disposal

What is the "book value" of an asset? How is the amount of gain (or loss) on disposal determined when an asset is sold or otherwise disposed of?

Will the amount of the cash inflow (proceeds from sale) that is generated by the sale of an asset at a gain be less than or greater than the net after-tax cash flow at the time of the sale? Why? What is the formula for computing the after-tax cash inflow from the sale of an asset when the asset is sold at a gain?

Will the amount of the cash inflow (proceeds from sale) that is generated by the sale of an asset at a loss be less than or greater than the net after-tax cash flow at the time of the sale? Why? What is the formula for computing the after-tax cash inflow from the sale of an asset when the asset is sold at a loss?

Investment in Working Capital

What is "working capital?" Why do some investment proposals require additional outlays for working capital?

RANKING INVESTMENT PROJECTS

> **LEARNING OBJECTIVE #6**
> *After studying this section of the chapter, you should be able to:*
> • Discuss the difficulty of ranking investment proposals, and use the profitability index.

If a project has a positive net present value, does this mean that the return projected for the project is less than, equal to, or greater than the company's cost of capital?

What is "capital rationing?" Why is capital rationing necessary?

Assume that the NPV of project A was less than that of project B, and that the IRR of project A was greater than that of project B. Why would the NPV and IRR methods of analysis yield different rankings for these two proposals?

What is the profitability index? What is the formula for calculating the profitability index of a project?

Is the profitability index a foolproof method for ranking investment proposals? Why or why not? If not, what criteria should be used?

ADDITIONAL METHODS FOR MAKING INVESTMENT DECISIONS

LEARNING OBJECTIVE #7

After studying this section of the chapter, you should be able to:

- Use the payback method and accounting-rate-of-return method to evaluate capital-investment projects.

Even though discounted-cash-flow decision models are conceptually superior, what other methods are used by managers to make investment decisions?

Payback Method

What is the "payback period?" What is the formula for calculating a project's payback period?

How is the payback period determined when a project has an uneven pattern of cash flows?

What are the two serious drawbacks of the use of the payback method? What are two reasons for its use?

Accounting-Rate-of-Return Method

What is the "accounting-rate-of-return method?" What is the formula for calculating a project's accounting rate of return?

Why do some managers prefer to compute the accounting rate of return using the average amount invested in a project rather than the project's full cost?

What is the relationship between the accounting rate of return (using initial investment), the accounting rate of return (using average investment), and the project's internal rate of return?

ESTIMATING CASH FLOWS: THE ROLE OF ACTIVITY-BASED COSTING

Why do activity-based costing systems generally improve the ability of an analyst to estimate the cash flows associated with a proposed project?

Why is the evaluation of a proposed investment in advanced manufacturing equipment especially complex?

APPENDIX TO CHAPTER 17: IMPACT OF INFLATION

LEARNING OBJECTIVE #8
Determine whether or not you are responsible for this appendix. If so, after studying this section of the chapter, you should be able to:
- Explain the impact of inflation on a capital-budgeting analysis.

How does the "real" interest rate differ from the "nominal" interest rate? Why must cash flows in nominal dollars be deflated in order to convert them to cash flows in real dollars? How is the deflation process performed?

Two Capital-Budgeting Approaches under Inflation

What are two approaches to capital-budgeting analysis that consider the impact of inflation? Which approach provides the correct conclusion?

SELF-TEST QUESTIONS AND EXERCISES

MATCHING

Match each of the key terms listed below with the appropriate textbook definition:

___	1.	Accounting-rate-of-return Method	___ 6.	Nominal interest rate*
___	2.	After-tax cash flow	___ 7.	Payback period
___	3.	Depreciation tax shield	___ 8.	Profitability index (or excess present value index)
___	4.	Modified Accelerated Cost Recovery System (MACRS)	___ 9.	Real dollars*
___	5.	Nominal dollars*	___ 10.	Real interest rate*
			___ 11.	Working capital

* This key term is included in the appendix to the chapter.

A. The cash flow expected after all tax implications have been taken into account.

B. The measure used for an actual cash flow that is observed.

C. The amount required for a project's after-tax cash inflows to accumulate to an amount that covers the initial investment.

D. The present value of a project's future cash flows (exclusive of the initial investment), divided by the initial investment.

E. A measure that reflects an adjustment for the purchasing power of a monetary unit.

F. A percentage formed by taking a project's average incremental revenue minus its average incremental expenses (including depreciation and income taxes) and dividing by the project's initial investment.

G. Current assets minus current liabilities.

H. The real interest rate plus an additional premium to compensate investors for inflation.

I. The depreciation schedule specified by the United States tax code, as modified by recent changes in the tax laws.

J. The reduction in a firm's income-tax expense due to the depreciation expense associated with a depreciable asset.

K. The underlying interest rate in the economy, which includes compensation to an investor for the time value of money and the risk of an investment.

TRUE-FALSE QUESTIONS

For each of the following statements, enter a T or F in the blank to indicate whether the statement is true or false.

___1. If the tax rate is 40 percent and taxable sales revenue is $8,000, then the corresponding after-tax cash inflow is $3,200.

___2. Some cash flows do not appear on the income statement.

___3. It is usually disadvantageous for a business to take tax deductions as early as allowable under the tax law.

___4. Current tax law requires that the same depreciation method be used for both tax purposes and external reporting purposes.

___5. Income-tax payments must be considered in any discounted cash-flow analysis.

___6. The number of years of depreciation specified by the tax code is the same as an asset's useful life.

___7. If the tax rate is 40 percent and tax-deductible cash expenses amount to $12,000, then the after-tax cash outflow is $7,200.

___8. The cash flow resulting from the purchase of an asset affects income but has no direct tax consequences.

___9. Under MACRS depreciation computations, an asset's salvage value is not subtracted in computing the asset's depreciation basis.

___10. If tax-deductible depreciation expense is $6,000 and the tax rate is 40 percent, the corresponding reduced cash outflow is $3,600.

___11. Working-capital increases needed to support an investment project should not be included in discounted-cash-flow analysis.

___12. In general, no valid method exists for ranking independent investment projects with positive net present values.

___13. If the NPV of an investment is negative, the profitability index will also be negative.

___14. The payback-period method puts the focus on the profitability of the investment.

___15. The payback method cannot be used on investment projects with uneven cash flows.

___16. If the payback method is used in capital-budgeting analysis, it should be used in conjunction with discounted-cash-flow analysis.

___17. The payback method is widely used in practice.

___18. (Appendix) Using cash flows measured in real dollars and a nominal interest rate to determine the nominal discount rate provides a correct capital-budgeting analysis.

___19. Evidence from management accounting practice suggests that the most widely used investment evaluation technique is NPV.

___20. (Appendix) A correct capital-budgeting analysis consists of using cash flows measured in real dollars and a real interest rate to determine the real discount rate.

FILL-IN-THE-BLANK QUESTIONS

For each of the following statements, fill in the blank to properly complete the statement.

1.   A(n)_____is the cash flow expected after all tax implications have been considered.

2.   The reduction in income taxes due to depreciation expense is called a(n) _____.

3.   The main concept underlying discounted-cash-flow analysis is the _____.

4.   A(n) _____method is any method under which an asset is depreciated more quickly in the early part of its life than it would be using straight-line depreciation.

5.   The _____of an asset is defined as the asset's acquisition cost minus the accumulated depreciation on the asset.

6.   The MACRS optional straight-line depreciation method assumes that assets are placed into service _____through the tax year.

7.   The present value of future cash flows from a project divided by the initial investment is called the _____.

8.   When an asset is sold for more than its current book value, a(n) _____is recorded.

9.   The _____of an investment project is the time needed for the after-tax cash inflows from the project to accumulate to an amount that covers the original investment.

10. The _____method puts the focus on the incremental accounting income that results from a project.

11. When an asset is sold for less than its current book value, a(n)_____ is recorded.

12. (Appendix) The _____ is the underlying interest rate, which includes compensation to investors for the time value of money and the risk of investment.

13. (Appendix) A cash flow measured in _____ dollars is the actual cash flow we observe.

14. (Appendix) The _____ is a rate which includes the real interest rate plus an additional premium to compensate investors for inflation.

15. (Appendix) A cash flow measured in _____ reflects an adjustment for the dollar's purchasing power.

MULTIPLE-CHOICE QUESTIONS

Circle the best answer or response.

1. Consider the following statements and determine which statement(s) is (are) true.

   I.   If the NPV of an investment project is positive, the profitability index is less than 1.
   II. If the NPV of an investment is 0, the profitability index equals 1.

   (a) Only I
   (b) Only II
   (c) Both I and II
   (d) Neither I nor II

2. The Parsley Company is considering the purchase of a machine costing $8,424 which will provide the annual cost saving of $5,200. The tax rate is 40 percent. The payback period in years for this investment proposal is
   (a) 1.62.
   (b) 1.9.
   (c) 2.25.
   (d) 2.7.

3. Which of the following is *not* a disadvantage of the payback method?
   (a) It ignores the salvage value of the investment.
   (b) It does not use after-tax cash flows.
   (c) It ignores the time value of money.
   (d) It fails to consider a project's profitability beyond the payback period.

4. The Weaver Company has just sold a truck for $7,500. The truck presently has a book value of $10,200. The tax rate is 40 percent. The cash flow resulting from the tax implications of the loss on disposal of the truck is
   (a) $1,080 inflow.
   (b) $1,080 outflow.
   (c) $1,620 inflow.
   (d) $1,620 outflow.

5.   Consider the following statements about the accounting-rate-of-return method and determine which statement(s) is (are) true.

   I.   The method does not consider the time value of money.
   II. The method provides a simple way of screening investment proposals.

   (a) Only I
   (b) Only II
   (c) Both I and II
   (d) Neither I and II

6.   An investment project has a net present value of $9,700. The initial outlay for the investment is $48,500. The profitability index for this investment is
   (a) 1.2.
   (b) 5 0
   (c) 0.2.
   (d) impossible to determine from the information given.

7.   The Corley Company has just sold a computer for $2,700. The book value of the computer at the time of sale is $1,200. The tax rate is 40 percent. The cash flow resulting from the tax implications of the gain on disposal of the computer is
   (a) $600 inflow.
   (b) $600 outflow.
   (c) $900 inflow.
   (d) $900 outflow.

EXERCISES

Record your answers to each part of the exercises in the space provided. Show your work. (You may need to refer to the MACRS table in the text to complete these exercises.)

Exercise 17.1

The Luther Company has recently bought industrial tools amounting to $78,000. This investment falls into the 3-year property class under the MACRS. The tax rate is 40 percent and the company's after-tax cost of capital is 14 percent.

(a) Compute the total present value of all the cash flows resulting from the depreciation tax shield of this investment assuming that depreciation is computed using the MACRS table percentages.

(b) Repeat part (a) assuming that depreciation is computed using the optional straight-line method.

(c) Which of the two methods in parts (a) and (b) makes the biggest contribution to the NPV calculation?

Exercise 17.2

The Jewett Company has just purchased a new copy machine for $64,000. This machine is in the 5-year MACRS property class and will be depreciated using MACRS table percentages. The useful life of this machine is 6 years, and it will be worthless at the end of 6 years. The company anticipates that the annual revenue from this machine will be $45,000 and that annual expenses, excluding depreciation and taxes, will be $12,000. The tax rate is 40 percent.

 (a) Prepare a schedule similar to Exhibit 17-10 in the text and then compute the average annual income.

(b) Use the information in part (a) to determine the accounting rate of return based on the initial investment in the denominator.

Exercise 17.3

(Note: Ignore income taxes in solving this problem.) The Van Dorn Community Library is considering the purchase of a bookmobile truck costing $83,000. This truck is expected to produce annual cash operating inflows of $23,000. The truck will have a useful life of 5 years and will have a salvage value of $6,000 at the end of 5 years. The library's cost of capital is 12 percent.

(a) Find the profitability index of this investment. Should the bookmobile be bought?

(b) Suppose that the bookmobile will need extra working capital of $9,000 if it is purchased. This working capital would be released at the end of the bookmobile's useful life. Under these circumstances, what is the net present value of this investment? Should the bookmobile be bought in this case?

Exercise 17.4

The Tryon Company makes a product called a nump in its Stubenville plant. It is contemplating the purchase of two robots for its Assembly Department which would revolutionize the production methods in a department that is presently doing its work manually. In order to keep pace with its competition in an age of high-tech production, the management of Tryon believes it is necessary to give serious consideration to the possibility of buying these two robots. In order to help management make a well-informed decision about these robots, the company accountant has gathered the following data:

Purchase cost of the two robots now	$793,200
Cost of physical installation of the robots	42,900
Other costs related to robot installation	8,500
Incremental yearly cost in maintenance and energy costs	96,100
Additional yearly costs of MIS and computer support	85,300
Salvage value of both robots in 8 years	12,000
Useful life of both robots	8 years

These robots are in the 7-year MACRS property class and would be depreciated using MACRS tables for tax purposes. Tryon's tax rate is 40 percent, and its after-tax cost of capital is 18 percent. One of the concerns troubling management is that if in fact these two robots are purchased, 16 laborers currently in the Assembly Department will have to be laid off. At Tryon laborers work 2,000 hours per year at an average wage of $12.45. There is another firm located 8 miles from Tryon that has indicated it probably would be willing to offer these laborers somewhat similar employment in the event they were discharged from Tryon. The average wage of these laborers will be stable over the next 8 years.

(a) Find the net present value of the two robots.

(b) Find the profitability index of this investment.

(c) Should the robots be purchased on economic grounds?

SOLUTIONS TO SELF-TEST QUESTIONS AND EXERCISES

MATCHING

1.	F	7.	C
2.	A	8.	D
3.	J	9.	E
4.	I	10.	K
5.	B	11.	G
6.	H		

TRUE-FALSE QUESTIONS

1.   F   It is $8,000 x (1 - .4) = $4,800.
2.   T
3.   F   It is usually advantageous to take tax deductions as early as possible.
4.   F   The law allows different methods for tax purposes and external reporting purposes.
5.   T
6.   F   The number of years specified by the tax code is usually different from an asset's useful life.
7.   T
8.   F   The cash flow resulting from the purchase of an asset does not immediately affect income.
9.   T
10.   F   It is $6,000 x .4 = $2,400. They should be included in the analysis.
11.   F   They should be included in the analysis.
12.   T
13.   F   It will be less than 1 and hence could be positives
14.   F   It puts the focus on liquidity.
15.   F   It can be used with uneven cash flows.
16.   T
17.   T
18.   F   For a correct analysis, nominal dollars should be used with a nominal interest rate.
19.   F   The illustration from management-accounting practice in the text at the end of the chapter indicates that the payback method is most widely used.
20.   T

FILL-IN-THE-BLANK QUESTIONS

1.   after-tax cash flow
2.   depreciation tax shield
3.   time value of money
4.   accelerated
5.   book value
6.   halfway
7.   profitability index
8.   gain on disposal
9.   payback period
10.   accounting-rate-of-return
11.   loss on disposal

12. real interest rate
13. nominal
14. nominal interest rate
15. real dollars

MULTIPLE-CHOICE QUESTIONS

1. **(b)** If NPV is positive, the profitability index exceeds 1.
2. **(d)** $8,424/($5,200 x .6) = 2.7 years.
3. **(b)** The payback method does use after-tax cash flows.
4. **(a)** ($10,200 - $7,500) x .4 = $1,080. Since there is a loss, this is an inflow.
5. **(c)**
6. **(a)** Present value of future flows = $48,500 + $9,700 = $58,200; profitability index = $58,200/$48,500 = 1.2.
7. **(b)** ($2,700 - $1,200) x .4 = $600. Since there is a gain, this is an outflow.

EXERCISES

Exercise 17.1

(a)

Cost of tools = $78,000; 3-year MACRS property class.

Year	MACRS %	Depreciation Deduction	Depreciation Tax Shield	Table III Factor	Present Value of Tax Shield
1	33.33	$25,997	$10,399	.877	$ 9,120
2	44.45	34,671	13,868	.769	10,664
3	14.81	11,552	4,621	.675	3,119
4	7.41	5,780	2,312	.592	1,369
		$78,000			$24,272

Total present value = $24,272

(b)

Straight-line depreciation = $78,000/3 = $26,000

Year	Depreciation Deduction	Depreciation Tax Shield	Table III Factor	Present Value of Tax Shield
1	$13,000	$ 5,200	.877	$ 4,560
2	26,000	10,400	.769	7,998
3	26,000	10,400	.675	7,020
4	13,000	5,200	.592	3,078
	$78,000			$22,656

Total present value = $22,656

(c)

The MACRS table percentage method makes the biggest contribution to the NPV calculation, since it gives the largest present value of tax-shield inflows.

Exercise 17.2

(a)

Asset cost = $64,000

Year	Sales Revenue	Operating Expenses*	MACRS Depreciation	Income Before Taxes	Income Taxes	Net Income
1	$45,000	$12,000	$12,800	$20,200	$ 8,080	$12,120
2	45,000	12,000	20,480	12,520	5,008	7,512
3	45,000	12,000	12,288	20,712	8,285	12,427
4	45,000	12,000	7,373	25,627	10,251	15,376
5	45,000	12,000	7,373	25,627	10,251	15,376
6	45,000	12,000	3,686	29,314	11,726	17,588
			$64,000			$80,399

*Excluding depreciation and taxes

Average annual income = $80,399/6 = $13,400

(b)

Accounting rate of return = $13,400/$64,000 = 20.94%

Exercise 17.3

(a)

Item	Dollar Amount	Present Value Factor	Present Value of Cash Flow
Initial cost (now)	$(83,000)	1.000	$(83,000)
Annual cash operating inflows	23,000	3.605	82,915
Salvage value (year 5)	6,000	.567	3,402
Net present value			$ 3,317

Profitability index = ($82,915 + $3,402)/$83,000 = 1.040. The bookmobile should be bought since the profitability index exceeds 1. (Also, NPV > 0.)

(b)

Item	Dollar Amount	Present Value Factor	Present Value of Cash Flow
Initial cost (now)	$(83,000)	1.000	$(83,000)
Working capital needed(now)	(9,000)	1.000	(9,000)
Annual cash operating inflows	23,000	3.605	82,915
Salvage value (year 5)	6,000	.567	3,402
Working capital released (year 5)	9,000	.567	5,103
Net present value			$ (580)

Since NPV < 0 in this case, the bookmobile should not be purchased on economic grounds.

Exercise 17.4

Computation of annual operating cash flows:

Saving in direct labor costs	
(2,000 x $12.45 x 16)	$ 398,400
Incremental maintenance and energy costs	(96,100)
Cost of MIS and computer support	(85,300)
Annual cash operating inflows	$217,000

After-tax annual operating inflows 217,000 x .6 = $130,200
After-tax inflow from salvage value 12,000 x .6 = $7,200
Total initial cost = $844,600

Computation of present value of depreciation tax shield:

Year	MACRS %	Depreciation	Tax Shield	PV Factor	Present Value
1	14.29	$120,693	$48,277	.847	$ 40,891
2	24.49	206,843	82,737	.718	59,405
3	17.49	147,721	59,088	.609	35,985
4	12.49	105,491	42,196	.516	21,773
5	8.93	75,423	30,169	.437	13,184
6	8.92	75,338	30,135	.370	11,150
7	8.93	75,423	30,169	.314	9,473
8	4.46	37,669	15,068	.266	4,008
		$844,601*			$195,869

*The $1 error is due to rounding.

(a)

Item	Dollar Amount	Present Value Factor	Present Value of Cash Flow
Purchase cost (now)	$(793,200)	1.000	$(793,200)
Physical Installation (now)	(42,900)	1.000	(42,900)
Other costs (now)	(8,500)	1.000	(8,500)
Annual cash operating inflows	130,200	4.078	530,956
Total depreciation tax shield	—	—	195,869
Salvage value (year 8)	7,200	.266	1,915
			$(115,860)

(b)

Profitability index = $844,600 - $115,860/$844,600 = 0.863

(c)

No, since NPV < 0; also, profitability index <1.

IDEAS FOR YOUR STUDY TEAM

1. Rewrite each of the definitions of the key terms that appear at the end of the chapter using your own words. Imagine that you are trying to explain each key term to a friend who has not taken any accounting classes. Then, get together with the other members of your study team and compare your definitions.

Accounting-rate-of-return method

After-tax cash flow

Depreciation tax shield

Modified Accelerated Cost Recovery System (MACRS)

Nominal dollars

Nominal interest rate

Payback period

Profitability index (or excess present value index)

Real dollars

Real interest rate

Working capital

2. Try to predict the types of questions, exercises and problems that you will encounter on the quizzes and exams that cover this chapter. Review the *Read and Recall Questions* and the *Self-Test Questions and Exercises* that are set forth in this Study Guide. Work through the end-of-chapter review problem(s), if applicable, and the end-of-chapter questions, exercises and problems that were assigned by your instructor. As you perform these tasks, identify the terms, concepts, formulas, etc. that you are responsible for knowing. After you develop the list of questions, exercises and problems that you expect to encounter on quizzes and exams, review the learning objectives that appear at the beginning of the chapter in your textbook to ensure that you have not overlooked anything significant. After you have completed your review of your list, get together with the other members of your study team and compare your predictions.

CHAPTER 18
ALLOCATION OF SUPPORT ACTIVITY
COSTS AND JOINT COSTS

CHAPTER FOCUS SUGGESTIONS

You were introduced to cost allocation in Chapter 12. This chapter extends those concepts to cover the allocation of service department costs and joint cost allocation. You should know how to use each of the various methods covered in the chapter.

READ AND RECALL QUESTIONS

SECTION 1: SERVICE DEPARTMENT COST ALLOCATION

LEARNING OBJECTIVE #1
After studying this section of the chapter, you should be able to:
- Allocate service department costs using the direct method, step-down method, or reciprocal-services method (appendix).

What is a "service department?" Why must all service department costs be allocated to the production departments in which the goods or services are produced?

What does it mean if two service departments exhibit "reciprocal services?"

Direct Method

Under the direct method, how are each service department's costs allocated to the production departments? What information is ignored by this method?

Step-Down Method

What is the first step in the step-down method? How are the various departments ordered when this method is used? How are each service department's costs allocated to other departments using this method?

How much of service department A's costs would be allocated to service Department B assuming that service department A provides services to department B but follows department B in the sequence?

Reciprocal-Services Method

What is "reciprocal service?"

Fixed versus Variable Costs

Why might the failure to distinguish between fixed and variable costs result in unfair cost allocation among the using departments?

Dual Cost Allocation

What method of allocating fixed and variable costs separately can be used with either the direct method or the step-down method of allocation? What basis is used to allocate variable costs? What basis is used to allocate fixed costs?

What is one limitation of the use of dual cost allocation? How can this behavioral problem be prevented?

Allocate Budgeted Costs

When service department costs are allocated to production departments, why should budgeted service department costs be used? Why shouldn't actual costs be used?

What four steps should be taken when allocating budgeted service department costs?

THE NEW MANUFACTURING ENVIRONMENT

What happens to the extent of service department cost allocations in the new manufacturing environment, which is characterized by the JIT philosophy and CIM systems?

LEARNING OBJECTIVE #3

After studying this section of the chapter, you should be able to:

- Explain the difference between two-stage cost allocation with departmental overhead rates and activity-based costing (ABC).

The Rise of Activity-Based Costing

Why does an activity-based costing approach generally provide a much more accurate cost for each of the organization's products or services? How does this approach differ from two-stage allocation with departmental overhead rates?

SECTION 2: JOINT PRODUCT COST ALLOCATION

LEARNING OBJECTIVE #4

After studying this section of the chapter, you should be able to:

- Allocate joint costs among joint products using each of the following techniques: physical-units method, relative-sales-value method, and net-realizable-value method.

What is a "joint production process?" What are "joint products?" What is the cost of the input and the joint production process called? What is the "split-off point?"

After studying this section of the chapter, you should be able to:
- Describe the purposes for which joint cost allocations is useful and those for which it is not.

Allocating Joint Costs

Why is allocation of joint product cost to the joint products that result from the joint production process necessary?

What are the three methods that are commonly used for allocating joint product costs?

How are costs allocated using the physical-units method?

How are costs allocated using the relative-sales-value method?

How are costs allocated using the net-realizable-value method? What is the "net realizable value" of each final product?

Which of the three methods is least preferable? Why?

What is a "by-product?" What are the two approaches for allocating cost to the by-product?

APPENDIX TO CHAPTER 18: RECIPROCAL SERVICES METHOD

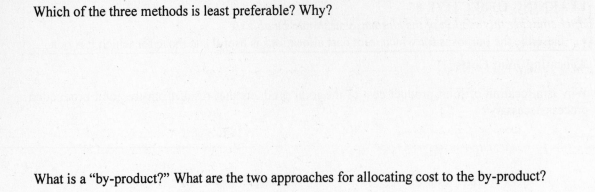

LEARNING OBJECTIVE #1
Determine whether or not you are responsible for this appendix. If so, after studying this section of the chapter, you should be able to:
• Allocate service department costs using the reciprocal-services method.

Why is the reciprocal-services method more accurate than the direct and step-down methods?

SELF-TEST QUESTIONS AND EXERCISES

MATCHING

Match each of the key terms listed below with the appropriate textbook definition:

___	1. By-product	___	8. Physical-units method
___	2. Direct method	___	9. Reciprocal service
___	3. Dual cost allocation	___	10. Reciprocal-services method
___	4. Joint production process	___	11. Relative-sales-value method
___	5. Joint products	___	12. Service department
___	6. Net realizable value	___	13. Split-off point
___	7. Net-realizable value method	___	14. Step-down method

A. A joint product's final sales value less any separable costs incurred after the split-off point.

B. A product from a joint process with very little value relative to the other joint products.

C. A method of service department cost allocation in which service department costs are allocated first to service departments and then to production departments.

D. A method in which joint costs are allocated to the joint products in proportion to their physical quantities.

E. A method of service department cost allocation which accounts for the mutual provision of reciprocal services among all service departments.

F. A production process that results in two or more joint products.

G. A method in which joint costs are allocated to the joint products in proportion to their total sales values at the split-off point.

H. The outputs of a joint production process.

I. An approach to service department cost allocation in which variable costs are allocated in proportion to short-term usage and fixed costs are allocated in proportion to long-term usage.

J. A method in which joint costs are allocated to the joint products in proportion to the net realizable value of each joint product.

K. A subunit in an organization that is not involved directly in producing the organization's output of goods or services.

L. The mutual provision of service by two service departments to each other.

M. The point in a joint production process at which the joint products become identifiable as separate products.

N. A method of service department cost allocation in which service department costs are allocated directly to the production departments.

TRUE-FALSE QUESTIONS

For each of the following statements, enter a T or F in the blank to indicate whether the statement is true or false.

___**1.** Service departments are unimportant in non-manufacturing organizations.

___**2.** In order to determine the cost of goods in an organization, all legitimate service department costs must be allocated to producing departments where these goods are made.

___**3.** The direct method does not ignore the fact that some service departments provide services to other service departments.

____4. Department size would not be a proper allocation base for allocating service department costs to producing departments.

____5. The primary purpose of cost allocation is to ensure that all costs incurred by the firm ultimately are assigned to its products or services.

____6. Cost allocations under the step-down method are the same regardless of how the service departments are sequenced in the allocation process.

____7. When fixed and variable costs are not distinguished in a service department cost allocation method, unfair cost allocations can result among the producing departments.

____8. The dual-allocation method can be used in conjunction with both the direct method and the step-down method.

____9. When allocating service department costs to producing departments, actual service department costs should be used.

____10. Service department cost allocations are used more extensively in advanced manufacturing systems than in traditional manufacturing systems.

____11. Joint cost allocations are necessary for inventory valuation and income determination.

____12. All joint products are salable at split-off.

____13. The breakdown of costs by activity in an ABC system is much finer than a breakdown by departments in traditional cost allocation.

____14. (Appendix) The reciprocal-services cost allocation method fully accounts for the mutual provision of services among all the service departments.

____15. (Appendix) The reciprocal-services cost allocation method cannot be used in conjunction with the dual-allocation approach.

FILL-IN-THE-BLANK QUESTIONS

For each of the following statements, fill in the blank to properly complete the statement.

1. A(n) _____ is a unit in an organization that is not involved directly in producing the organization's goods and services.

2. Under the _____ method, each service department's costs are allocated only among the producing departments.

3. The _____ method of service department cost allocation gives partial recognition of the fact that some service departments render services to other service departments.

4. The mutual provision of service among service departments is called _____ services.

5. Under the dual-allocation method, variable costs are allocated on the basis of _____ usage of the service department's output.

6. Under the dual-allocation method, fixed costs are allocated on the basis of _____ usage of the service department's output.

7. A joint production process results in at least two products called _____.

8. The common costs incurred in a joint production process before split-off are called _____.

9. The _____ of a final product made by a joint production process is its sales value after further processing less any separable costs incurred after the split-off point.

10. The _____ method of joint cost allocation is based on the relative sales value of each joint product at the split-off point.

11. A product from a joint process with a small sales value relative to that of other joint products is called a(n) _____.

MULTIPLE-CHOICE QUESTIONS

Circle the best answer or response.

1. Which of the followings *not* a proper step in allocating service department costs to producing departments?
   (a) Computing variances between budgeted and actual service department costs
   (b) Using variances to help control service department costs
   (c) Closing out service department costs against the period's income
   (d) Allocating the service department's actual costs to the producing departments

2. Consider the following statements about joint-cost allocation methods and determine which statement(s) is (are) true.

   I. The physical-units method is not based on economic characteristics of the joint products.
   II. These methods are useful in managerial decision problems about selling joint products at split-off instead of further processing them before sale.

   (a) Only I
   (b) Only II
   (c) Both I and II
   (d) Neither I nor II

3. A common practice in accounting for a by-product of a joint production process is to
   (a) add the cost of the by-product to the joint cost before allocating the joint cost.
   (b) subtract the net realizable value of the by-product from the joint cost before allocating the joint cost.
   (c) subtract the cost of the by-product from the joint cost before allocating the joint cost.
   (d) add the net realizable value of the by-product to the joint cost before allocating the joint cost.

4. A service department has costs of $15,000. Producing Department X uses 35 percent of the service department's output, and Producing Department Y uses the rest of the service department's output. Under the direct method, the portion of the service department's cost allocated to Producing Department Y is
   (a) $5,250.
   (b) $6,750.
   (c) $9,750.
   (d) $1 1,250.

18-9

EXERCISES

Record your answers to each part of the exercises in the space provided. Show your work.

Exercise 18.1

Sommer's Realty is a large real estate firm that has two revenue-producing departments: Residential and Commercial. It also has two service departments, Personnel and Computing. The usage of the service departments' output last year was as follows:

	Provider of Service	
User of Service	**Personnel**	**Computing**
Personnel	--	10%
Computing	15%	--
Residential	40%	30%
Commercial	45%	60%

The budgeted costs last year for the service departments were as follows:

Personnel	$138,000
Computing	195,000

(a) Allocate the costs of the service departments to the revenue-generating departments by the direct method.

(b) Allocate the costs of the service departments to the revenue-generating departments by the step-down method, allocating personnel costs first and then computing costs.

Exercise 18.2

The Ramsey Company has three producing departments—Fabricating, Assembly, and Finishing. The company has one service department—Energy. The following data are available for March:

Department	Energy Used (in kWh)	Long-Run Monthly Average Usage (in kWh)
Fabricating	15,000	18,000
Assembly	12,000	6,000
Finishing	3,000	6,000

Costs of Energy Department:

	Actual	Budgeted
Variable	$15,000	$12,000
Fixed	5,400	6,000

(a) Compute the total cost variance for the Energy Department.

(b) Use the dual-allocation method to allocate the budgeted energy costs to the producing departments. Find the total allocated amount for each producing department.

Exercise 18.3

The Armstrong Company produces products X-200 and Z-450 from a joint production process. Each of these products can be sold at split-off or processed further. Costs of processing further are all variable and are traceable directly to the individual products. In 19x3 the joint costs of production were $40,000 and both products were processed beyond split-off. Additional data for 19x3 are as follows:

Product	Units Made	Sales Value At Split-off	Further Processing Data Sales Value	Separable Costs
X-200	5,000	$18,750	$32,500	$8,750
Z-450	3,000	21,000	27,000	6,000

Allocate the joint costs of production to the joint products and find the total unit cost of each product using

(a) The physical-units method based on volume of production

(b) The relative-sales-value method

(c) The net-realizable-value method

Exercise 18.4

(Appendix) Sun Valley Hospital is a small hospital which renders health care and performs X rays on its patients. All other services needed for patients are performed at nearby independent facilities. The hospital has two service departments—Maintenance and Administration. Budget data for July are as follows:

Department	Producer of Service Maintenance	Producer of Service Administration	Budgeted Costs
Maintenance	--	15%	$50,000
Administration	10%	--	70,000
Health Care	80%	80%	90,000
X ray	10%	5%	10,000

(a) Find the final total costs (both indirect and direct) of the Health Care and X ray departments using the reciprocal-services cost allocation method.

(b) Suppose that a certain health care procedure has direct costs of $12.00 for labor and $21.00 for supplies. Find an appropriate total cost for this procedure which includes a charge for the allocated indirect costs of the service departments.

SOLUTIONS TO SELF-TEST QUESTIONS AND EXERCISES

MATCHING

1.	B	7.	J	13.	M
2.	N	8.	D	14.	C
3.	I	9.	L		
4.	F	10.	E		
5.	H	11.	G		
6.	A	12.	K		

TRUE-FALSE QUESTIONS

1. F They are also very important segments in nonmanufacturing factoring organizations such as hospitals.
2. T
3. F It does ignore the fact that some service departments serve other service departments.
4. F Department size could possibly be a proper allocation base.
5. T
6. F They are different, depending on how the service departments are sequenced.
7. T
8. T
9. F Budgeted service department costs should be used.
10. F They are used less.
11. T
12. F Some joint products are marketable only after further processing.
13. T
14. T
15. F It can be used in conjunction with the dual-allocation method.

FILL-IN-THE-BLANK QUESTIONS

1. service department
2. direct
3. step-down
4. reciprocal
5. short-run
6. long-run average
7. joint products
8. joint costs
9. net realizable value
10. relative-sales-value
11. by-product

MULTIPLE-CHOICE QUESTIONS

1. (d) The budgeted costs should be allocated to the producing departments.
2. (a) Joint-cost allocation methods are irrelevant for the seller-process-further decision problem.
3. (b) The other choices are all false.
4. (c) $15,000 x .65 = $9,750.

EXERCISES

Exercise 18.1

(a)

Service Department	Cost to Be Allocated	Revenue-Generating Departments			
		Residential		Commercial	
		Fraction	Amount	Fraction	Amount
Personnel	$138,000	40/85	$ 64,941	45/85	$ 73,059
Computing	195,000	1/3	65,000	2/3	130,000
			$129,941		$203,059

(b)

	Service Departments		Producing Departments	
	Personnel	Computing	Residential	Commercial
Costs prior to allocation	$138,000	$195,000		
Allocation of personnel costs	138,000	20,700(15%)	$ 55,200(40%)	$ 2,100(45%)
Allocation of computing costs		$215,700	71,900 (1/3)	143,800 (2/3)
Total allocated costs			$127,100	$205,900

Exercise 18.2

(a)

Total cost variance = $20,400 - $18,000 = $2,400 unfavorable

(b)

Cost Type	Amount to be Allocated	Producing Departments		
		Fabricating	Assembly	Finishing
Variable	$12,000	$6,000 (15/30)	$4,800 (12/30)	$1,200 (3/30)
Fixed	6,000	3,600 (18/30)	1,200 (6/30)	1,200 (6/30)
Totals	$18,000	$9,600	$6,000	$2,400

Exercise 18.3

(a)

Physical-units method:

Product	Units Made	Relative Proportion	Allocated Joint Cost	Separable Costs	Total Cost	Unit Cost
X-00	5,000	5/8	$25,000	$8,750	$33,750	$6.75
Z-450	3,000	3/8	15,000	6,000	21,000	7.00
	8,000					

(b)

Relative-sales-value method:

Product	Units Made	Sales Value At Split-off	Relative Proportion	Allocated Joint Cost	Separable Costs	Total Cost	Unit Cost
X-200	5,000	$18,750	.4717	$18,868	$8,750	$27,618	$5.52
Z-450	3,000	21,000	.5283	21,132	6,000	27,132	9.04
		$39,750					

(c)

Net-realizable-value method:

Product	Units Made	Sales Value after Further Processing	Separable Costs	Net Realizable Value	Relative Proportion	Allocated Cost	Total Cost	Unit Cost
X-200	5,000	$32,500	$8,750	$23,750	.5307	$21,228	$29,978	$6.00
Z-450	3,000	27,000	6,000	21,000	.4693	18,772	24,772	8.26
				$44,750				

Exercise 18.4

(a)

Let M and A be the redistributed costs of Maintenance and Administration, respectively, after receiving each other's cost allocations. Then: $M = 50,000 + 0.15A$ and $A = 70,000 + 0.10M$.

Solving these equations simultaneously, we obtain $M = \$61,421.10$ and $A = \$76,142.10$.

Total final cost of Health Care = $\$90,000 + 0.80(\$61,421.10) + 0.80(\$76,142.10) = \$200,051$

Total final cost of X-ray = $\$10,000 + 0.10(\$61,421.10) + 0.05(\$76,142.10) = \$19,949$

(b)

Portion of Health Care's final cost that is indirect (from service department allocations):
$200,051 -$90,000 = $110,051.

Rate for indirect costs of Health Care = $110,051/$90,000 = 1.2228 = 122.28%

Cost of given Health Care procedure:

Direct costs		
Labor	$12.00	
Materials	21.00	$33.00
Indirect costs: 1.2228 x $33		40.35
Total cost for procedure		$73.35

IDEAS FOR YOUR STUDY TEAM

1. Rewrite each of the definitions of the key terms that appear at the end of the chapter using your own words. Imagine that you are trying to explain each key term to a friend who has not taken any accounting classes. Then, get together with the other members of your study team and compare your definitions.

By-product

Direct method

Dual cost allocation

Joint production process

Joint products

Net realizable value

Net-realizable-value method

Physical-units method

Reciprocal service

Reciprocal-services method

Relative-sales-value method

Service department

Split-off point

Step-down method

2.   Try to predict the types of questions, exercises and problems that you will encounter on the quizzes and exams that cover this chapter. Review the *Read and Recall Questions* and the *Self-Test Questions and Exercises* that are set forth in this Study Guide. Work through the end-of-chapter review problem(s), if applicable, and the end-of-chapter questions, exercises and problems that were assigned by your instructor. As you perform these tasks, identify the terms, concepts, formulas, etc. that you are responsible for knowing. After you develop the list of questions, exercises and problems that you expect to encounter on quizzes and exams, review the learning objectives that appear at the beginning of the chapter in your textbook to ensure that you have not overlooked anything significant. After you have completed your review of your list, get together with the other members of your study team and compare your predictions.

CHAPTER FOCUS SUGGESTIONS

This chapter compares and contrasts absorption, variable, and throughput costing. In absorption costing, direct-material costs, direct-labor costs, and *all* manufacturing-overhead costs (i.e., variable and fixed) are applied to production. As such, product costs determined under absorption costing include fixed manufacturing-overhead costs. In variable costing, only direct-material costs, direct-labor costs, and *variable* manufacturing-overhead costs are applied to production. As such, product costs determined under variable costing do not include fixed manufacturing-overhead costs; such costs are treated as period costs and expensed as incurred. Variable costing is consistent with CVP analysis; absorption costing is not. Throughput costing, on the other hand, assigns only the unit-level spending for direct costs as the cost of products or services. You will need to be familiar with income statements prepared under all three methods.

READ AND RECALL QUESTIONS

LEARNING OBJECTIVE #1
After studying this section of the chapter, you should be able to:
- Explain the accounting treatment of fixed manufacturing overhead under absorption and variable costing.

Product Costs

What is "absorption costing" (or full costing)? Which types of costs are treated as inventoriable costs (or product costs) when absorption costing is used?

How does variable costing differ from absorption costing? Which types of costs are treated as inventoriable costs (or product costs) when variable costing is used?

When are fixed overhead costs expensed when variable costing is used? When are fixed overhead costs expensed when absorption costing is used?

LEARNING OBJECTIVE #2
After studying this section of the chapter, you should be able to:
- Prepare an income statement under absorption costing.

Absorption-Costing Income Statement

Which types of costs are categorized as period costs on an absorption-costing income statement?

Which line on the absorption-costing income statement includes fixed manufacturing-overhead costs?

LEARNING OBJECTIVE #3
After studying this section of the chapter, you should be able to:
- Prepare an income statement under variable costing

Variable-Costing Income Statement

How does the format of a variable-costing income statement differ from that of an absorption-costing income statement? What subtotal is used on a variable-costing income statement to highlight the separation of variable and fixed costs?

Where do fixed overhead costs appear on a variable-costing income statement?

LEARNING OBJECTIVE #4

After studying this section of the chapter, you should be able to:
• Reconcile reported income under absorption and variable costing.

Reconciling Income under Absorption and Variable Costing

If there is no change in inventory during the year, will the amount of net income reported on an absorption-costing income statement be less than, equal to, or greater than the amount of net income reported on a variable-costing income statement? Why?

If inventory increases during the year, will the amount of net income reported on an absorption-costing income statement be less than, equal to, or greater than the amount of net income reported on a variable-costing income statement? Why?

If inventory decreases during the year, will the amount of net income reported on an absorption-costing income statement be less than, equal to, or greater than the amount of net income reported on a variable-costing income statement? Why?

What formula can be used to reconcile the net income amounts reported under absorption-costing and variable-costing?

LEARNING OBJECTIVE #5

After studying this section of the chapter, you should be able to:

• Explain the implications of absorption and variable costing for cost-volume-profit analysis.

Cost-Volume-Profit Analysis

What formula is used to compute the break-even point in units?

If the number of units required to break-even (as calculated using the formula above) equaled the number of units produced and sold during the year, would net income be zero on the variable-costing income statement for the year? Why or why not?

Would net income be zero if the number of units produced was not equal to the number of units sold (that is, if there was a change in inventory) during the year? Why or why not?

If the number of units required to break-even (as calculated using the formula above) equaled the number of units produced and sold during the year, would net income be zero on the absorption-costing income statement for the year? Why or why not?

Again, would net income be zero if the number of units produced was not the same as the number of units sold during the year? Why or why not?

Evaluation of Absorption and Variable Costing

Why do many mangers prefer to use absorption-costing data for pricing decisions? Why do others argue that a product's variable costs provide a better basis for pricing decisions?

Which method (absorption costing or variable costing) is required by generally accepted accounting principles for external-reporting purposes?

Which method (absorption costing or variable costing) is required for reporting income for tax purposes?

Will the differences between net income reported using absorption costing and that reported using variable costing be smaller or larger in a JIT environment? Why?

LEARNING OBJECTIVES #6 & #7
After studying this section of the chapter, you should be able to:
- Explain the rationale behind throughput costing.
- Prepare an income statement under throughput costing.

What is throughput costing?

Why do many managers advocate throughput costing?

APPENDIX TO CHAPTER 19: EFFECT OF THE VOLUME VARIANCE UNDER ABSORPTION AND VARIABLE COSTING

LEARNING OBJECTIVE #8
Determine whether or not you are responsible for this appendix. If so, after studying this section of the chapter, you should be able to:
- Explain the effect of the volume variance under absorption and variable costing.

What is the formula for calculating the fixed-overhead volume variance?

If planned production equals actual production, is there a fixed-overhead volume variance when variable costing is used? Why or why not?

If planned production is less than actual production, is there a fixed-overhead volume variance when variable costing is used? Why or why not?

If planned production is more than actual production, is there a fixed-overhead volume variance when variable costing is used? Why or why not?

If planned production equals actual production, is there a fixed-overhead volume variance when absorption costing is used? Why or why not?

If planned production is less than actual production, is there a fixed-overhead volume variance when absorption costing is used? Why or why not?

If planned production is more than actual production, is there a fixed-overhead volume variance when absorption costing is used? Why or why not?

SELF-TEST QUESTIONS AND EXERCISES

MATCHING

Match each of the key terms listed below with the appropriate textbook definition:

___ 1. Absorption (or full) costing
___ 2. Throughput costing
___ 3. Variable (or direct) costing

A. A method of product costing in which only variable manufacturing overhead is included as a product cost that flows through the manufacturing accounts (i.e., Work-in-Process Inventory, Finished-Goods Inventory, and Cost of Goods Sold). Fixed manufacturing overhead is treated as a period cost.

B. A method of product costing in which both variable and fixed manufacturing overhead are included in the product costs that flow through the manufacturing accounts (i.e., Work-in-Process Inventory, Finished-Goods Inventory, and Cost of Goods Sold).

C. A method of product costing that assigns only the unit-level spending for direct costs as the cost of products or services.

TRUE-FALSE QUESTIONS

For each of the following statements, enter a T or F in the blank to indicate whether the statement is true or false.

___1. Absorption costing is consistent with CVP analysis.
___2. In a JIT environment, the income differences under absorption and variable costing will be insignificant.
___3. (Appendix) In standard absorption costing, a fixed volume variance that is favorable is subtracted from gross margin in the income statement.

FILL-IN-THE-BLANK QUESTIONS

For each of the following statements, fill in the blank to properly complete the statement.

1. In a(n) _____–costing system, fixed manufacturing-overhead is inventoried.

2. In a(n) _____–costing system, fixed manufacturing-overhead is treated as a period cost.

3. Generally accepted accounting principles require that income reporting be based on _____costing.

MULTIPLE-CHOICE QUESTIONS

Circle the best answer or response.

1. Consider the following statements: I – Proponents of absorption costing argue that to include fixed cost in the inventoried cost of a product will overstate the cost of the product. II Defenders of variable costing argue that the fixed-cost component of a product's absorption-costing value has no future service potential. Which statement(s) is (are) true?
   (a) Only I
   (b) Only II
   (c) Both I and II
   (d) Neither I nor II

2. The Harkness Company makes and sells a single product. The March 1 inventory was 3,000 units, and the March 31 inventory was 5,000 units. If the predetermined fixed-overhead rate is $12 per unit, then the reported income for March under absorption costing in relation to variable costing is
   (a) $24,000 less.
   (b) $24,000 more.
   (c) $60,000 less.
   (d) $60,000 more

EXERCISES

Record your answers to each part of the exercises in the space provided. Show your work.

Exercise 19.1

The Stearns Company makes and sells a single product and had the following data for February:

Units sold	6,500
Variable manufacturing overhead	$23,750
Finished-goods inventory, February 1	none
Variable selling and administrative expenses	$ 3,900
Direct materials used	$37,500
Planned production (in units)	12,500
Fixed selling and administrative expenses	$27,100
Fixed manufacturing overhead	$28,750
Units produced	12,500
Direct labor incurred	$20,000

There were no work-in-process inventories on February 1 or February 28.

(a) Compute the cost of the finished-goods inventory using:

(1) Absorption costing

(2) Variable costing

(b) Determine the difference in the amount of net income that would be reported for February between the two methods.

SOLUTIONS TO SELF-TEST QUESTIONS AND EXERCISES

MATCHING

1. **B**
2. **C**
3. **A**

TRUE-FALSE QUESTIONS

1. **F** It is inconsistent with CVP analysis; variable costing is consistent with CVP analysis.
2. **T**
3. **F** It is added to gross margin.

FILL-IN-THE-BLANK QUESTIONS

1. absorption
2. variable
3. absorption

MULTIPLE-CHOICE QUESTIONS

1. **(b)** Statement I is not true at all.
2. **(b)** $12 x (5,000 – 3,000) = $24,000

EXERCISES

Exercise 19.1

Finished-goods inventory, February 28, in units = 0 + 12,500 - 6,500 = 6,000

Manufacturing costs for February:

Direct materials	$ 37,500
Direct labor	20,000
Variable manufacturing overhead	23,750
Total variable product cost	$ 81,250
Fixed manufacturing overhead	28,750
Total product cost	$110,000

(a)

Unit product cost under absorption costing: $110,000/12,500 = $8.80

Finished-goods inventory, February 28, under absorption costing is valued at:

$8.80 x 6,000 = $52,800

(b)

Unit product cost under variable costing: $81,250/12,500 = $6.50

Finished-goods inventory, February 28, under variable costing is valued at:

$6.50 x 6,000 = $39,000

(c)

The higher income will be obtained under absorption costing because ending inventory of finished goods is valued higher by $13,800 under absorption costing than under variable costing. Note that 6,000 x $2.30 = $13,800, where $2.30 is the fixed-overhead rate.

IDEAS FOR YOUR STUDY TEAM

1. Rewrite each of the definitions of the key terms that appear at the end of the chapter using your own words. Imagine that you are trying to explain each key term to a friend who has not taken any accounting classes. Then, get together with the other members of your study team and compare your definitions.

Absorption (or full) costing

Throughput costing

Variable (or direct) costing

2. Try to predict the types of questions, exercises and problems that you will encounter on the quizzes and exams that cover this chapter. Review the *Read and Recall Questions* and the *Self-Test Questions and Exercises* that are set forth in this Study Guide. Work through the end-of-chapter review problem(s), if applicable, and the end-of-chapter questions, exercises and problems that were assigned by your instructor. As you perform these tasks, identify the terms, concepts, formulas, etc. that you are responsible for knowing. After you develop the list of questions, exercises and problems that you expect to encounter on quizzes and exams, review the learning objectives that appear at the beginning of the chapter in your textbook to ensure that you have not overlooked anything significant. After you have completed your review of your list, get together with the other members of your study team and compare your predictions.

3. Now that the course is over, take a few minutes to "recap." List at least ten things that you learned in this course that you truly believe you will use sometime in the future (in another course, during an internship you have lined up, when you are succeeding in the career that you are striving for, or in your life outside of work). Maybe you are already using some of the things that you have learned! Be specific; indicate *how* you will use what you have learned. (That is, don't just jot down, "How to compute variances.") Then, get together with the other members of your study team, and compare your lists.